Taste of Home

HOW TO COOK
(just about) Anything

TASTE OF HOME BOOKS • RDA ENTHUSIAST BRANDS, LLC • MILWAUKEE, WI

1610 N. 2nd St., Suite 102,
Milwaukee WI 53212-3906

Visit us at tasteofhome.com for other Taste of Home books and products.

International Standard Book Number:
979-8-88977-156-2

Content Director: Mark Hagen
Creative Director: Raeann Thompson
Associate Creative Director: Jami Geittmann
Senior Editor: Christine Rukavena
Senior Art Director: Courtney Lovetere
Manager, Production Design: Satyandra Raghav
Senior Print Publication Designer: Bipin Balakrishnan
Print Production Artist: Nandini Mittal
Deputy Editor, Copy Desk: Ann M. Walter
Senior Copy Editor: Elizabeth Pollock Bruch
Copy Editor: Rayan Naqash
Associate Copy Editor: Rachana Rana

Cover Photography
Photographer: Mark Derse
Set Stylist: Stephanie Marchese
Food Stylist: Sue Draheim

Pictured on front cover:
Citrus-Herb Roast Chicken, p.193; Carolina-Style Pork Barbecue, p. 155; Slow-Cooker Spaghetti & Meatballs, p. 171; Dark Chocolate Cream Pie, p. 311

Pictured on back cover:
On-the-Go Breakfast Muffins, p. 15; Lasagna Deliziosa, p. 220; Snowflake Doughnuts, p. 97; Upstate Minestrone, p. 85; Smoked Salmon Dip, p. 41

Printed in China
3 5 7 9 10 8 6 4

CONTENTS

Icons throughout help make the most of your time and resources:

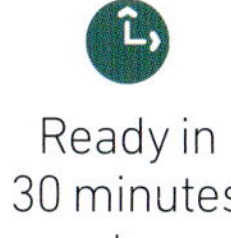

Ready in 30 minutes or less

5 or fewer ingredients (may also call for salt, pepper, water, oil)

Made in a slow cooker

Made in a Dutch oven

BASIC KNIFE SKILLS

Discover the essential knives for your collection, and learn about knife care and handling, plus key cutting techniques

COMMON CUTTING & CHOPPING TECHNIQUES

MINCING AND CHOPPING

- Holding the chef's knife with a power grip (see p. 5), rest the fingers of your other hand on the top of the blade near the tip.
- Using the handle to guide and apply pressure, move the knife in an arc across the food with a rocking motion until food is chopped to the desired size.

DICING AND CUBING VEGETABLES

- Using a chef's knife, trim each side of the vegetable, squaring it off. Cut lengthwise into evenly spaced strips. The narrower the strips, the smaller the pieces will be.
- Stack the strips and cut lengthwise into uniformly sized smaller strips.
- Arrange the square-shaped strips into a pile and cut widthwise into uniform cubes.

MAKING BIAS OR DIAGONAL CUTS

- Holding a chef's or paring knife at an angle to the food, slice as thick or thin as desired, using a control grip (see p. 5). This cutting technique is often used in stir-fry recipes.

MAKING JULIENNE STRIPS

- Using a chef's knife, cut a thin strip from 1 side of vegetable. Turn so the vegetable sits flat.
- Cut vegetable into thin, even slices of the desired length (usually 2 in.).
- Stack the slices and cut lengthwise into thin strips.

CUTTING WEDGES

- Using a chef's knife or serrated knife, cut the produce in half from stem end to blossom end. Lay halves cut side down on a cutting board. Cut each half vertically into thirds.

ZESTING

- Pull a citrus zester or rasp across limes, lemons or oranges, being careful not to remove the bitter white pith; chop strips into fine pieces if desired. Or use the finest side of a box grater.

▲ **Mincing** Pieces no larger than ⅛ in.

◀ **Chopping** ¼-to ½-in. pieces

◀ **Bias/Diagonal Cuts** Size of pieces based on desired length and thickness

◀ **Cubing** ½-to-1-in. uniform pieces

▶ **Dicing** ⅛-to-¼-in. uniform pieces

▶ **Julienne Strips** Pieces roughly 2 in. long

◀ **Wedges** Cut wedges in half to obtain desired thickness

▲ **Zesting** The sharp teeth of the smallest holes on a box grater yield very fine pieces of citrus zest

ESSENTIAL CUTLERY

Good knives are a must for any well-equipped kitchen. Here are the basics for building your collection.

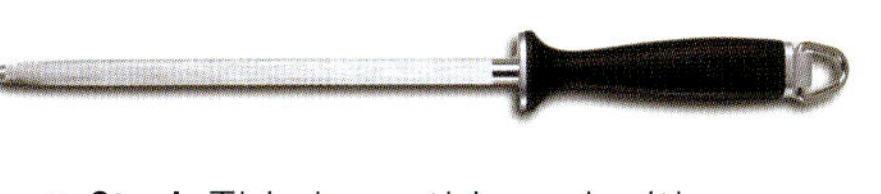

▲ **Steel:** This long, thin rod with a handle is used to smooth out small rough spots on the edge of a knife blade and to reset the edge. After the steel, you might use a whetstone or electric sharpener to hone your knives.

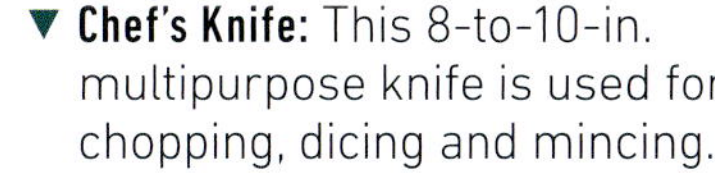

▼ **Chef's Knife:** This 8-to-10-in. multipurpose knife is used for chopping, dicing and mincing.

▲ **Serrated or Bread Knife:** This knife's serrated blade is used for slicing breads, cakes and delicate foods like tomatoes. An 8-in. blade is most versatile, but a range of lengths is available.

▼ **Paring Knife:** This 3-to 4-in. knife is used for peeling, mincing and slicing small foods.

▼ **Kitchen Shears:** This versatile tool is used to snip fresh herbs, disjoint chicken, trim pastry and more.

KNIFE CARE

• To keep knives sharp, cut foods on a soft plastic or wooden cutting board. Ceramic, granite, metal and other hard surfaces will dull the blades.

• Always wash and dry knives by hand immediately after use. Never let them soak in water or wash in the dishwasher.

• Store knives in a slotted wooden block or on a magnetic rack especially designed for knives. Proper storage will protect knife edges, keep blades sharper for longer and guard against injury.

KEEPING SHARP

Rest the tip of the steel on the work surface. Hold your knife at a 20-degree angle to the steel. Start with the heel of the blade against the steel and draw the blade up across the steel until you reach the tip of the knife. Repeat 5 times on both sides of knife blade. Repeat as needed.

1

2

GRIP BASICS

Every cook should master these 2 key grips:

1) POWER GRIP: Choking up on the knife blade yields more strength and speed for tasks like chopping hard vegetables and cutting through bone.

2) CONTROL GRIP: Gently hold the knife handle and treat the blade as an extension of your fingertips for fine, precision tasks.

KITCHEN EQUIPMENT & FOOD SAFETY

Build your collection with the following pieces, then expand to include items as desired from the sidebar on p. 7. The basic pieces for every kitchen include:

COOKWARE

▲ 1-qt. and 3-qt. saucepans with lids

◀ 8-in. or 9-in. saute/omelet pan

◀ 10-in. skillet

◀ 10-in. or 12-in. skillet with lid

▶ 5-to-8-qt. Dutch oven with lid

▼ Roaster with a meat rack

BAKEWARE

◀ 13x9-in. baking pan and/or dish (3 qt.)

▶ 9x5-in. and 8x4-in. loaf pans

◀ 15x10x1-in. baking pans

▶ 12-cup muffin pan (standard size)

MEASURING TOOLS

◀ Liquid measuring cups

▼ Dry measuring cups

◀ Measuring spoons

THERMOMETER

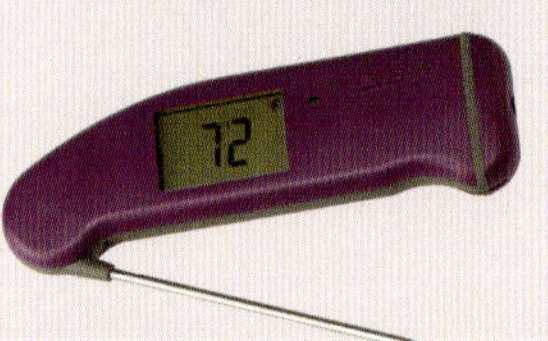

▲ **Thermometer** An instant-read thermometer is a great time-saver and helps you cook with precision. But other styles work fine too.

FOOD SAFETY

To ensure that the food you serve is safe from harmful pathogens, follow these basic but important rules:

KEEP IT CLEAN: Hot, soapy water is a must for hands, knives, work surfaces, cutting boards and utensils used in food preparation. All items, including hands, should be washed before and after touching raw food.

Sanitize cutting boards with a solution of 1 tsp. chlorine bleach to 1 qt. water. Let solution stand on the cutting board several minutes before rinsing clean. Air-dry the board or thoroughly dry it with clean paper towels.

KEEP FOODS SEPARATE: Don't cross-contaminate by allowing the juices or flesh of raw meat to come into contact with other foods. Wash any utensils used in preparation of raw meat in hot, soapy water before using with other foods. Don't reuse packaging materials, such as foam meat trays or plastic wrap.

Also, do not rinse raw poultry, meat or seafood before cooking. Proper cooking will kill any surface bacteria. Washing raw foods could contaminate the sink, which could then transfer bacteria to other foods or utensils if not immediately cleaned and sanitized.

KEEP IT AT THE RIGHT TEMPERATURE: Keep hot foods hot and cold foods cold. Use warming trays and chafing dishes to keep hot foods at 140° or higher. Use ice to keep cold food at 40° or cooler. Don't keep foods at room temperature for longer than 2 hours (or 1 hour on hot days).

TEMPERATURE DONENESS GUIDELINES

Always cook foods to the proper temperature

TEMPERATURE	WHAT'S COOKING?
135°	Medium-rare: Beef, lamb
140°	Medium: Beef, pork, lamb
140°	Fully cooked ham
145°	Pork, fresh ham (minimum internal temperature)
145°	Medium-well: Beef, lamb
160°	Ground beef, ground pork, ground veal, ground lamb, veal
160°	Egg dishes
165°	Ground chicken, ground turkey, boneless chicken breast, boneless turkey breast, sausages
165°	Casseroles, leftovers, stuffing
170°	Chicken and turkey bone-in breasts, boneless chicken thighs
170°-175°	Whole chicken, whole turkey, bone-in thighs and drumsticks, legs, wings; pheasant
180°	Duck, goose (minimum internal temperature)

EXPANDING YOUR TOOLKIT

Once you have the basic knives, cookware, bakeware, measuring tools and thermometer, consider adding the following items:

- Apple corer
- Box grater
- Cake pans (10-in. round)
- Can and bottle opener
- Citrus juicer
- Citrus zester
- Colander
- Corkscrew
- Cutting boards
- Dough cutter/scraper
- Egg slicer
- Ladles, large and small
- Meat fork
- Meat mallet/tenderizer
- Metal skewers
- Metal strainer or sieve
- Mixer
- Mixing bowls
- Mixing spoons
- Pancake turners
- Pastry bags and tips
- Pastry blender
- Pastry brushes
- Pepper mill
- Pie pans
- Pizza cutter
- Potato masher
- Rolling pin
- Salad spinner
- Slotted spoon
- Spatulas, rubber and metal
- Storage and freezer containers
- Textiles: Dishcloths, towels, hot pads, oven mitts
- Thermometers: Candy/deep-fat, oven, refrigerator/freezer
- Tongs
- Utility knife
- Vegetable peeler
- Whisks
- Wire cooling racks

how to cook ...

BREAKFAST

MILLION DOLLAR BACON, PAGE 13

BANANA PANCAKE FOR ONE

Get a delicious start to the day with this tender, hearty pancake. Try coconut or almond extract in place of vanilla for a fun change of pace.
—Carmen Bolar, Bronx, NY

TAKES: 15 MIN. • **MAKES:** 1 PANCAKE

- ¼ cup plus 1 Tbsp. all-purpose flour
- ½ tsp. baking powder
- 1 medium ripe banana, mashed
- 1 large egg, lightly beaten, room temperature
- ½ tsp. vanilla extract
- Optional: Maple syrup and banana slices

DID YOU KNOW?

Bananas start ripening as soon as they're picked because ethylene gas escapes from their stems. Wrapping the stems with tape, food wrap or foil slows this process—you may notice taped stems in grocery stores.

1. In a small bowl, combine flour and baking powder. In another bowl, combine mashed banana, egg and vanilla; stir into the dry ingredients just until moistened.

2. Pour batter onto a hot griddle coated with cooking spray; turn when bubbles form on top and the pancake is golden brown on one side. Cook until second side is golden brown. If desired, serve with syrup and banana slices.

1 SERVING 325 cal., 6g fat (2g sat. fat), 186mg chol., 313mg sod., 57g carb. (15g sugars, 4g fiber), 12g pro.

LOADED HUEVOS RANCHEROS

This is a unique and tasty version of huevos rancheros. It's similar to cowboy hash, with potatoes replacing the traditional corn tortillas.
—Joan Hallford, North Richland Hills, TX

PREP: 15 MIN. + STANDING • **COOK:** 20 MIN. • **MAKES:** 4 SERVINGS

- 1 poblano pepper
- ½ lb. fresh chorizo or bulk spicy pork sausage
- 4 cups frozen O'Brien potatoes, thawed
- ½ cup shredded pepper jack cheese
- 1 tsp. smoked paprika
- ½ tsp. kosher salt
- ½ tsp. garlic powder
- ½ tsp. pepper
- 4 large eggs
- Optional: Salsa, sour cream and minced fresh cilantro

1. Place poblano pepper on a foil-lined baking sheet. Broil 4 in. from heat until skin blisters, rotating with tongs until all sides are blistered and blackened, about 5 minutes. Immediately place pepper in a small bowl; cover and let stand for 20 minutes.

2. Peel off and discard charred skin. Remove stem and seeds. Finely chop pepper; set aside.

3. In same skillet, cook chorizo over medium heat until cooked through, 6-8 minutes, breaking into crumbles; drain. Add potatoes; cook and stir until potatoes are tender, 8-10 minutes. Stir in cheese, paprika, salt, garlic powder and pepper.

4. With back of a spoon, make 4 wells in potato mixture. Break an egg in each well. Cook, covered, on medium-low until egg whites are completely set and yolks begin to thicken but are not hard, 5-7 minutes. Serve with roasted pepper and, if desired, salsa, sour cream and fresh cilantro.

NOTE Wear disposable gloves when cutting hot peppers; the oils can burn skin. Avoid touching your face.

1 SERVING 426 cal., 26g fat (10g sat. fat), 251mg chol., 1114mg sod., 20g carb. (2g sugars, 3g fiber), 24g pro.

BLUEBERRY OATMEAL

We love homemade oatmeal, and this delicious, blueberry-topped oatmeal recipe is delightful. It's so tasty that it could be eaten for dessert as well.
—Lesley Robeson, Casper, WY

TAKES: 10 MIN. • **MAKES:** 2 SERVINGS

- 1¾ cups 2% milk
- 1 cup quick-cooking oats
- ⅛ tsp. salt
- ⅓ cup packed brown sugar
- ½ tsp. ground cinnamon
- ¾ cup fresh or frozen blueberries, thawed

In a small saucepan, bring milk to a boil. Stir in oats and salt. Cook over medium heat until thickened, 1-2 minutes, stirring occasionally. Stir in brown sugar and cinnamon. Divide between 2 serving bowls; top with blueberries.

1 CUP 455 cal., 7g fat (3g sat. fat), 16mg chol., 271mg sod., 89g carb. (57g sugars, 7g fiber), 13g pro.

RASPBERRY OATMEAL Substitute ¾ cup raspberries for the blueberries.

READER REVIEW

"Excellent oatmeal! I'm dieting, so I changed a few things to make it healthier. I used 1 cup water and ¾ cup skim milk and cut the brown sugar to 2 Tbsp. It was still sweet and delicious. I didn't miss the additional brown sugar at all."

—GUEST2327, TASTEOFHOME.COM

MILLION DOLLAR BACON

These spicy-sweet bacon strips aren't only delicious—with their maple syrup glaze, they're also attractive. Baking them in the oven in a foil-lined pan makes cleanup a breeze.
—Taste of Home *Test Kitchen*

PREP: 10 MIN. • **BAKE:** 25 MIN. • **MAKES:** 1 DOZEN

- ⅔ cup packed brown sugar
- ½ tsp. crushed red pepper flakes
- ½ tsp. cayenne pepper
- ½ tsp. coarsely ground pepper
- 1 lb. thick-sliced bacon strips
- ½ cup maple syrup

1. Preheat oven to 350°. Line a 15x10x1-in. pan with foil. Combine the brown sugar, red pepper flakes, cayenne and pepper. Dip bacon strips in sugar mixture; place in prepared pan.

2. Bake 20-25 minutes or until browned and crisp. Remove from the oven, drizzle with maple syrup. Return pan to oven and bake for 5 minutes longer or until bacon looks glossy but dry. Transfer bacon to a cooling rack (do not use paper towels as they will stick to the bacon). Serve warm.

1 PIECE 101 cal., 5g fat (2g sat. fat), 10mg chol., 253mg sod., 11g carb. (10g sugars, 0 fiber), 4g pro.

ON-THE-GO BREAKFAST MUFFINS

My family frequently requests these muffins. I usually prepare them on Sunday nights, so when we're running late on weekday mornings, the kids can grab these to eat on the bus.
—Irene Wayman, Grantsville, UT

PREP: 30 MIN. • **BAKE:** 15 MIN. • **MAKES:** 1½ DOZEN

- 1 lb. bulk Italian sausage
- 7 large eggs, divided use
- 2 cups all-purpose flour
- ⅓ cup sugar
- 3 tsp. baking powder
- ½ tsp. salt
- ½ cup 2% milk
- ½ cup canola oil
- 1 cup shredded cheddar cheese, divided

1. Preheat the oven to 400°. In a large nonstick skillet, cook the sausage over medium heat for 6-8 minutes or until no longer pink, breaking into crumbles. Remove with a slotted spoon; drain on paper towels. Wipe skillet clean.

2. In a small bowl, whisk 5 eggs. Pour into same skillet; cook and stir over medium heat until thickened and no liquid egg remains. Remove from heat.

3. In a large bowl, whisk flour, sugar, baking powder and salt. In another bowl, whisk remaining eggs, milk and oil until blended. Add to flour mixture; stir just until moistened. Fold in ⅔ cup cheese, sausage and scrambled eggs.

4. Fill greased or paper-lined muffin cups three-fourths full. Sprinkle tops with remaining cheese. Bake until a toothpick inserted in the center comes out clean, 12-15 minutes. Cool 5 minutes before removing from pans to wire racks. Serve warm.

FREEZE OPTION Freeze cooled muffins in an airtight container. To use, microwave each muffin on high for 45-60 seconds or until heated through.

1 MUFFIN 238 cal., 16g fat (4g sat. fat), 93mg chol., 357mg sod., 15g carb. (4g sugars, 0 fiber), 8g pro.

PEANUT BUTTER GRANOLA MINI BARS

Kids will flip over this deliciously sweet snack! After all, what's not to love about a batch of peanut butter-honey oatmeal bars? And at fewer than 100 calories each, you can afford to have seconds.
—Vivian Levine, Summerfield, FL

PREP: 20 MIN. • **BAKE:** 15 MIN. • **MAKES:** 3 DOZEN

- ½ cup reduced-fat creamy peanut butter
- ⅓ cup honey
- 1 large egg, room temperature
- 2 Tbsp. canola oil
- 1 tsp. vanilla extract
- 3½ cups old-fashioned oats
- ½ cup packed brown sugar
- ¾ tsp. salt
- ⅓ cup peanut butter chips
- ⅓ cup miniature semisweet chocolate chips

1. Preheat oven to 350°. In a large bowl, beat peanut butter, honey, egg, oil and vanilla until blended. Combine oats, brown sugar and salt; add to the peanut butter mixture and mix well. Stir in chips. (Batter will be sticky.)

2. Press into a greased 13x9-in. baking pan. Bake until mixture is set and edges are lightly browned, 12-15 minutes. Cool on a wire rack. Cut into bars.

1 BAR 96 cal., 4g fat (1g sat. fat), 5mg chol., 78mg sod., 14g carb. (8g sugars, 1g fiber), 3g pro. **DIABETIC EXCHANGES** 1 starch, 1 fat.

READER REVIEW

"I made these as a post-workout snack/breakfast, and I added some pureed honey-roasted peanuts and chocolate and peanut butter protein powder. They are amazing, filling and perfect to start off my day!"

—JENNA092, TASTEOFHOME.COM

EGGS BENEDICT CASSEROLE

Here's a casserole as tasty as eggs Benedict but without the hassle. Simply assemble the ingredients ahead and bake it the next morning for an elegant breakfast or brunch.

—Sandie Heindel, Liberty, MO

PREP: 25 MIN. + CHILLING • **BAKE:** 45 MIN. • **MAKES:** 12 SERVINGS (1⅔ CUPS SAUCE)

- 12 oz. Canadian bacon, chopped
- 6 English muffins, split and cut into 1-in. pieces
- 8 large eggs
- 2 cups 2% milk
- 1 tsp. onion powder
- ¼ tsp. paprika

HOLLANDAISE SAUCE

- 4 large egg yolks
- ½ cup heavy whipping cream
- 2 Tbsp. lemon juice
- 1 tsp. Dijon mustard
- ½ cup butter, melted
- Minced chives, optional

CUSTOMIZE YOUR BENEDICT

Swap Canadian bacon for smoked salmon, crab, ham, breakfast sausage or a different type of bacon. Add vegetables like asparagus, mushrooms, red peppers, tomatoes or sauteed spinach for a Florentine twist.

1. Place half the bacon in a greased 3-qt. or 13x9-in. baking dish; top with English muffin pieces and the remaining bacon. In a large bowl, whisk eggs, milk and onion powder; pour over the top. Cover and refrigerate overnight.

2. Preheat the oven to 375°. Remove the casserole from refrigerator while oven heats. Sprinkle top with paprika. Bake, covered, for 35 minutes. Uncover; bake for 10-15 minutes longer or until a knife inserted in the center comes out clean.

3. For sauce, in top of a double boiler or a metal bowl over simmering water, whisk egg yolks, heavy cream, lemon juice and mustard until blended; cook until mixture is just thick enough to coat a metal spoon and temperature reaches 160°, whisking constantly. Reduce the heat to very low. Slowly drizzle in melted butter, whisking constantly. Serve immediately with the casserole. If desired, sprinkle with minced chives.

1 PIECE WITH ABOUT 2 TBSP. SAUCE
286 cal., 19g fat (10g sat. fat), 256mg chol., 535mg sod., 16g carb. (4g sugars, 1g fiber), 14g pro.

PUMPKIN & CHICKEN SAUSAGE HASH

This can be served as a side or main dish. I like to serve it topped with poached or fried eggs for breakfast.

—Valerie Donn, Gaylord, MI

PREP: 15 MIN. • **COOK:** 25 MIN. • **MAKES:** 4 SERVINGS

- 2 Tbsp. olive oil
- 2 cups cubed fresh pumpkin or butternut squash
- ¼ tsp. salt
- ¼ tsp. pepper
- ½ cup chopped onion
- 1 pkg. (12 oz.) fully cooked apple chicken sausage links or flavor of your choice, cut into ½-in. slices
- 1 cup sliced fresh mushrooms
- ½ cup chopped sweet red pepper
- ½ cup chopped green pepper
- 1 tsp. garlic powder
- ¼ cup minced fresh parsley

In a large skillet, heat oil over medium heat. Add pumpkin; sprinkle with salt and pepper. Cook and stir until crisp-tender, 8-10 minutes. Add onion; cook for 3 minutes longer. Add the sausage, mushrooms, red and green peppers and garlic powder. Cook and stir until pumpkin is tender, 10-12 minutes. Top with fresh parsley before serving.

1 SERVING 260 cal., 14g fat (3g sat. fat), 60mg chol., 634mg sod., 19g carb. (13g sugars, 2g fiber), 16g pro. **DIABETIC EXCHANGES** 2 lean meat, 1½ fat, 1 starch.

NOTES

SLOW-COOKER BREAKFAST CASSEROLE

Here's a breakfast casserole that's easy to cook. I can make it the night before and it's ready in the morning. It's the perfect recipe when I have weekend guests.
—Ellie Stutheit, Las Vegas, NV

PREP: 25 MIN. • **COOK:** 7 HOURS • **MAKES:** 12 SERVINGS

- 1 pkg. (30 oz.) frozen shredded hash brown potatoes
- 1 lb. bulk pork sausage, cooked and drained
- 1 medium onion, chopped
- 1 can (4 oz.) chopped green chiles
- 1½ cups shredded cheddar cheese
- 12 large eggs
- 1 cup 2% milk
- ½ tsp. salt
- ½ tsp. pepper

In a greased 5- or 6-qt. slow cooker, layer half the potatoes, sausage, onion, chiles and cheese. Repeat layers. In a large bowl, whisk eggs, milk, salt and pepper; pour over top. Cover and cook on low for 7-9 hours or until the eggs are set.

1 CUP 272 cal., 16g fat (7g sat. fat), 242mg chol., 466mg sod., 16g carb. (3g sugars, 1g fiber), 15g pro.

PANCAKE & WAFFLE MIX

This terrific blend provides the ease of a boxed pancake mix with the homemade goodness of light, fluffy pancakes and waffles.
—Deb Poitz, Fort Morgan, CO

TAKES: 10 MIN. • **MAKES:** 11 CUPS MIX (ABOUT 7 BATCHES PANCAKES OR 4 BATCHES WAFFLES)

- 8 cups all-purpose flour
- 2 cups buttermilk blend powder
- ½ cup sugar
- 8 tsp. baking powder
- 4 tsp. baking soda
- 2 tsp. salt

ADDITIONAL INGREDIENTS FOR PANCAKES

- 1 large egg, room temperature
- 1 cup water
- 2 Tbsp. canola oil

ADDITIONAL INGREDIENTS FOR WAFFLES

- 3 large eggs, separated, room temperature
- 2 cups water
- ¼ cup canola oil

In a large bowl, combine the first 6 ingredients with a wire whisk. Store in an airtight container in refrigerator up to 6 months.

TO PREPARE PANCAKES: In a medium bowl, beat egg, water and oil. Whisk in 1½ cups pancake & waffle mix. Let stand for 5 minutes. Pour batter by ⅓ cupfuls onto a lightly greased hot griddle; turn when bubbles form on top of pancakes. Cook until second side is golden brown. **Makes:** about 6 pancakes per batch.

TO PREPARE WAFFLES: In a large bowl, beat the egg yolks, water and oil. Stir in 2½ cups pancake & waffle mix just until moistened. In a bowl, beat the egg whites until stiff peaks form; fold into the batter. Bake in a preheated waffle maker according to manufacturer's directions until golden brown. **Makes:** about 13 (4-in.) waffles per batch.

3 PANCAKES 170 cal., 6g fat (1g sat. fat), 39mg chol., 23g carb. (6g sugars, 1g fiber), 5g pro. **2 WAFFLES** 295 cal., 12g fat (2g sat. fat), 91mg chol., 598mg sod., 37g carb. (8g sugars, 1g fiber), 10g pro.

CAMPER'S BREAKFAST HASH

When we go camping with family and friends, I always make this hearty breakfast. It's a favorite at home too.
—*Linda Krivanek, Oak Creek, WI*

TAKES: 25 MIN. • **MAKES:** 8 SERVINGS

- ¼ cup butter, cubed
- 2 pkg. (20 oz. each) refrigerated shredded hash brown potatoes
- 1 pkg. (7 oz.) frozen fully cooked breakfast sausage links, thawed and cut into ½-in. pieces
- ¼ cup chopped onion
- ¼ cup chopped green pepper
- 12 large eggs, lightly beaten
- Salt and pepper to taste
- 1 cup shredded cheddar cheese

1. In a deep 12-in. cast-iron or other heavy skillet, melt butter. Add potatoes, sausage, onion and green pepper. Cook, uncovered, over medium heat until the potatoes are lightly browned, turning once, 15-20 minutes.

2. Push potato mixture toward edge of pan. Pour eggs into center of pan. Cook and stir over medium heat until eggs are completely set. Season with salt and pepper. Reduce heat; stir eggs into the potato mixture. Top with cheddar cheese; cover and cook until cheese is melted, 1-2 minutes.

1 CUP 376 cal., 27g fat (12g sat. fat), 364mg chol., 520mg sod., 17g carb. (2g sugars, 1g fiber), 18g pro.

READER REVIEW

"I make this recipe a lot at our house! I use smoked sausage or kielbasa. If there is leftover corn or green beans from a previous meal, I toss it in too! This is a versatile recipe."

—PAPACULLOP, TASTEOFHOME.COM

BAKED OATMEAL

You may think you're biting into a warm-from-the-oven oatmeal cookie when you taste this breakfast treat. Just add milk to get your morning off to the perfect start.
—Arlene Riehl, Dundee, NY

PREP: 10 MIN. • **BAKE:** 40 MIN. • **MAKES:** 9 SERVINGS

- 3 cups quick-cooking oats
- 1 cup packed brown sugar
- 2 tsp. baking powder
- 1 tsp. salt
- 1 tsp. ground cinnamon
- 2 large eggs, room temperature
- 1 cup whole milk
- ½ cup butter, melted
- Additional milk

1. Preheat the oven to 350°. In a large bowl, combine oats, brown sugar, baking powder, salt and cinnamon. In another bowl, whisk eggs, milk and butter. Stir into oat mixture until blended.

2. Spoon into a greased 9-in. square baking pan. Bake for 40-45 minutes or until set. Serve warm with milk.

1 SERVING 318 cal., 14g fat (7g sat. fat), 78mg chol., 492mg sod., 43g carb. (25g sugars, 3g fiber), 7g pro.

APPLE-RAISIN BAKED OATMEAL Stir in 1 chopped medium apple, ⅓ cup raisins and ⅓ cup chopped walnuts. Transfer to baking pan. Bake as directed.

FRUITY BAKED OATMEAL Stir in 1 chopped medium apple, ⅓ cup chopped peaches and ⅓ cup blueberries. Transfer to baking pan. Bake as directed.

VANILLA FRENCH TOAST

We discovered this recipe in Mexico. We couldn't figure out what made the French toast so delicious and flavorful until we learned the secret was vanilla—one of Mexico's most popular flavorings. Since then, we've added a touch of vanilla to our waffle and pancake recipes, and it makes all the difference.

—Joe and Bobbi Schott, Castroville, TX

TAKES: 25 MIN. • **MAKES:** 6 SERVINGS

- 4 large eggs, lightly beaten
- 1 cup 2% milk
- 2 Tbsp. sugar
- 2 tsp. vanilla extract
- ⅛ tsp. salt
- 12 slices day-old sandwich bread
- Optional toppings: Butter, maple syrup, fresh berries and confectioners' sugar

1. In a shallow dish, whisk together first 5 ingredients. Preheat a greased griddle over medium heat.

2. Dip bread into egg mixture, allowing to soak 30 seconds on each side. Cook on griddle until golden brown on both sides. Serve with toppings as desired.

2 PIECES 218 cal., 6g fat (3g sat. fat), 127mg chol., 376mg sod., 30g carb. (9g sugars, 1g fiber), 10g pro. **DIABETIC EXCHANGES** 2 starch, 1 medium-fat meat.

SHAKSHUKA

Shakshuka is a dish made of poached eggs with tomatoes, onion and cumin. I learned about it while traveling, and it's now my favorite way to eat eggs.
—Ezra Weeks, Calgary, AB

TAKES: 30 MIN. • **MAKES:** 4 SERVINGS

- 2 Tbsp. olive oil
- 1 medium onion, chopped
- 1 garlic clove, minced
- 1 tsp. ground cumin
- 1 tsp. pepper
- ½ to 1 tsp. chili powder
- ½ tsp. salt
- 1 tsp. Sriracha chili sauce or hot pepper sauce, optional
- 2 medium tomatoes, chopped
- 4 large eggs
- Chopped fresh cilantro
- Whole pita breads, toasted

1. In a large heavy skillet, heat oil over medium heat. Add onion; cook and stir until tender, 4-6 minutes. Add garlic, seasonings and, if desired, chili sauce; cook 30 seconds longer. Add tomatoes; cook until mixture is thickened, stirring occasionally, 3-5 minutes.

2. With back of spoon, make 4 wells in vegetable mixture; break 1 egg into each well. Cook, covered, until egg whites are completely set and yolks begin to thicken but are not hard, 4-6 minutes. Sprinkle with cilantro; serve with pita bread.

1 SERVING 159 cal., 12g fat (3g sat. fat), 186mg chol., 381mg sod., 6g carb. (3g sugars, 2g fiber), 7g pro. **DIABETIC EXCHANGES** 1½ fat, 1 medium-fat meat, 1 vegetable.

ABOUT SHAKSHUKA

This North African–Middle Eastern dish features eggs poached in a spiced tomato sauce. A hearty, one-skillet meal, it's perfect for breakfast or brunch. Serve shakshuka with pitas, rustic bread, couscous or toast.

HAM & CHEESE QUICHE

When I was expecting our daughter, I made and froze these cheesy quiches as well as several other dishes. After her birth, it was nice to have dinner waiting in the freezer when my husband and I were too tired to cook.
—Christena Palmer, Green River, WY

PREP: 20 MIN. • **BAKE:** 35 MIN. • **MAKES:** 2 QUICHES (6 SERVINGS EACH)

- 2 sheets refrigerated pie crust
- 2 cups diced fully cooked ham
- 2 cups shredded sharp cheddar cheese
- 2 tsp. dried minced onion
- 4 large eggs
- 2 cups half-and-half cream
- ½ tsp. salt
- ¼ tsp. pepper

1. Preheat oven to 400°. Unroll pie crusts into two 9-in. pie plates; flute edges. Line unpricked the pie crusts with a double thickness of heavy-duty foil. Fill with pie weights, dried beans or uncooked rice. Bake 10-12 minutes or until light golden brown. Remove foil and weights; bake 3-5 minutes longer or until bottom is golden brown. Cool on wire racks.

2. Divide ham, cheese and onion between the crusts. In a large bowl, whisk eggs, cream, salt and pepper until blended. Pour into crusts. Cover edges loosely with foil. Bake until a knife inserted in center comes out clean, 35-40 minutes. Let stand 5-10 minutes before cutting.

FREEZE OPTION Cover and freeze the unbaked quiche. To use, remove from the freezer 30 minutes before baking (do not thaw). Preheat the oven to 350°. Place quiche on a baking sheet; cover edge loosely with foil. Bake as directed, increasing time as necessary, until a knife inserted in the center comes out clean.

NOTE Let the pie weights cool before storing. Beans and rice may be reused for pie weights but not for cooking.

1 PIECE 349 cal., 23g fat (12g sat. fat), 132mg chol., 596mg sod., 20g carb. (3g sugars, 0 fiber), 13g pro.

QUICK SAUSAGE GRAVY

I thought everyone knew how to make sausage gravy until my husband George and I served it for a breakfast we hosted. It disappeared quickly, and everyone who tried it asked for the recipe.
—Joan Daumeyer, Blanchester, OH

TAKES: 20 MIN. • **MAKES:** 6 SERVINGS

- 1 lb. bulk pork sausage
- ¼ cup all-purpose flour
- 2 cups whole milk
- ¼ tsp. pepper

SAUSAGE GRAVY TIPS

How do you store leftover gravy? Gravy will last for 3-5 days when stored in an airtight container in the fridge.

What are some variations of this gravy recipe? Try adding different seasonings like sage, red pepper flakes, garlic or onion powder, or a few dashes of hot pepper sauce.

What can you serve with sausage gravy? Serve gravy over split hot biscuits, with fried potatoes or eggs on the side.

In a large skillet over medium heat, cook sausage until no longer pink, 5-7 minutes, breaking into crumbles; drain, reserving 3 Tbsp. drippings in pan with cooked sausage. Stir in flour. Gradually add milk. Bring to a boil; cook and stir until thickened, about 1 minute. Stir in pepper.

1 SERVING 253 cal., 19g fat (7g sat. fat), 49mg chol., 495mg sod., 9g carb. (4g sugars, 0 fiber), 11g pro.

how to cook ...

POPULAR SNACKS

SMOKED SALMON DIP, PAGE 41

BUFFALO CHICKEN DIP

Buffalo wing sauce, cream cheese, and ranch or blue cheese dressing make a lively party dip. Everywhere I take this, people want the recipe.
—Belinda Gibson, Dry Ridge, KY

TAKES: 30 MIN. • **MAKES:** ABOUT 2 CUPS

- 1 pkg. (8 oz.) cream cheese, softened
- 1 cup chopped cooked chicken breast
- ½ cup Buffalo wing sauce
- ½ cup ranch or blue cheese salad dressing
- 2 cups shredded Colby-Monterey Jack cheese
- French bread baguette slices, celery ribs or tortilla chips

1. Preheat oven to 350°. Spread cream cheese into an ungreased shallow 1-qt. baking dish. Layer with chicken, wing sauce and salad dressing. Sprinkle with cheese.

2. Bake, uncovered, until cheese is melted, 20-25 minutes. Serve with baguette slices.

2 TBSP. 152 cal., 13g fat (7g sat. fat), 36mg chol., 409mg sod., 2g carb. (1g sugars, 0 fiber), 7g pro.

READER REVIEW

"Fantastic! I made 2 batches, 1 with ranch and 1 with blue cheese, for a summer get-together. I loved the blue cheese one! The ranch was really good too—it's just what you prefer. Both pans were scraped clean!"

—MICHELE511, TASTEOFHOME.COM

JALAPENO POPPER SPREAD

I've been told by fellow partygoers that this recipe tastes exactly like a jalapeno popper. I like that it can be made without much fuss.

—Ariane McAlpine, Penticton, BC

PREP: 10 MIN. • **BAKE:** 25 MIN. • **MAKES:** 16 SERVINGS

- 2 pkg. (8 oz. each) cream cheese, softened
- 1 cup mayonnaise
- ½ cup shredded Monterey Jack cheese
- ¼ cup canned chopped green chiles
- ¼ cup canned diced jalapeno peppers
- 1 cup shredded Parmesan cheese
- ½ cup panko bread crumbs
- Sweet red and yellow pepper pieces and corn chips

POPPER SPREAD TIPS

• Regular dry bread crumbs stand in just fine for panko.

• Monterey Jack is a phenomenal melting cheese. If you want a little extra spice, use pepper jack instead.

In a large bowl, beat the first 5 ingredients until blended; spread into an ungreased 9-in. pie plate. Sprinkle with Parmesan cheese; top with bread crumbs. Bake at 400° until lightly browned, 25-30 minutes. Serve with peppers and chips.

¼ CUP 239 cal., 23g fat (9g sat. fat), 43mg chol., 304mg sod., 3g carb. (1g sugars, 0 fiber), 5g pro.

BAKED EGG ROLLS

These egg rolls are low in fat, but the crispiness from baking will fool some into thinking they were fried!
—Barbara Lierman, Lyons, NE

PREP: 30 MIN. • **BAKE:** 10 MIN. • **MAKES:** 16 SERVINGS

- 2 cups grated carrots
- 1 can (14 oz.) bean sprouts, drained
- ½ cup chopped water chestnuts
- ¼ cup chopped green pepper
- ¼ cup chopped green onions
- 1 garlic clove, minced
- 2 cups finely diced cooked chicken
- 4 tsp. cornstarch
- 1 Tbsp. water
- 1 Tbsp. light soy sauce
- 1 tsp. canola oil
- 1 tsp. brown sugar
- Pinch cayenne pepper
- 16 egg roll wrappers
- Cooking spray

1. Coat a large skillet with cooking spray; heat pan over medium heat. Add the first 6 ingredients; cook and stir until the vegetables are crisp-tender, about 3 minutes. Add chicken; heat through.

2. In a small bowl, combine cornstarch, water, soy sauce, oil, brown sugar and cayenne until smooth; stir into chicken mixture. Bring to a boil. Cook and stir 2 minutes or until thickened; remove from the heat.

3. Spoon ¼ cup chicken mixture on the bottom third of 1 egg roll wrapper; fold sides toward the center and roll tightly. (Keep remaining wrappers covered with a damp paper towel until ready to use.) Place seam side down on a baking sheet coated with cooking spray. Repeat.

4. Spritz tops of egg rolls with cooking spray. Bake at 425° for 10-15 minutes or until lightly browned.

FREEZE OPTION Freeze cooled egg rolls in a freezer container, separating layers with waxed paper. To use, reheat rolls on a baking sheet in a preheated 350° oven until crisp and heated through.

1 EGG ROLL 146 cal., 2g fat (0 sat. fat), 18mg chol., 250mg sod., 22g carb. (1g sugars, 1g fiber), 9g pro. **DIABETIC EXCHANGES** 1½ starch, 1 lean meat, ½ fat.

HOT ARTICHOKE-SPINACH DIP

One taste of this outrageously delicious dip and your guests will not stop eating it until it's gone. The savory blend of artichokes, spinach and Parmesan cheese is positively addictive! It taste even better if you make it the night before and chill it in the fridge before baking.
—Michelle Krzmarzick, Torrance, CA

TAKES: 30 MIN. • **MAKES:** 3 CUPS

- 1 pkg. (8 oz.) cream cheese, softened
- ½ cup grated Parmesan cheese
- ¼ cup mayonnaise
- 1 garlic clove, minced
- 1 tsp. dried basil
- ¼ tsp. garlic salt
- ¼ tsp. pepper
- 1 can (14 oz.) water-packed artichoke hearts, rinsed, drained and chopped
- ½ cup frozen chopped spinach, thawed and squeezed dry
- ¼ cup shredded mozzarella cheese
- Assorted crackers

Preheat oven to 350°. In a large bowl, combine the first 7 ingredients; mix well. Stir in artichokes and spinach. Transfer to a greased 9-in. pie plate. Sprinkle with the mozzarella cheese. Bake, uncovered, 20-25 minutes or until the dip is bubbly and the edge is lightly browned. Serve with the crackers.

2 TBSP. 68 cal., 6g fat (3g sat. fat), 13mg chol., 139mg sod., 2g carb. (0 sugars, 0 fiber), 2g pro.

HOT SPINACH DIP TIPS

What can you serve with this dip? Pair the creamy spinach dip with fresh veggies, garlic bread, pita or tortilla chips for a perfect balance of textures.

Can you make this dip in advance? Yes! Prep it a day ahead, refrigerate and bake when ready. Add a few minutes to ensure it's hot and bubbly.

What ingredient swaps work well in this recipe? Use 5 oz. cooked, well-blotted fresh spinach instead of frozen. For a lighter version, swap in reduced-fat cream cheese and light mayonnaise.

SWEET & TANGY CHICKEN WINGS

I love the convenience of slow-cooker recipes for get-togethers. Start these wings a few hours ahead of time and you'll have fantastic appetizers ready when your guests arrive.
—*Ida Tuey, South Lyon, MI*

PREP: 20 MIN. • **COOK:** 2¼ HOURS • **MAKES:** 2 DOZEN

- 12 chicken wings (about 2½ lbs.)
- ½ tsp. salt, divided
- Dash pepper
- 1½ cups ketchup
- ¼ cup packed brown sugar
- ¼ cup red wine vinegar
- 2 Tbsp. Worcestershire sauce
- 1 Tbsp. Dijon mustard
- 1 tsp. minced garlic
- 1 tsp. liquid smoke, optional
- Optional: Sliced jalapeno peppers, finely chopped red onion and sesame seeds

1. Using a sharp knife, cut through the 2 wing joints; discard wingtips. Sprinkle chicken with a dash of salt and pepper. Broil 4-6 in. from the heat until golden brown, 6-8 minutes on each side. Transfer to a greased 5-qt. slow cooker.

2. Combine the ketchup, brown sugar, vinegar, Worcestershire sauce, mustard, garlic, liquid smoke if desired, and the remaining salt; pour over wings. Toss to coat.

3. Cover and cook on low until chicken is tender, 2-3 hours. If desired, top with jalapenos, onion and sesame seeds to serve.

FREEZE OPTION Freeze cooled fully cooked wings in freezer containers. To use, partially thaw in refrigerator overnight. Reheat wings in a foil-lined 15x10x1-in. baking pan in a preheated 325° oven until heated through, covering if necessary to prevent browning. Serve as directed.

1 PIECE 74 cal., 3g fat (1g sat. fat), 14mg chol., 282mg sod., 7g carb. (6g sugars, 0 fiber), 5g pro.

SLOW-COOKER CHAI TEA

A wonderful sweet and spicy aroma wafts from the slow cooker as this fragrant and flavorful tea cooks.
—Crystal Jo Bruns, Iliff, CO

PREP: 20 MIN. • **COOK:** 8 HOURS • **MAKES:** 12 SERVINGS (3 QT.)

- 15 slices fresh gingerroot (about 3 oz.)
- 3 cinnamon sticks (3 in.)
- 25 whole cloves
- 15 cardamom pods, lightly crushed
- 3 whole peppercorns
- 3½ qt. water
- 8 black tea bags
- 1 can (14 oz.) sweetened condensed milk

1. Place first 5 ingredients on a double thickness of cheesecloth. Gather corners of cloth to enclose the seasonings; tie securely with string. Place spice bag in water in a 5- or 6-qt. slow cooker. Cook, covered, on low 8 hours. Discard spice bag.

2. Add tea bags; steep, covered, 3-5 minutes according to taste. Discard tea bags. Stir in milk; heat through. Serve warm.

1 CUP 109 cal., 3g fat (2g sat. fat), 11mg chol., 50mg sod., 19g carb. (18g sugars, 0 fiber), 3g pro.

CRISPY CRAB RANGOON

My husband loved the appetizers we had at P.F. Chang's so much that I was determined to make them at home. After several more trips to that eatery to taste them again, I had them perfected! I often prepare the filling earlier in the day to save time later.
—*Cathy Blankman, Warroad, MN*

TAKES: 30 MIN. • **MAKES:** 16 APPETIZERS

- 3 oz. cream cheese, softened
- 2 green onions, finely chopped
- ¼ cup finely chopped imitation crabmeat
- 1 tsp. minced garlic
- 16 wonton wrappers
- Oil for frying
- Sweet-and-sour sauce

RANGOON MAKING TIPS

How do you keep crab rangoon from exploding? The amount of filling called for per rangoon may seem a little skimpy, but overfilling the wrappers can cause them to burst when frying. Be sure to press out any air bubbles so pressure does not build up inside. Also, freezing the dumplings for 15 minutes before cooking may help keep them intact.

How do you fry crab rangoon? Use a high smoke point oil such as canola or peanut oil. Heat oil to 375° and add dumplings in small batches to keep the oil's temperature high.

1. In a small bowl, beat cream cheese until smooth. Stir in the green onion, crab and garlic.

2. Place about 1½ tsp. filling in center of a wonton wrapper. (Keep remaining wrappers covered with a damp paper towel until ready to use.) Moisten edges with water; fold opposite corners over filling and press to seal. Repeat.

3. In an electric skillet, heat 1 in. oil to 375°. Fry the wontons, in batches, until golden brown, about 1 minute on each side. Drain on paper towels. Serve with sweet-and-sour sauce.

1 RANGOON 61 cal., 4g fat (1g sat. fat), 6mg chol., 77mg sod., 5g carb. (0 sugars, 0 fiber), 1g pro.

SMOKED SALMON DIP

There are plenty of ways to enjoy salmon dips, from smearing it on bagels for brunch to serving it with crackers at a party. No matter how you serve this salmon dip, it's sure to become a favorite.
—Taste of Home *Test Kitchen*

TAKES: 15 MIN. • **MAKES:** 2½ CUPS

- 12 oz. cream cheese, cubed
- ¼ cup sour cream
- 3 green onions, chopped (white parts only)
- 2 Tbsp. capers, drained
- 2 Tbsp. mayonnaise
- 4 oz. smoked salmon or lox
- 1 Tbsp. dill weed
- 1 Tbsp. lemon juice
- ¼ tsp. hot pepper sauce
- ⅛ tsp. pepper
- Assorted crackers

Place the first 10 ingredients in a food processor; cover and process until smooth. Refrigerate, covered, until serving. Serve with crackers.

2 TBSP. 83 cal., 8g fat (4g sat. fat), 21mg chol., 121mg sod., 1g carb. (1g sugars, 0 fiber), 2g pro.

NOTES

QUESO DIP

Thick, cheesy and creamy, this queso is perfect for dipping. I use mild chiles and salsa, but if you like more heat, you can kick it up with medium-heat varieties. Serve it over eggs and omelets for breakfast or pasta with a sprinkle of bacon for a Mexican-American mac and cheese.
—Kallee Krong-McCreery, Escondido, CA

TAKES: 20 MIN. • **MAKES:** 2½ CUPS

- 1 cup heavy whipping cream
- ½ cup sour cream
- 2 oz. cream cheese, softened
- 1 tsp. cornstarch
- 1 Tbsp. water
- 2 oz. pepper jack cheese, shredded
- ½ cup shredded Oaxaca or Monterey Jack cheese
- 1 can (4 oz.) chopped green chiles
- ¾ tsp. garlic salt
- Optional: Chopped tomatoes and sliced serrano pepper

1. In a small saucepan, heat whipping cream over medium heat. Add sour cream and cream cheese; cook and stir until smooth.

2. In a small bowl, whisk cornstarch and water until smooth; stir into saucepan. Bring to a boil; cook and stir until slightly thickened, about 1 minute.

3. Reduce heat to low. Stir in shredded cheeses, green chiles and garlic salt. Cook and stir until cheese is melted. If desired, garnish with tomato and serrano pepper. Serve warm.

¼ CUP 172 cal., 17g fat (10g sat. fat), 52mg chol., 289mg sod., 2g carb. (1g sugars, 0 fiber), 4g pro.

SPARKLING GINGER LEMONADE

Chill out with this delightful cooler, perfect for springtime bridal showers or hot summer days on the deck. It's a quick fix you'll stir up time and again.
—Jodi Blubaugh, Eagle Mountain, UT

PREP: 20 MIN. + COOLING • **MAKES:** 5 SERVINGS

2 cups water
1 cup honey
2 Tbsp. minced fresh gingerroot
2 cups club soda, chilled
1 cup lemon juice
Ice cubes
Optional: Lemon slices and fresh mint

READER REVIEW

"We are huge fans of ginger ale and lemonade at our house, so this recipe was great for us. One cup of honey was a bit too much for us, so we cut it back some—but otherwise, we loved it!"

—LPHJKITCHEN, TASTEOFHOME.COM

1. In a saucepan, bring the water, honey and ginger to a boil. Remove from heat; cover and steep for 10 minutes. Strain, discarding ginger. Cool completely.

2. Transfer to a pitcher; stir in soda and lemon juice. Serve over ice. Garnish with lemon slices and fresh mint if desired.

1 CUP 217 cal., 0 fat (0 sat. fat), 0 chol., 23mg sod., 59g carb. (56g sugars, 0 fiber), 0 pro.

BABA GANOUSH

Baba ganoush (also spelled baba ghanoush or baba ghanouj) is a Lebanese dip made with roasted eggplant. It's typically served as a starter with pita bread or fresh vegetables.
—Nithya Narasimhan, Chennai, India

PREP: 15 MIN. • **BAKE:** 20 MIN. + COOLING • **MAKES:** 1 CUP

- 1 medium eggplant
- 2 Tbsp. olive oil, divided
- 1 tsp. salt, divided
- ½ tsp. paprika
- 2 Tbsp. tahini
- 1 garlic clove, minced
- 1 tsp. lemon juice
- Chopped fresh parsley

1. Preheat oven to 450°. Cut eggplant in half lengthwise. Place cut side up on an ungreased baking sheet. Brush 1 Tbsp. olive oil over the cut sides. Sprinkle with ½ tsp. salt and paprika. Bake until dark golden brown, 20-25 minutes. Remove eggplant from pan to a wire rack to cool completely.

2. Peel skin from eggplant; discard. Put flesh into a food processor and pulse to mash; transfer to bowl. Stir in the tahini, garlic, lemon juice and remaining ½ tsp. salt. Spoon into serving dish. Drizzle with remaining 1 Tbsp. olive oil. Sprinkle with parsley and additional paprika.

2 TBSP. 74 cal., 6g fat (1g sat. fat), 0 chol., 297mg sod., 5g carb. (2g sugars, 2g fiber), 1g pro.

GO NUTS

These snacks are the perfect nosh during prep time, while watching the game or as an on-the-go fuel.

CHOCOLATE-RASPBERRY MACADAMIA NUTS

In a food processor, process 1 oz. **freeze-dried raspberries** to a fine powder; add 3 Tbsp. **confectioners' sugar** and pulse to combine. Stir together 2 cups toasted **almonds** and 3 oz. melted **dark chocolate**. Add raspberry mixture; toss to coat. Spread nuts on a parchment-lined sheet pan; let stand until set.

ROSEMARY-GRAPEFRUIT CASHEWS

Stir together 2 Tbsp. ruby red **grapefruit juice**, 1 Tbsp. grated **grapefruit zest** and 1 Tbsp. minced fresh **rosemary**. Add 2 cups **cashews**; stir to combine. Spread on a parchment-lined baking sheet. Bake at 350° until fragrant and nuts start to brown, 8-10 minutes. Cool in pan on a wire rack.

OLD BAY MIXED NUTS

Stir together 2 Tbsp. **butter**, 2 tsp. **seafood seasoning** and **lemon zest**, and ½ tsp. **pepper sauce**. Add 2 cups **mixed nuts**; stir to combine. Spread on a parchment-lined baking sheet. Bake at 350° until fragrant and nuts start to brown, 12-15 minutes. Cool in pan on a wire rack.

MOJITO HAZELNUTS

Combine 3 Tbsp. **honey**, 4 tsp. **lime zest** and 1 tsp. **dried mint**. Add 2 cups **hazelnuts**; stir to combine. Spread on a parchment-lined baking sheet. Bake at 350° until fragrant and nuts start to brown, 8-10 minutes. Cool in pan on a wire rack.

SRIRACHA-MOLASSES PECANS

Stir together 3 Tbsp. **maple syrup** and 3 Tbsp. **Sriracha chili sauce**. Add 2 cups **pecan halves**; stir to combine. Spread on a parchment-lined baking sheet. Bake at 350° until fragrant and nuts start to brown, 8-10 minutes. Cool in pan on a wire rack.

FRUIT SALSA WITH CINNAMON CHIPS

I first made this fresh, fruity salsa for a family baby shower. Everyone wanted the recipe. Now, someone makes this juicy snack for just about every family gathering—and I have to keep reminding everyone who introduced it!
—Jessica Robinson, Indian Trail, NC

TAKES: 30 MIN. • **MAKES:** 20 SERVINGS (2½ CUPS SALSA, 80 CHIPS)

- 1 cup finely chopped fresh strawberries
- 1 medium navel orange, peeled and finely chopped
- 3 medium kiwifruit, peeled and finely chopped
- 1 can (8 oz.) unsweetened crushed pineapple, drained
- 1 Tbsp. lemon juice
- 1½ tsp. sugar

CINNAMON CHIPS

- 10 flour tortillas (8 in.)
- ¼ cup butter, melted
- ⅓ cup sugar
- 1 tsp. ground cinnamon

1. In a small bowl, combine the first 6 ingredients. Cover and refrigerate until serving.

2. For chips, brush tortillas with butter; cut each into 8 wedges. Combine sugar and cinnamon; sprinkle over wedges. Place on ungreased baking sheets.

3. Bake at 350° for 5-10 minutes or just until crisp. Serve with fruit salsa.

2 TBSP. SALSA WITH 4 CHIPS 134 cal., 4g fat (2g sat. fat), 6mg chol., 136mg sod., 22g carb. (7g sugars, 2g fiber), 2g pro.

ANTIPASTO KABOBS

My husband and I met at a cooking class. We have loved creating menus and entertaining ever since. These do-ahead appetizers are a favorite to serve.
—Denise Hazen, Cincinnati, OH

PREP: 35 MIN. + MARINATING • **MAKES:** 40 APPETIZERS

- 1 pkg. (9 oz.) refrigerated cheese tortellini
- 40 pimiento-stuffed olives
- 40 large pitted ripe olives
- ¾ cup Italian salad dressing
- 40 thin slices pepperoni
- 20 thin slices hard salami, halved

1. Cook tortellini according to package directions; drain and rinse in cold water. In a large bowl, combine the tortellini, olives and salad dressing. Toss to coat; cover and refrigerate for 4 hours or overnight.

2. Drain the mixture, discarding the marinade. For each appetizer, thread a stuffed olive, a folded pepperoni slice, a tortellini, a folded salami piece and a ripe olive on a toothpick or short skewer.

1 KABOB 66 cal., 5g fat (1g sat. fat), 9mg chol., 315mg sod., 4g carb. (0 sugars, 0 fiber), 2g pro.

EASY DEVILED EGGS

This recipe comes from the Durbin Inn, a well-known restaurant in Rushville, Indiana, from the 1920s until it closed in the late '70s. The eggs are delicious, and it's easy to make more for larger gatherings.
—*Margaret Sanders, Indianapolis, IN*

TAKES: 15 MIN. • **MAKES:** 1 DOZEN

- 6 hard-boiled large eggs
- 2 Tbsp. mayonnaise
- 1 tsp. sugar
- 1 tsp. white vinegar
- 1 tsp. prepared mustard
- ½ tsp. salt
- Optional: Paprika and minced chives

READER REVIEW

"Served these for people to graze on Easter afternoon, and they were gobbled up so quickly! Love this recipe. Not too sweet, lots of flavor."
—MOKOPILI, TASTEOFHOME.COM

Slice eggs in half lengthwise; remove yolks and set whites aside. In a small bowl, mash yolks with a fork. Add the mayonnaise, sugar, vinegar, mustard and salt; mix well. Stuff or pipe into egg whites. If desired, sprinkle with paprika and chives. Refrigerate until serving.

1 EGG HALF 55 cal., 4g fat (1g sat. fat), 94mg chol., 146mg sod., 1g carb. (1g sugars, 0 fiber), 3g pro.

BACON-CHEDDAR DEVILED EGGS To mashed yolks, add ¼ cup mayonnaise, 2 cooked and crumbled bacon strips, 1 Tbsp. finely shredded cheddar cheese, 1½ tsp. honey mustard and ⅛ tsp. pepper. Stuff as directed.

PICNIC STUFFED EGGS To mashed yolks, add ¼ cup mayonnaise, 2 Tbsp. drained sweet pickle relish, 1½ tsp. honey mustard, ½ tsp. garlic salt, ¼ tsp. Worcestershire sauce and ⅛ tsp. pepper. Stuff as directed.

SANTA FE DEVILED EGGS To mashed yolks, add 3 Tbsp. each mayonnaise and canned chopped green chiles, 1½ tsp. chipotle pepper in adobo sauce and ¼ tsp. garlic salt. Stuff as directed. Garnish each with 1 tsp. salsa and a sliver of ripe olive.

CRAB-STUFFED DEVILED EGGS Make 12 hard-boiled eggs. To mashed yolks, add 1 can (6 oz.) crabmeat (drained, flaked and cartilage removed), ⅔ cup mayonnaise, ½ cup finely chopped celery, ½ cup slivered almonds, 2 Tbsp. finely chopped green pepper and ½ tsp. salt. Stuff as directed.

PEPPER POPPERS

These creamy stuffed jalapenos have some bite. They may be the most popular treats I make! My husband is always hinting that I should make a batch.
—Lisa Byington, Johnson City, NY

PREP: 25 MIN. • **BAKE:** 15 MIN. • **MAKES:** ABOUT 2 DOZEN

- 1 pkg. (8 oz.) cream cheese, softened
- 1 cup shredded sharp cheddar cheese
- 1 cup shredded Monterey Jack cheese
- 6 bacon strips, cooked and crumbled
- ¼ tsp. salt
- ¼ tsp. garlic powder
- ¼ tsp. chili powder
- 1 lb. fresh jalapenos, halved lengthwise and seeded
- ½ cup dry bread crumbs
- Sour cream, onion dip or ranch salad dressing

CAN'T STAND THE HEAT?

Here are a few tricks to make your poppers less spicy.

- Start by inspecting them at the store. Some say that peppers with tiny little cracks in the skin may be spicier than those with smooth skins.
- Thoroughly remove the seeds and membranes, which contain most of the heat-producing capsaicin.
- Soak the prepped jalapenos in cold water for 15-20 minutes before draining and proceeding with the recipe.
- Serve your poppers with a cool, creamy ranch dressing or sour cream to reduce the heat's impact on the tongue.

1. Preheat oven to 325°. In a large bowl, combine the cream cheese, cheddar cheese, Monterey Jack cheese, bacon and seasonings; mix well. Spoon about 2 Tbsp. into each pepper half. Roll in the bread crumbs.

2. Place in a greased 15x10x1-in. baking pan. Bake, uncovered, until cheese is melted and peppers are heated through, 15-20 minutes. Serve with sour cream, dip or dressing.

FREEZE OPTION After rolling in bread crumbs, cover and freeze the unbaked stuffed peppers on waxed paper-lined baking sheets until firm. Transfer to a resealable freezer container; return to freezer. To use, bake peppers as directed, increasing time by 3-4 minutes.

NOTE Wear disposable gloves when cutting hot peppers; the oils can burn skin. Avoid touching your face.

1 POPPER 94 cal., 7g fat (4g sat. fat), 20mg chol., 167mg sod., 4g carb. (1g sugars, 1g fiber), 4g pro.

BACON CHEESEBURGER SLIDERS

I created this dish to fill two pans because these sliders disappear fast. Just cut the recipe in half if you want to make only one batch.
—Nick Iverson, Denver, CO

PREP: 20 MIN. • **BAKE:** 20 MIN. • **MAKES:** 2 DOZEN

- 2 pkg. (17 oz. each) Hawaiian sweet rolls
- 22 slices American or cheddar cheese, divided
- 2 lbs. ground beef
- 1 cup chopped onion
- 1 can (14½ oz.) diced tomatoes with garlic and onion, drained
- 1 Tbsp. Dijon mustard
- 1 Tbsp. Worcestershire sauce
- ¾ tsp. salt
- ¾ tsp. pepper
- 24 bacon strips, cooked and broken into 1-in. pieces

GLAZE

- 1 cup butter, cubed
- ¼ cup packed brown sugar
- 4 tsp. Worcestershire sauce
- 2 Tbsp. Dijon mustard
- 2 Tbsp. sesame seeds

CUSTOMIZE YOUR SLIDERS

• **Switch the meat:** If you'd prefer a lighter meat, swap the beef for ground chicken or turkey. Additionally, you can use mushrooms and black beans in place of the burger if you prefer a meatless option.

• **Add toppings:** Favorite slider toppings include pickles, banana peppers and green peppers. Sliced tomatoes are tasty too.

1. Preheat the oven to 350°. Without separating rolls, cut each package of rolls horizontally in half; arrange bottom halves in 2 greased 13x9-in. baking pans. In each pan, place 5 slices of cheese on bottom halves of rolls. Bake until cheese is melted, 3-5 minutes.

2. In a large skillet, cook beef and onion over medium heat until beef is no longer pink and onion is tender, 6-8 minutes breaking beef into crumbles; drain. Stir in tomatoes, mustard, Worcestershire sauce, salt and pepper. Cook and stir until combined, 1-2 minutes.

3. Spoon beef mixture evenly over rolls; top with bacon and remaining cheese. Replace tops.

4. For the glaze, in a microwave-safe bowl, combine the butter, brown sugar, Worcestershire sauce and mustard. Microwave, covered, on high until butter is melted, stirring occasionally. Drizzle or brush over rolls; sprinkle with sesame seeds. Bake, uncovered, until golden brown and heated through, 20-25 minutes.

1 SLIDER 380 cal., 24g fat (13g sat. fat), 86mg chol., 628mg sod., 21g carb. (9g sugars, 2g fiber), 18g pro.

HOMEMADE EGGNOG

After one sip, folks will know this smooth and creamy holiday staple is homemade, not a store-bought variety. If desired, add a half cup rum or brandy.

—Pat Waymire, Yellow Springs, OH

PREP: 15 MIN. • **COOK:** 30 MIN. + CHILLING • **MAKES:** 12 SERVINGS (3 QT.)

12 large eggs
1½ cups sugar
½ tsp. salt
8 cups whole milk, divided
2 Tbsp. vanilla extract
1 tsp. ground nutmeg
2 cups heavy whipping cream
Additional nutmeg, optional

1. In a heavy saucepan, whisk together eggs, sugar and salt. Gradually add 4 cups milk; cook and stir over low heat until a thermometer reads 160°-170°, 30-35 minutes. Do not allow to boil. Immediately transfer to a large bowl.

2. Stir in vanilla, nutmeg and remaining milk. Place bowl in an ice-water bath, stirring until milk mixture is cool. (If mixture separates, process in a blender until smooth.) Refrigerate, covered, until cold, at least 3 hours.

3. To serve, beat cream until soft peaks form. Whisk gently into cooled milk mixture. If desired, sprinkle with additional nutmeg before serving.

1 CUP 411 cal., 25g fat (14g sat. fat), 247mg chol., 251mg sod., 35g carb. (35g sugars, 0 fiber), 13g pro.

ROASTED CURRY CHICKPEAS

We coated chickpeas with simple seasonings to make a low-fat snacking sensation. It rivals the types sold in stores, with just a few ingredients.
—Taste of Home *Test Kitchen*

TAKES: 30 MIN. • **MAKES:** 1 CUP

- 1 can (15 oz.) chickpeas or garbanzo beans
- 2 Tbsp. olive oil
- 1 tsp. salt
- ¼ tsp. pepper
- 2 tsp. curry powder
- ½ tsp. crushed red pepper flakes

Preheat oven to 450°. Rinse and drain chickpeas. Place on paper towels and pat dry. Place in a greased 15x10x1-in. baking pan; drizzle with oil and sprinkle with seasonings. Toss to coat. Bake until crispy and golden brown, 25-30 minutes.

¼ CUP 162 cal., 9g fat (1g sat. fat), 0 chol., 728mg sod., 17g carb. (3g sugars, 5g fiber), 4g pro.

NOTES

BLUE-RIBBON BEEF NACHOS

Chili powder and sassy salsa season a zesty mixture of ground beef and refried beans that's sprinkled with green onion, tomatoes and olives.
—Diane Hixon, Niceville, FL

TAKES: 25 MIN. • **MAKES:** 6 SERVINGS

- 1 lb. ground beef
- 1 small onion, chopped
- 1 can (16 oz.) refried beans
- 1 jar (16 oz.) salsa
- 1 can (6 oz.) ripe olives, chopped
- ½ cup shredded cheddar cheese
- 1 green onion, chopped
- 2 Tbsp. chili powder
- 1 tsp. salt
- Tortilla chips
- Optional toppings: Sliced ripe olives, chopped green onions and diced tomatoes

In a large skillet, cook the beef and onion over medium heat until meat is no longer pink, breaking beef into crumbles; drain. Stir in next 7 ingredients; heat through. Serve over tortilla chips. Top with olives, onions and tomatoes if desired.

1 SERVING 294 cal., 14g fat (6g sat. fat), 53mg chol., 1353mg sod., 19g carb. (5g sugars, 9g fiber), 20g pro.

NACHO TIPS

How do you keep nachos from getting soggy? Add wet toppings such as salsa and sour cream just before serving, or serve them on the side. Use real shredded cheese instead of processed cheese sauce to keep the chips crisp.

What toppings work best on nachos? Try classic toppings such as guacamole, sour cream, and jalapenos. Swap ground beef for shredded chicken and use Monterey Jack instead of cheddar for a fresh twist.

What can I do with leftover nachos? Store toppings and beef separately in airtight containers and use within 2 days. Reheat assembled nachos in the oven to restore their crispiness.

WONTON RAVIOLI

I created this recipe as a quick yet elegant meal. But it also works well as an appetizer. You can substitute ingredients to your liking.
—Jenny Johnson, White Bear Lake, MN

PREP: 30 MIN. • **BAKE:** 10 MIN./BATCH • **MAKES:** 44 APPETIZERS

- 1 lb. ground beef
- ⅓ cup chopped onion
- ½ tsp. minced garlic
- ½ tsp. dried oregano
- ½ tsp. dried basil
- 88 wonton wrappers
- 2¾ cups shredded part-skim mozzarella cheese
- 2 Tbsp. butter, melted
- Grated Parmesan cheese, optional
- Spaghetti sauce, warmed

1. In a large skillet, cook the beef, onion and garlic over medium heat until meat is no longer pink, 5-7 minutes, breaking beef into crumbles; drain. Stir in oregano and basil.

2. Preheat oven to 350°. Place 8 wonton wrappers on a greased baking sheet; top each with 1 Tbsp. meat mixture and 1 Tbsp. mozzarella cheese. Moisten edges with water; top with another wonton wrapper. Press edges with a fork to seal. Repeat with remaining wrappers, meat mixture and cheese.

3. Brush wontons with butter. Sprinkle with Parmesan cheese if desired. Bake until golden brown, 10-12 minutes. Serve with spaghetti sauce.

1 PIECE 86 cal., 3g fat (1g sat. fat), 12mg chol., 135mg sod., 10g carb. (0 sugars, 0 fiber), 5g pro. **DIABETIC EXCHANGES** ½ starch, ½ lean meat.

NOTES

PEPPERONI PINWHEELS

These golden brown snacks have lots of pepperoni flavor. They're easy to make, and they taste so good!
—Vikki Rebholz, West Chester, OH

PREP: 20 MIN. • **BAKE:** 15 MIN. • **MAKES:** 2 DOZEN

- ½ cup diced pepperoni
- ½ cup shredded part-skim mozzarella cheese
- ¼ tsp. dried oregano
- 1 large egg, separated
- 1 tube (8 oz.) refrigerated crescent rolls

1. Preheat oven to 375°. In a small bowl, combine pepperoni, cheese, oregano and egg yolk. In another small bowl, whisk the egg white until foamy; set aside. Separate crescent dough into 4 rectangles; seal perforations.

2. Spread pepperoni mixture over each rectangle to within ¼ in. of edges. Roll up jelly-roll style, starting with a short side; pinch seams to seal. Cut each into 6 slices.

3. Place cut side down on greased baking sheets; brush tops with egg white. Bake until golden brown, 12-15 minutes. Serve warm. Refrigerate leftovers.

2 PIECES 122 cal., 8g fat (3g sat. fat), 26mg chol., 291mg sod., 8g carb. (2g sugars, 0 fiber), 4g pro.

MEXICAN SHRIMP COCKTAIL

It's up to you how to enjoy this cocktail—eat it with a spoon as a chilled appetizer, or use tortilla chips or crackers for scooping.
—Taste of Home *Test Kitchen*

PREP: 30 MIN. + CHILLING • **MAKES:** 8 SERVINGS

- 2 qt. water
- 1 medium white onion, sliced
- 6 garlic cloves, smashed
- 2¼ tsp. salt, divided
- 1 tsp. whole peppercorns
- 1 lb. uncooked shrimp (31-40 per lb.), peeled and deveined
- 2 medium tomatoes, seeded and finely chopped
- 1 small cucumber, seeded and chopped
- ½ cup finely chopped red onion
- 1 jalapeno pepper, seeded and finely chopped
- 1 cup Clamato juice, chilled
- ½ cup chopped fresh cilantro
- ¼ cup ketchup
- 2 Tbsp. lime juice
- 1 tsp. hot pepper sauce
- 1 medium ripe avocado, cubed

1. In a large saucepan, combine the water, onion slices, garlic, 2 tsp. salt and peppercorns. Bring to a boil. Add shrimp. Cook until the shrimp just turn pink, 2-3 minutes. Drain; immediately drop shrimp into bowl of ice water. Discard the onion, garlic and peppercorns. Drain shrimp.

2. In a large bowl, combine the shrimp, tomatoes, cucumber, red onion and jalapeno. In another bowl, whisk the Clamato, cilantro, ketchup, lime juice, hot pepper sauce and remaining ¼ tsp. salt; pour over shrimp mixture. Stir to coat. Gently stir in avocado.

NOTE Wear disposable gloves when cutting hot peppers; the oils can burn skin. Avoid touching your face.

¾ CUP 105 cal., 4g fat (1g sat. fat), 69mg chol., 413mg sod., 8g carb. (5g sugars, 2g fiber), 10g pro.

SWEET-SOUR CHICKEN DIPPERS

Since you can chop up all the ingredients the night before, this can be ready in about 30 minutes. So it's a great appetizer for parties.
—Kari Kelley, Plains, MT

PREP: 40 MIN. • **COOK:** 10 MIN. • **MAKES:** 4 DOZEN APPETIZERS

- 1 can (8 oz.) crushed pineapple
- 1½ cups sugar
- 1 can (14½ oz.) diced tomatoes, undrained
- ½ cup white vinegar
- ½ cup chopped onion
- ½ cup chopped green pepper
- 1 Tbsp. soy sauce
- ¼ tsp. ground ginger
- 1 Tbsp. cornstarch

CHICKEN

- 1 cup all-purpose flour
- 1 cup cornstarch
- 2 tsp. baking powder
- 2 tsp. baking soda
- 2 tsp. sugar
- 1⅓ cups cold water
- Oil for deep-fat frying
- 1½ lbs. boneless skinless chicken breasts, cut into chunks

1. Drain pineapple, reserving juice. In a large saucepan, combine the sugar, tomatoes, vinegar, onion, green pepper, soy sauce, ginger and pineapple. Simmer for 20 minutes.

2. Meanwhile, in a small bowl, combine cornstarch and the reserved pineapple juice until smooth; add to the tomato mixture. Bring to a boil; cook and stir 2 minutes or until thickened. Remove from the heat; set aside.

3. For batter, in a small bowl, combine the flour, cornstarch, baking powder, baking soda, sugar and water until smooth.

4. In a deep-fat fryer, heat the oil to 375°. Dip chicken pieces in batter; drop into oil and fry 3-5 minutes on each side or until golden brown and juices run clear. Serve immediately with sweet-sour sauce.

1 PIECE WITH 4 TSP. SAUCE 79 cal., 2g fat (0 sat. fat), 8mg chol., 113mg sod., 12g carb. (8g sugars, 0 fiber), 3g pro.

CHICKEN DIPPER TIPS

How do you ensure chicken nuggets fry evenly? Cut chicken into uniform pieces and heat oil to 375° before frying. Work in small batches, allowing the oil to return to temperature between rounds for crisp, even cooking.

How do you store and reheat fried sweet and sour chicken? Cool completely before storing in an airtight container for up to 2 days. Reheat on a wire rack over a baking sheet at 400° for 10 minutes to restore crispiness.

What are good appetizers to serve with sweet and sour chicken? You can pair the nuggets with crispy egg rolls, crab rangoon or a light cucumber salad to create a well-rounded spread.

how to cook ... SOUPS & STEWS

CHEESEBURGER SOUP, PAGE 87

QUICK POTATO CORN CHOWDER

This can be a meal in itself if you want! It works in every season, so enjoy it year-round.
—Lucia Johnson, Massena, NY

TAKES: 30 MIN. • **MAKES:** 8 SERVINGS (2 QT.)

- 1 medium onion, chopped
- 1 Tbsp. olive oil
- 2 cans (14½ oz. each) chicken broth
- 3 large Yukon Gold potatoes, peeled and cubed
- 1 can (15¼ oz.) whole kernel corn, drained
- 1 cup 2% milk, divided
- ½ tsp. salt
- ½ tsp. pepper
- ⅓ cup all-purpose flour
- Minced fresh parsley, optional

1. In a large saucepan, cook and stir onion in oil over medium heat until tender. Add broth and potatoes; bring to a boil. Reduce the heat; cover and simmer for 10-15 minutes or until potatoes are tender.

2. Stir in corn, ½ cup milk, salt and pepper. In a small bowl, whisk flour and remaining milk until smooth. Stir into soup; return to a boil. Cook and stir for 2-3 minutes or until thickened. Sprinkle with parsley if desired.

1 CUP 176 cal., 3g fat (1g sat. fat), 5mg chol., 759mg sod., 31g carb. (7g sugars, 3g fiber), 5g pro.

APPLE CIDER BEEF STEW

We start craving this comforting stew as soon as the weather gets crisp and Nebraska's apple orchards start selling fresh cider. Its subtle sweetness is a welcome change from other stews. We enjoy it with biscuits, sliced apples and cheddar cheese.

—Joyce Glaesemann, Lincoln, NE

PREP: 30 MIN. • **COOK:** 1¾ HOURS • **MAKES:** 8 SERVINGS

- 2 lbs. beef stew meat, cut into 1-in. cubes
- 2 Tbsp. canola oil
- 3 cups apple cider or juice
- 1 can (14½ oz.) reduced-sodium beef broth
- 2 Tbsp. cider vinegar
- 1½ tsp. salt
- ¼ to ½ tsp. dried thyme
- ¼ tsp. pepper
- 3 medium potatoes, peeled and cubed
- 4 medium carrots, cut into ¾-in. pieces
- 3 celery ribs, cut into ¾-in. pieces
- 2 medium onions, cut into wedges
- ¼ cup all-purpose flour
- ¼ cup water
- Fresh thyme sprigs, optional

1. In a Dutch oven, brown beef on all sides in oil over medium-high heat; drain. Add cider, broth, vinegar, salt, thyme and pepper; bring to a boil. Reduce heat; cover and simmer for 1¼ hours.

2. Add potatoes, carrots, celery and onions; return to a boil. Reduce heat; cover and simmer for 30-35 minutes or until beef and vegetables are tender.

3. Combine flour and water until smooth; stir into stew. Bring to a boil; cook and stir for 2 minutes or until thickened. If desired, serve with fresh thyme.

1 CUP 330 cal., 12g fat (3g sat. fat), 72mg chol., 628mg sod., 31g carb. (14g sugars, 2g fiber), 24g pro. **DIABETIC EXCHANGES** 3 lean meat, 1½ starch, 1 vegetable.

EASY SHRIMP RAMEN

You probably already have many of the ingredients for this shrimp ramen in your pantry. This 30-minute garlic and ginger dish makes for a great weeknight dinner.
—Taste of Home *Test Kitchen*

TAKES: 30 MIN. • **MAKES:** 4 SERVINGS

- 2 Tbsp. canola oil
- ½ lb. sliced baby portobello mushrooms
- 1 large carrot, shredded
- 4 garlic cloves, minced
- 2 tsp. minced fresh gingerroot
- 1 carton (32 oz.) chicken broth
- 1 Tbsp. soy sauce
- 2 tsp. sesame oil
- 1 lb. uncooked shrimp (31-40 per lb.), peeled and deveined
- 2 pkg. (3 oz. each) ramen noodles (any flavor)
- 4 green onions, chopped
- Chopped fresh cilantro, optional

1. In a large saucepan, heat oil over medium heat. Add mushrooms and carrot; cook and stir for 6-8 minutes or until mushrooms are tender. Stir in garlic and ginger; cook 1 minute longer.

2. Stir in broth, soy sauce and sesame oil. Bring to a boil. Add shrimp and ramen (discard seasoning packets or save for another use). Simmer until shrimp turn pink and the noodles are tender, 4-6 minutes. Garnish with green onions and, if desired, cilantro.

1½ CUPS 413 cal., 19g fat (5g sat. fat), 138mg chol., 1394mg sod., 34g carb. (3g sugars, 2g fiber), 26g pro.

READER REVIEW

"I found this recipe quick and easy to make—and satisfying and delicious too! I didn't use mushrooms because I didn't have any. Instead, I used diced red pepper and edamame. My whole family enjoyed the flavors ... almost like eating at our local Chinese buffet! I give this 5 stars for sure!"

—BICKTASW, TASTEOFHOME.COM

GRANDMA'S CHICKEN & DUMPLING SOUP

I've enjoyed making this rich soup for over 40 years. Every time I serve it, I remember my grandma, who was very special to me and known as a terrific cook.
—Paulette Balda, Prophetstown, IL

PREP: 20 MIN. + COOLING • **COOK:** 2¼ HOURS • **MAKES:** 12 SERVINGS (3 QT.)

- 1 broiler/fryer chicken (3½ to 4 lbs.), cut up
- 2¼ qt. cold water
- 5 chicken bouillon cubes
- 6 whole peppercorns
- 3 whole cloves
- 1 can (10½ oz.) condensed cream of chicken soup, undiluted
- 1 can (10½ oz.) condensed cream of mushroom soup, undiluted
- 1½ cups chopped carrots
- 1 cup fresh or frozen peas
- 1 cup chopped celery
- 1 cup chopped peeled potatoes
- ¼ cup chopped onion
- 1½ tsp. seasoned salt
- ¼ tsp. pepper
- 1 bay leaf

DUMPLINGS

- 2 cups all-purpose flour
- 4 tsp. baking powder
- 1 tsp. salt
- ¼ tsp. pepper
- 1 large egg, beaten
- 2 Tbsp. butter, melted
- ¾ to 1 cup 2% milk
- Snipped fresh parsley, optional

1. Place the chicken, water, bouillon, peppercorns and cloves in a stockpot. Cover and bring to a boil; skim foam. Reduce heat; simmer, covered, until the chicken is tender, 45-60 minutes. Strain broth; return to stockpot.

2. Remove chicken and set aside until cool enough to handle. Remove meat from bones; discard bones and skin. Cut chicken into chunks. Cool broth; skim off fat.

3. Return chicken to the stockpot with soups, vegetables and seasonings; bring to a boil. Reduce heat; cover and simmer for 1 hour. Uncover; increase heat to a gentle boil. Discard bay leaf.

4. For dumplings, combine the dry ingredients in a medium bowl. Stir in egg, butter and enough milk to make a moist stiff batter. Drop by teaspoonfuls into soup. Cover and cook without lifting lid, 18-20 minutes. If desired, sprinkle with parsley.

1 CUP 333 cal., 14g fat (5g sat. fat), 79mg chol., 1447mg sod., 28g carb. (4g sugars, 3g fiber), 22g pro.

FRENCH ONION SOUP

I've also made this savory soup in a slow cooker for a fuss-free meal. It cooks on low for 3-4 hours.
—Denise Hruz, Germantown, WI

TAKES: 30 MIN. • **MAKES:** 9 SERVINGS (2¼ QT.)

- ¼ cup butter, cubed
- 4 large onions, sliced
- ¼ cup sugar
- 2 Tbsp. all-purpose flour
- 2 cans (14½ oz. each) reduced-sodium beef broth
- 2 cans (10½ oz. each) condensed French onion soup
- 2 cups water
- ½ cup grated Parmesan cheese
- 9 slices French bread (½ in. thick)
- 9 Tbsp. shredded part-skim mozzarella cheese
- Chopped fresh thyme, optional

1. In a Dutch oven over medium-high heat, melt butter. Add onions; saute until tender. Add sugar; cook and stir until lightly browned. Stir in flour until blended; gradually add broth, soup and water. Bring to a boil. Reduce the heat; cover and simmer for 10 minutes. Stir in Parmesan cheese.

2. Meanwhile, place bread on a baking sheet. Broil 4 in. from heat until toasted, about 2 minutes on each side. Sprinkle with mozzarella; broil until cheese is melted, about 2 minutes. Ladle soup into bowls; top each serving with a cheese toast. If desired, top with fresh thyme.

1 CUP WITH 1 CHEESE TOAST 192 cal., 9g fat (5g sat. fat), 26mg chol., 875mg sod., 22g carb. (11g sugars, 2g fiber), 7g pro.

CONTEST-WINNING ROASTED TOMATO SOUP

Just before the first frost of the season, we gather up all of the tomatoes from my mom's garden to create this flavorful soup. Although it sounds like a lot of garlic, when it's roasted, the garlic becomes mellow and almost sweet. We serve this soup with toasted bread spread with pesto.
—Kaitlyn Lerdahl, Madison, WI

PREP: 25 MIN. • **COOK:** 40 MIN. • **MAKES:** 6 SERVINGS

- 15 large tomatoes (5 lbs.), seeded and quartered
- ¼ cup plus 2 Tbsp. canola oil, divided
- 8 garlic cloves, minced
- 1 large onion, chopped
- 2 cups water
- 1 tsp. salt
- ½ tsp. crushed red pepper flakes, optional
- ½ cup heavy whipping cream
- Fresh basil leaves, optional

1. Preheat oven to 400°. Place tomatoes in a greased 15x10x1-in. baking pan. Combine ¼ cup oil and garlic; drizzle over tomatoes. Toss to coat. Bake for 15-20 minutes or until softened, stirring occasionally. Remove and discard skins.

2. Meanwhile, in a Dutch oven, saute onion in remaining 2 Tbsp. oil until tender. Add tomatoes, water, salt and, if desired, pepper flakes. Bring to a boil. Reduce heat; cover and simmer until flavors are blended, about 30 minutes. Cool slightly.

3. In a blender, process soup in batches until smooth. Return to pan. Stir in cream and heat through. Sprinkle with basil if desired.

FREEZE OPTION Cool soup and transfer to freezer containers. Freeze for up to 3 months. To use, thaw in the refrigerator overnight. Place in a large saucepan; heat through. Garnish with basil if desired.

1 CUP 276 cal., 22g fat (6g sat. fat), 27mg chol., 421mg sod., 19g carb. (11g sugars, 5g fiber), 4g pro.

NOTES

CHEESY HAM CHOWDER

My five children all agree that this soothing recipe is wonderful. The soup is full of potatoes, carrots and ham. The best part is that I can get it on the table in only a half hour of hands-on time.
—Jennifer Trenhaile, Emerson, NE

PREP: 30 MIN. • **COOK:** 30 MIN. • **MAKES:** 10 SERVINGS (2½ QT.)

- 10 bacon strips, diced
- 1 large onion, chopped
- 1 cup diced carrots
- 3 Tbsp. all-purpose flour
- 3 cups whole milk
- 1½ cups water
- 2½ cups cubed potatoes
- 1 can (15¼ oz.) whole kernel corn, drained
- 2 tsp. chicken bouillon granules
- Pepper to taste
- 3 cups shredded cheddar cheese
- 2 cups cubed fully cooked ham
- Minced fresh parsley, optional

1. In a Dutch oven, cook the bacon over medium heat until crisp. Using a slotted spoon, remove to paper towels to drain. In drippings, saute onion and carrots until tender. Stir in flour until blended. Gradually add milk and water. Bring to a boil; cook and stir for 2 minutes or until thickened.

2. Add the potatoes, corn, bouillon and pepper. Reduce heat; simmer, uncovered, 20 minutes or until potatoes are tender. Add cheese and ham; heat until cheese is melted. Stir in bacon. If desired, garnish with parsley and additional bacon.

1 CUP 404 cal., 26g fat (12g sat. fat), 76mg chol., 1081mg sod., 20g carb. (8g sugars, 3g fiber), 22g pro.

LOUISIANA GUMBO

Gumbo is a stew-like dish made with meat or seafood, tomatoes, bell peppers and okra. You can serve it with hot pepper sauce on the side so guests can add their own heat.
—Gloria Mason, Springhill, LA

PREP: 20 MIN. • **COOK:** 1¾ HOURS + COOLING • **MAKES:** 12 SERVINGS (3 QT.)

- 1 broiler/fryer chicken (3 to 3½ lbs.), cut up
- 2 qt. water
- ¾ cup all-purpose flour
- ½ cup canola oil
- ½ cup sliced green onions
- ½ cup chopped onion
- ½ cup chopped green pepper
- ½ cup chopped sweet red pepper
- ½ cup chopped celery
- 2 garlic cloves, minced
- ½ lb. smoked sausage, cut into 1-in. cubes
- ½ lb. fully cooked ham, cut into ¾-in. cubes
- ½ lb. fresh or frozen uncooked shrimp, peeled and deveined
- 1 cup fresh or frozen sliced okra
- 1 can (16 oz.) kidney beans, rinsed and drained
- ½ tsp. salt
- ¼ tsp. pepper
- ¼ tsp. hot pepper sauce
- Sliced green onions, optional

1. Place chicken and water in a Dutch oven; bring to a boil. Reduce heat; cover and simmer for 30-45 minutes or until chicken is tender.

2. Remove chicken; cool. Reserve 6 cups broth. Remove chicken from bones; cut into bite-sized pieces.

3. In a Dutch oven or soup kettle, mix flour and oil until smooth; cook and stir over medium-low heat for 2-3 minutes or until browned. Stir in onions, peppers, celery and garlic; cook for 5 minutes or until vegetables are tender. Stir in the sausage, ham and reserved broth and chicken. Cover; simmer for 45 minutes.

4. Add shrimp, okra, beans, salt, pepper and hot pepper sauce; cover and simmer for 2-4 minutes or until shrimp turn pink. If desired, serve with green onions and additional hot pepper sauce.

1 CUP 397 cal., 24g fat (5g sat. fat), 97mg chol., 643mg sod., 15g carb. (2g sugars, 3g fiber), 30g pro.

PERFECT GUMBO CONSISTENCY

This gumbo is thickened with a roux—equal parts of fat and flour. If you desire a thicker consistency, whisk in a little more roux. If you use fresh sliced okra, it will also help thicken the gumbo. Alternatively, mix 1-2 Tbsp. cornstarch with a few Tbsp. of cold water, stir it in, and boil for 1-2 minutes. Many people enjoy serving their gumbo over hot, cooked rice—this creates a hearty texture too.

VEGETARIAN SPLIT PEA SOUP

Even the pickiest pea soup lover will request this version time and again. It's thick and well seasoned, and packs a nutritional punch with plenty of fiber and protein. It's wonderful when served with a slice of crusty French bread.
—Michele Doucette, Stephenville, NL

PREP: 15 MIN. • **COOK:** 1½ HOURS • **MAKES:** 7 SERVINGS

- 6 cups vegetable broth
- 2 cups dried green split peas, rinsed
- 1 medium onion, chopped
- 1 cup chopped carrots
- 2 celery ribs with leaves, chopped
- 2 garlic cloves, minced
- ½ tsp. dried marjoram
- ½ tsp. dried basil
- ¼ tsp. ground cumin
- ½ tsp. salt
- ¼ tsp. pepper
- Optional: Shredded carrots and sliced green onions

1. In a large saucepan, combine first 9 ingredients; bring to a boil. Reduce heat; cover and simmer until peas are tender, about 1 hour, stirring occasionally.

2. Add salt and pepper; cook 10 minutes longer. Remove soup from the heat; cool slightly. Process in batches in a blender or food processor until smooth; return to pan and heat through. If desired, garnish with carrots and green onions.

1 CUP 227 cal., 1g fat (0 sat. fat), 0 chol., 771mg sod., 42g carb. (7g sugars, 15g fiber), 14g pro.

NOTES

PASTA E FAGIOLI

My husband enjoys my version of this soup so much that he stopped ordering it at restaurants. He'd rather savor this homemade soup. It's so easy to make, yet hearty enough to be a full dinner.
—Brenda Thomas, Springfield, MO

TAKES: 30 MIN. • **MAKES:** 5 SERVINGS

- ½ lb. Italian turkey sausage links, casings removed, crumbled
- 1 small onion, chopped
- 1½ tsp. canola oil
- 1 garlic clove, minced
- 2 cups water
- 1 can (15½ oz.) great northern beans, rinsed and drained
- 1 can (14½ oz.) diced tomatoes, undrained
- 1 can (14½ oz.) reduced-sodium chicken broth
- ¾ cup uncooked elbow macaroni
- ¼ tsp. pepper
- 1 cup fresh spinach leaves, cut as desired
- 5 tsp. shredded Parmesan cheese

1. In a large saucepan, cook sausage over medium heat until no longer pink; drain, remove from pan and set aside. In the same pan, saute onion in oil until tender. Add garlic; saute 1 minute longer.

2. Add water, beans, tomatoes, broth, macaroni and pepper; bring to a boil. Cook, uncovered, 8-10 minutes or until macaroni is tender.

3. Reduce heat to low; stir in sausage and spinach. Cook until spinach is wilted, 2-3 minutes. Garnish with cheese.

1⅓ CUPS 228 cal., 7g fat (1g sat. fat), 29mg chol., 841mg sod., 27g carb. (4g sugars, 6g fiber), 16g pro. **DIABETIC EXCHANGES** 1½ starch, 1 vegetable, 1 lean meat, ½ fat.

YANKEE BEAN SOUP

Bacon, molasses and onion add great flavor to my special bean soup. A friend from Massachusetts gave me the recipe years ago, and I've made it countless times since then.
—Ann Nace, Perkasie, PA

PREP: 30 MIN. + STANDING • **COOK:** 1¾ HOURS • **MAKES:** 6 SERVINGS

- 1½ cups dried navy beans
- ½ lb. sliced bacon, diced
- ¾ cup chopped onion
- ½ cup chopped carrot
- ⅓ cup chopped celery leaves
- 4 cups water
- 2 cups milk
- 2 tsp. molasses
- 1½ tsp. salt

1. Place beans in a Dutch oven; add water to cover by 2 in. Bring to a boil; boil for 2 minutes. Remove from the heat; cover and let stand for 1 hour.

2. Drain and rinse beans, discarding the liquid. Set beans aside. In the same pan, cook bacon over medium heat until crisp. Using a slotted spoon, remove bacon to paper towels; drain, reserving 2 Tbsp. drippings.

3. In drippings, saute onion until tender. Stir in carrot and celery leaves. Return beans to pan. Add water. Bring to a boil. Reduce heat; cover and simmer until beans are tender, 1¾-2 hours.

4. Stir in the milk, molasses, salt and bacon. Remove about 2½ cups of soup; cool slightly. Place in a blender or food processor; cover and process until pureed. Return to pan; heat through.

1 CUP 315 cal., 10g fat (4g sat. fat), 22mg chol., 847mg sod., 40g carb. (10g sugars, 13g fiber), 18g pro.

CHICKEN POTPIE SOUP

My grandmother handwrote a cookbook; she created this amazing pie crust, and I added the delicious soup for it.
—*Karen LeMay, Seabrook, TX*

PREP: 20 MIN. + CHILLING • **COOK:** 20 MIN. • **MAKES:** 6 SERVINGS. (2¼ QT.)

- 2 cups all-purpose flour
- 1¼ tsp. salt
- ⅔ cup shortening
- 5 to 6 Tbsp. 2% milk

SOUP

- 2 Tbsp. butter
- 1 cup cubed peeled potatoes
- 1 cup chopped sweet onion
- 2 celery ribs, chopped
- 2 medium carrots, chopped
- ½ cup all-purpose flour
- ½ tsp. salt
- ¼ tsp. pepper
- 3 cans (14½ oz. each) chicken broth
- 2 cups shredded cooked chicken
- 1 cup frozen petite peas
- 1 cup frozen corn

1. In a large bowl, mix flour and salt; cut in shortening until crumbly. Gradually add milk, tossing with a fork until dough holds together when pressed. Shape into a disk; refrigerate, covered, 30 minutes or overnight.

2. Preheat the oven to 425°. On a lightly floured surface, roll the dough to ⅛-in. thickness. Using a floured 2½-in heart-shaped or round cutter, cut 18 shapes. Place 1 in. apart on ungreased baking sheets. Bake for 8-11 minutes or until golden brown. Cool on a wire rack.

3. For soup, heat butter in a Dutch oven over medium-high heat. Add potatoes, onion, celery and carrots; cook and stir for 5-7 minutes or until onion is tender.

4. Stir in the flour, salt and pepper until blended; gradually whisk in chicken broth. Bring to a boil over medium-high heat, stirring occasionally. Reduce heat; simmer, uncovered, 8-10 minutes or until potatoes are tender. Stir in remaining ingredients; heat through. Serve with pie crust toppers.

1½ CUPS SOUP WITH 3 TOPPERS 614 cal., 30g fat (9g sat. fat), 57mg chol., 1706mg sod., 60g carb. (7g sugars, 5g fiber), 23g pro.

SLOW-COOKED CHILI

This hearty chili can cook for up to 10 hours on low in the slow cooker. It's so good to come home to its wonderful aroma after a long day away.
—Sue Call, Beech Grove, IN

PREP: 20 MIN. • **COOK:** 8 HOURS • **MAKES:** 10 SERVINGS (2½ QT.)

- 2 lbs. lean ground beef (90% lean)
- 2 cans (16 oz. each) kidney beans, rinsed and drained
- 2 cans (14½ oz. each) diced tomatoes, undrained
- 1 can (8 oz.) tomato sauce
- 2 medium onions, chopped
- 1 medium green pepper, chopped
- 2 garlic cloves, minced
- 2 Tbsp. chili powder
- 1 tsp. salt
- 1 tsp. pepper
- Optional: Shredded cheddar cheese, sliced green onions, chopped red onion, sliced jalapeno peppers and sour cream

1. In a large skillet, cook the beef over medium heat for 10-12 minutes or until no longer pink, breaking into crumbles; drain.

2. Transfer to a 5-qt. slow cooker. Add next 9 ingredients. Cover and cook on low for 8-10 hours. Serve with toppings as desired.

1 CUP 260 cal., 8g fat (3g sat. fat), 57mg chol., 712mg sod., 23g carb. (6g sugars, 7g fiber), 25g pro. **DIABETIC EXCHANGES** 3 lean meat, 1½ starch, 1 vegetable.

READER REVIEW

"I added a can of mild Rotel tomatoes with green chiles, and it was fantastic! We also topped each serving with sour cream. Delicious!"

—MEG, TASTEOFHOME.COM

CIOPPINO

If you're looking for a great seafood recipe for your slow cooker, this classic fish stew is just the ticket. It's brimming with clams, crab, fish and shrimp, and it is fancy enough to be an elegant meal.
—Lisa Moriarty, Wilton, NH

PREP: 20 MIN. • **COOK:** 4 HOURS 20 MIN. • **MAKES:** 8 SERVINGS (2½ QT.)

- 1 can (28 oz.) diced tomatoes, undrained
- 2 medium onions, chopped
- 3 celery ribs, chopped
- 1 bottle (8 oz.) clam juice
- 1 can (6 oz.) tomato paste
- ½ cup white wine or ½ cup vegetable broth
- 5 garlic cloves, minced
- 1 Tbsp. red wine vinegar
- 1 Tbsp. olive oil
- 1 to 2 tsp. Italian seasoning
- 1 bay leaf
- ½ tsp. sugar
- 1 lb. haddock fillets, cut into 1-in. pieces
- 1 lb. uncooked shrimp (41-50 per lb.), peeled and deveined
- 1 can (6 oz.) chopped clams, undrained
- 1 can (6 oz.) lump crabmeat, drained
- 2 Tbsp. minced fresh parsley

1. In a 4- or 5-qt. slow cooker, combine first 12 ingredients. Cook, covered, on low for 4-5 hours.

2. Stir in seafood. Cook, covered, until fish just begin to flake easily with a fork and shrimp turn pink, 20-30 minutes longer.

3. Remove bay leaf. Stir in parsley.

1¼ CUPS 205 cal., 3g fat (1g sat. fat), 125mg chol., 483mg sod., 15g carb. (8g sugars, 3g fiber), 29g pro. **DIABETIC EXCHANGES** 3 lean meat, 2 vegetable.

CUSTOMIZE IT!

This recipe is flexible—adjust it to your taste, budget and time. For a little more heat, add red pepper flakes or hot sauce. Instead of haddock, use cod, tilapia or another firm white fish. Boost the seafood with lobster, scallops, mussels or even octopus. When tomatoes are at their best, toss in diced ripe plum tomatoes. And for more flavor depth, add diced carrots, sliced fennel or a splash of dry vermouth or red wine—these are classic pairings with seafood and tomatoes.

CREAMY WHITE CHILI

I got this recipe from my sister-in-law, who made a big batch and served a crowd one night. It was a hit. Plus, it's quick and easy to make, which is helpful since I'm a college student. In all my years of cooking in 4-H, I've never had another dish get so many compliments.
—Laura Brewer, Lafayette, IN

PREP: 10 MIN. • **COOK:** 40 MIN. • **MAKES:** 7 SERVINGS

- 1 lb. boneless skinless chicken breasts, cut into ½-in. cubes
- 1 medium onion, chopped
- 1½ tsp. garlic powder
- 1 Tbsp. canola oil
- 2 cans (15½ oz. each) great northern beans, rinsed and drained
- 1 can (14½ oz.) chicken broth
- 2 cans (4 oz. each) chopped green chiles
- 1 tsp. salt
- 1 tsp. ground cumin
- 1 tsp. dried oregano
- ½ tsp. pepper
- ¼ tsp. cayenne pepper
- 1 cup sour cream
- ½ cup heavy whipping cream
- Optional: Tortilla chips, shredded cheddar cheese and sliced seeded jalapeno pepper

1. In a large saucepan, saute chicken, onion and garlic powder in oil until chicken is no longer pink. Add beans, broth, green chiles and seasonings. Bring to a boil. Reduce heat; simmer, uncovered, 30 minutes.

2. Remove from heat; stir in sour cream and heavy cream. If desired, top with tortilla chips, cheese and jalapenos.

1 CUP 334 cal., 16g fat (8g sat. fat), 81mg chol., 1045mg sod., 24g carb. (3g sugars, 7g fiber), 22g pro.

UPSTATE MINESTRONE

If you love vegetables, you'll find this minestrone especially satisfying. Keep the recipe in mind when you have a bounty of fresh garden produce.

—Yvonne Krantz, Mount Upton, NY

PREP: 25 MIN. • **COOK:** 1½ HOURS • **MAKES:** 8 SERVINGS

- 1 lb. Italian sausage links, cut into ½-in. slices
- 1 Tbsp. olive oil
- 1 cup finely chopped onion
- 1 cup sliced fresh carrots
- 1 garlic clove, finely minced
- 1 tsp. dried basil
- 2 cups shredded cabbage
- 2 small zucchini, sliced
- 2 cans (10½ oz. each) condensed beef broth, undiluted or 3 beef bouillon cubes plus 1½ cups water
- 1 can (14½ oz.) diced tomatoes, undrained
- ¼ tsp. salt
- ¼ tsp. pepper
- 1 can (15½ oz.) great northern beans, rinsed and drained
- Minced fresh parsley

1. In a Dutch oven, brown sausage in oil. Add onion, carrots, garlic and basil; cook for 5 minutes. Stir in cabbage, zucchini, broth, tomatoes, salt and pepper.

2. Bring to a boil. Reduce heat; cover and simmer for 1 hour. Add beans; cook for 20 minutes longer. Garnish with parsley.

FREEZE OPTION Freeze cooled soup in freezer containers. To use, partially thaw in refrigerator overnight. Heat through in a saucepan, stirring occasionally; add broth or water if necessary.

1 SERVING 236 cal., 14g fat (4g sat. fat), 31mg chol., 1329mg sod., 16g carb. (4g sugars, 5g fiber), 12g pro.

NOTES

CHEESEBURGER SOUP

A local restaurant serves a similar soup but wouldn't share its recipe with me. I developed my own, modifying a recipe I already had for potato soup. I was really pleased with the way this all-American dish turned out.
—Joanie Shawhan, Madison, WI

PREP: 30 MIN. • **COOK:** 25 MIN. • **MAKES:** 8 SERVINGS (2 QT.)

- ½ lb. ground beef
- 4 Tbsp. butter, divided
- ¾ cup chopped onion
- ¾ cup shredded carrots
- ¾ cup diced celery
- 1 tsp. dried basil
- 1 tsp. dried parsley flakes
- 1¾ lbs. (about 4 cups) cubed peeled potatoes
- 3 cups chicken broth
- ¼ cup all-purpose flour
- 8 to 16 oz. Velveeta, cubed
- 1½ cups whole milk
- ¾ tsp. salt
- ¼ to ½ tsp. pepper
- ¼ cup sour cream
- Optional: Onion rings and thinly sliced green onions

1. In a large saucepan over medium heat, cook and crumble beef until no longer pink, 6-8 minutes; drain and remove from pan. In same saucepan, melt 1 Tbsp. butter over medium heat. Saute onion, carrots, celery, basil and parsley until vegetables are tender, about 10 minutes. Add potatoes, broth and ground beef; bring to a boil. Reduce heat; simmer, covered, 10-12 minutes or until potatoes are tender.

2. Meanwhile, in a small skillet, melt the remaining 3 Tbsp. butter. Add flour; cook and stir until bubbly, 3-5 minutes. Add to soup; bring to a boil. Cook and stir for 2 minutes. Reduce heat to low. Stir in cheese, milk, salt and pepper; cook until cheese melts. Remove from heat; blend in sour cream. If desired, serve with onion rings and green onions.

1 CUP 354 cal., 20g fat (11g sat. fat), 70mg chol., 1012mg sod., 31g carb. (7g sugars, 3g fiber), 14g pro.

READER REVIEW

"One of the best soups I've ever tasted! It's absolutely delicious, and everyone loves it. I wish I had cooked some bacon for topping to go with green onions and sour cream. Next time I will."

—FLOYDPATSY, TASTEOFHOME.COM

RUSTIC ITALIAN TORTELLINI SOUP

This is my favorite soup recipe. It's quick to fix on a busy night and full of healthy, tasty ingredients. It originally called for spicy sausage links, but I've found that turkey sausage or even ground turkey breast works just as well.
—Tracy Fasnacht, Irwin, PA

PREP: 20 MIN. • **COOK:** 20 MIN. • **MAKES:** 6 SERVINGS (2 QT.)

- 3/4 lb. Italian turkey sausage links, casings removed
- 1 medium onion, chopped
- 6 garlic cloves, minced
- 2 cans (14 1/2 oz. each) reduced-sodium chicken broth
- 1 3/4 cups water
- 1 can (14 1/2 oz.) diced tomatoes, undrained
- 1 pkg. (9 oz.) refrigerated cheese tortellini
- 1 pkg. (6 oz.) fresh baby spinach, coarsely chopped
- 2 1/4 tsp. minced fresh basil or 3/4 tsp. dried basil
- 1/4 tsp. pepper
- Dash crushed red pepper flakes
- Shredded Parmesan cheese, optional

1. Crumble sausage into a Dutch oven; add onion. Cook and stir over medium heat until meat is no longer pink. Add garlic; cook 1 minute longer. Stir in broth, water and tomatoes. Bring to a boil.

2. Add tortellini; return to a boil. Cook for 5-8 minutes or until almost tender, stirring occasionally. Reduce heat; add spinach, basil, pepper and pepper flakes. Cook 2-3 minutes longer or until spinach is wilted and tortellini are tender. Serve with cheese if desired.

FREEZE OPTION Place individual portions of cooled soup in freezer containers and freeze. To use, partially thaw soup in the refrigerator overnight. Heat through in a saucepan, stirring occasionally; add broth if necessary.

1 1/3 CUPS 203 cal., 8g fat (2g sat. fat), 40mg chol., 878mg sod., 18g carb. (5g sugars, 3g fiber), 16g pro.

CREAMY ACCENT

To give this soup a rich consistency, add a splash of heavy cream at the end of cooking.

GOLDEN CLAM CHOWDER

My recipe makes it easy to enjoy homemade clam chowder any night of the week. Not only are the bits of crispy bacon very traditional, but they also make the soup feel rich and indulgent.
—Amanda Bowyer, Caldwell, ID

PREP: 20 MIN. • **COOK:** 20 MIN. • **MAKES:** 7 SERVINGS

- 2 celery ribs
- 2 medium carrots
- 1 medium onion
- 2 tsp. olive oil
- 4 garlic cloves, minced
- 4 medium potatoes, peeled and diced
- 2 cans (6½ oz. each) minced clams, undrained
- 1 bottle (8 oz.) clam juice
- 1 cup plus 1 Tbsp. water, divided
- 1 tsp. minced fresh thyme
- ½ tsp. salt
- ½ tsp. pepper
- 1 can (12 oz.) evaporated milk
- 2 tsp. cornstarch
- 2 bacon strips, cooked and crumbled

1. Finely chop celery, carrots and onion. In a Dutch oven, saute vegetables in oil until tender. Add garlic; cook 1 minute longer. Stir in the potatoes, clams, clam juice, 1 cup water, thyme, salt and pepper. Bring to a boil. Reduce the heat; cover and simmer for 12-15 minutes or until potatoes are tender.

2. Gradually stir in milk; heat through. Combine cornstarch and remaining 1 Tbsp. water until smooth; stir into chowder. Bring to a boil; cook and stir until thickened, about 2 minutes. Top with bacon and, if desired, additional fresh thyme.

1 CUP 195 cal., 5g fat (3g sat. fat), 27mg chol., 574mg sod., 28g carb. (8g sugars, 2g fiber), 10g pro. **DIABETIC EXCHANGES** 1 starch, 1 vegetable, 1 lean meat, 1 fat.

OLD-FASHIONED TURKEY NOODLE SOUP

Make the most of leftover turkey with a delicious homemade soup. Roasting the turkey bones, garlic and vegetables adds a rich flavor without added fat.
—Taste of Home *Test Kitchen*

PREP: 5 HOURS + CHILLING • **COOK:** 30 MIN. • **MAKES:** 10 SERVINGS (3¾ QT.)

BROTH

- 1 leftover turkey carcass (from a 12- to 14-lb. turkey)
- 2 cooked turkey wings, meat removed
- 2 cooked turkey drumsticks, meat removed
- 1 turkey neck bone
- 1 medium unpeeled onion, cut into wedges
- 2 small unpeeled carrots, cut into chunks
- 6 to 8 garlic cloves, peeled
- 4 qt. plus 1 cup cold water, divided

SOUP

- 3 qt. water
- 5 cups uncooked egg noodles
- 2 cups diced carrots
- 2 cups diced celery
- 3 cups cubed cooked turkey
- ¼ cup minced fresh parsley
- 2½ tsp. salt
- 2 tsp. dried thyme
- 1 tsp. pepper

1. Place turkey carcass, bones from wings and drumsticks, neck bone, onion, carrots and garlic in a 15x10x1-in. baking pan coated with cooking spray. Bake, uncovered, at 400° for 1 hour, turning once.

2. Transfer the carcass, bones and vegetables to an 8-qt. stockpot. Add 4 qts. cold water; set aside. Pour 1 cup cold water into baking pan, stirring to loosen browned bits. Add to pot. Bring to a boil. Reduce the heat; cover and simmer for 3-4 hours.

3. Cool slightly. Strain broth; discard bones and vegetables. Set stockpot in an ice-water bath until broth cools, stirring occasionally. Cover and refrigerate overnight.

4. Skim fat from broth. Cover and bring to a boil. Reduce the heat to a simmer. Meanwhile, in a Dutch oven, bring 3 qts. water to a boil. Add noodles and carrots; cook for 4 minutes. Add celery; cook for 5-7 minutes longer or until the noodles and vegetables are tender. Drain; add to simmering broth. Add cubed turkey; heat through. Stir in parsley, salt, thyme and pepper.

1½ CUPS 188 cal., 4g fat (1g sat. fat), 66mg chol., 670mg sod., 17g carb. (2g sugars, 2g fiber), 20g pro. **DIABETIC EXCHANGES** 2 lean meat, 1 starch.

MOROCCAN CHICKPEA STEW

When I served this spicy stew to friends, both vegetarians and meat lovers, they were thrilled with the abundance of squash, potatoes, tomatoes and zucchini.
—Cindy Beberman, Orland Park, IL

PREP: 20 MIN. • **COOK:** 30 MIN. • **MAKES:** 9 SERVINGS (2¼ QT.)

- 1 large onion, finely chopped
- 2 Tbsp. olive oil
- 1 Tbsp. butter
- 2 garlic cloves, minced
- 2 tsp. ground cumin
- 1 cinnamon stick (3 in.)
- ½ tsp. chili powder
- 4 cups vegetable broth
- 2 cups cubed peeled butternut squash
- 1 can (15 oz.) chickpeas or garbanzo beans, rinsed and drained
- 1 can (14½ oz.) diced tomatoes, undrained
- 1 medium red potato, cut into 1-in. cubes
- 1 medium sweet potato, peeled and cut into 1-in. cubes
- 1 medium lemon, thinly sliced
- ¼ tsp. salt
- 2 small zucchini, cubed
- 3 Tbsp. minced fresh cilantro

1. In a Dutch oven, saute onion in oil and butter until tender. Add the garlic, cumin, cinnamon stick and chili powder; saute 1 minute longer.

2. Stir in the broth, squash, chickpeas, tomatoes, potatoes, lemon and salt. Bring to a boil. Reduce heat; cover and simmer until potatoes and squash are almost tender, 15-20 minutes.

3. Add zucchini; return to a boil. Reduce heat; cover and simmer for 5-8 minutes or until vegetables are tender. Discard cinnamon stick and lemon slices. Stir in cilantro.

1 CUP 152 cal., 5g fat (1g sat. fat), 3mg chol., 621mg sod., 24g carb. (7g sugars, 5g fiber), 4g pro. **DIABETIC EXCHANGES** 1 starch, 1 vegetable, 1 fat.

SWISS POTATO SOUP

You have a few options when it comes to fixing this soup—it can also be made in the microwave or started in a slow cooker in the morning.

—Krista Musser, Orrville, OH

TAKES: 30 MIN. • **MAKES:** 4 SERVINGS (1 QT.)

- 5 bacon strips, diced
- 1 medium onion, chopped
- 2 cups water
- 4 medium potatoes, peeled and cubed
- 1½ tsp. salt
- ⅛ tsp. pepper
- ⅓ cup all-purpose flour
- 2 cups 2% milk
- 1 cup shredded Swiss cheese

1. In a large saucepan, cook bacon until crisp; remove to paper towels with a slotted spoon. Drain, reserving 1 Tbsp. drippings.

2. Saute onion in drippings until tender. Add water, potatoes, salt and pepper. Bring to a boil. Reduce heat; simmer, uncovered, until potatoes are tender, about 12 minutes.

3. Combine flour and milk until smooth; gradually stir into potato mixture. Bring to a boil; cook and stir for 2 minutes or until thickened and bubbly. Remove from heat; stir in cheese until melted. Sprinkle with bacon.

1 CUP 455 cal., 17g fat (9g sat. fat), 46mg chol., 1218mg sod., 57g carb. (12g sugars, 4g fiber), 21g pro.

how to cook ...
BREADS

BOSTON BROWN BREAD, PAGE 100

SNOWFLAKE DOUGHNUTS

My family never cared for doughnuts much until they tried these. Their light-as-a-feather texture and golden brown color are so appealing.

—Alice Dunkin, Rock River, WY

PREP: 20 MIN. + RISING • **COOK:** 5 MIN./BATCH • **MAKES:** 3 DOZEN

- 2 pkg. (¼ oz. each) active dry yeast
- 1 cup warm water (110° to 115°)
- 1¼ cups warm milk (110° to 115°)
- ½ cup canola oil
- 1 cup sugar
- ½ tsp. salt
- 3 large eggs, room temperature
- 6 cups all-purpose flour
- Oil for deep-fat frying
- Additional sugar or confectioners' sugar, optional

1. In a large bowl, dissolve the yeast in warm water. Add warm milk and oil. Add sugar, salt and eggs. Stir in flour (dough will be very sticky). Cover and let rise in a warm place until doubled, about 1 hour.

2. Stir dough down; roll out on a well-floured surface to ½-in. thickness. Cut with a 2½-in. cutter. Place on greased baking sheets; cover and let rise for 15-25 minutes.

3. In an electric skillet, deep-fat fryer or Dutch oven, heat the oil to 350°. Fry doughnuts, a few at a time, until golden brown on both sides. Drain on paper towels. If desired, roll in additional sugar or confectioners' sugar.

1 DOUGHNUT 175 cal., 8g fat (1g sat. fat), 16mg chol., 43mg sod., 22g carb. (6g sugars, 1g fiber), 3g pro.

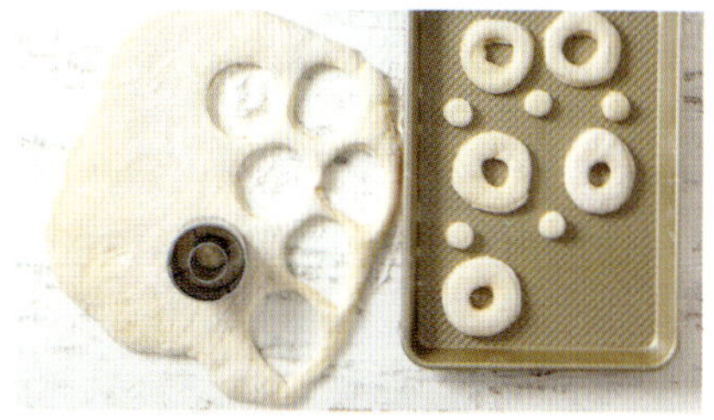

CARAMEL-PECAN STICKY BUNS

My mother used to make delicious cinnamon rolls when I was a child. Later, she taught my sister and me to make them. I've since added the caramel and pecans. These scrumptious buns are a huge hit wherever I take them.

—Judy Powell, Star, ID

PREP: 30 MIN. + RISING • **BAKE:** 30 MIN. • **MAKES:** 1 DOZEN

- 1 pkg. (¼ oz.) active dry yeast
- ¾ cup warm water (110° to 115°)
- ¾ cup warm 2% milk (110° to 115°)
- ¼ cup sugar
- 3 Tbsp. canola oil
- 2 tsp. salt
- 3¾ to 4¼ cups all-purpose flour

FILLING

- ¼ cup butter, softened
- ¼ cup sugar
- 3 tsp. ground cinnamon
- ¾ cup packed brown sugar
- ½ cup heavy whipping cream
- 1 cup coarsely chopped pecans

1. In a large bowl, dissolve the yeast in warm water. Add the milk, sugar, oil, salt and 1¼ cups flour. Beat on medium speed for 2-3 minutes or until smooth. Stir in enough remaining flour to form a soft dough.

2. Turn onto a floured surface; knead until smooth and elastic, 6-8 minutes. Place in a greased bowl, turning once to grease the top. Cover and let rise in a warm place until doubled, about 1 hour.

3. Punch dough down. Turn onto a lightly floured surface. Roll into an 18x12-in. rectangle. Spread butter to within ½ in. of edges. Combine sugar and cinnamon; sprinkle over butter. Roll up jelly-roll style, starting with a long side; pinch seam to seal. Cut into 12 slices.

4. Combine the brown sugar and cream; pour into a greased 13x9-in. baking pan. Sprinkle with pecans. Place rolls cut side down over pecans. Cover and let rise until doubled, about 1 hour.

5. Bake at 350° for 30-35 minutes or until well browned. Cool for 1 minute before inverting onto a serving platter.

1 STICKY BUN 405 cal., 19g fat (6g sat. fat), 26mg chol., 450mg sod., 55g carb. (23g sugars, 2g fiber), 6g pro.

LEMON BLUEBERRY BISCUITS

Lemon and blueberries make such a fresh and flavorful combination in all kinds of baked goods—including these delightful biscuits.
—Taste of Home *Test Kitchen*

PREP: 30 MIN. • **BAKE:** 15 MIN. • **MAKES:** 1 DOZEN

- 2 cups all-purpose flour
- ½ cup sugar
- 2 tsp. baking powder
- ½ tsp. baking soda
- ¼ tsp. salt
- 1 cup lemon yogurt
- 1 large egg, room temperature
- ¼ cup butter, melted
- 1 tsp. grated lemon zest
- 1 cup fresh or frozen blueberries

GLAZE

- ½ cup confectioners' sugar
- 1 Tbsp. lemon juice
- ½ tsp. grated lemon zest

1. Preheat oven to 400°. In a large bowl, whisk the first 5 ingredients. In another bowl, whisk lemon yogurt, egg, butter and lemon zest until blended. Add to flour mixture; stir just until moistened. Fold in blueberries.

2. Drop by ⅓ cupfuls 1 in. apart onto a greased baking sheet. Bake until light brown, 15-18 minutes.

3. In a small bowl, combine the glaze ingredients; stir until smooth. Drizzle over warm biscuits.

1 BISCUIT 193 cal., 5g fat (3g sat. fat), 29mg chol., 223mg sod., 35g carb. (18g sugars, 1g fiber), 4g pro.

READER REVIEW

"These are super quick and easy to make. I freeze them for breakfast, and they are also amazing with a scoop of vanilla ice cream."

—GUEST4873, TASTEOFHOME.COM

BOSTON BROWN BREAD

The rustic, old-fashioned flavor of this hearty bread is out of this world. Recipes like this remind me why I find cooking and baking not only fun, but very fulfilling.
—Sharon Delaney-Chronis, South Milwaukee, WI

PREP: 20 MIN. • **COOK:** 50 MIN. + STANDING • **MAKES:** 1 LOAF (12 PIECES)

- ½ cup cornmeal
- ½ cup whole wheat flour
- ½ cup rye flour
- ½ tsp. baking powder
- ½ tsp. baking soda
- ¼ tsp. salt
- 1 cup buttermilk
- ⅓ cup molasses
- 2 Tbsp. brown sugar
- 1 Tbsp. canola oil
- 3 Tbsp. chopped walnuts, toasted
- 3 Tbsp. raisins
- Cream cheese, softened, optional

1. In a large bowl, combine the first 6 ingredients. In another bowl, whisk the buttermilk, molasses, brown sugar and oil. Stir into the dry ingredients just until moistened. Fold in walnuts and raisins. Transfer to a greased 8x4-in. loaf pan; cover with foil.

2. Place pan on a rack in a boiling-water canner or other large, deep pot; add 1 in. hot water to pot. Bring to a gentle boil; cover and steam for 45-50 minutes or until a toothpick inserted in the center comes out clean, adding more water to the pot as needed.

3. Remove pan from pot; let stand for 10 minutes before removing bread from pan to a wire rack. Serve with cream cheese if desired.

1 PIECE 124 cal., 3g fat (0 sat. fat), 1mg chol., 145mg sod., 23g carb. (10g sugars, 2g fiber), 3g pro. **DIABETIC EXCHANGES** 1½ starch, ½ fat.

EASY BANANA BREAD

I look after several youngsters each day while their parents are at work. They come running when I announce it's time to cook. This bread is one of their favorite treats to help bake and eat.
—Sharon Ward, King Ferry, NY

PREP: 15 MIN. • **BAKE:** 50 MIN. + STANDING • **MAKES:** 1 LOAF (12 PIECES)

- ⅓ cup shortening
- ½ cup sugar
- 2 large eggs, room temperature
- 1¾ cups all-purpose flour
- 1 tsp. baking powder
- ½ tsp. baking soda
- ½ tsp. salt
- 1 cup mashed ripe bananas

1. In a large bowl, cream shortening and sugar. Beat in eggs. Combine flour, baking powder, baking soda and salt; add to the creamed mixture alternately with bananas, beating well after each addition. Pour into a greased 8x4-in. loaf pan.

2. Bake at 350° for 50-55 minutes or until a toothpick inserted in center comes out clean. Let stand for 10 minutes before removing from pan; cool on a wire rack.

1 PIECE 176 cal., 6g fat (2g sat. fat), 31mg chol., 203mg sod., 27g carb. (11g sugars, 1g fiber), 3g pro.

FAVORITE JALAPENO CORN MUFFINS

Honey butter tastes so yummy spread over these hot and snappy muffins. They're delicious with soups, stews and chili.
—*Mary Thomas, Hugo, MN*

PREP: 20 MIN. • **BAKE:** 15 MIN. • **MAKES:** 8 MUFFINS

- ½ cup all-purpose flour
- ½ cup cornmeal
- 4½ tsp. brown sugar
- ½ tsp. baking powder
- ¼ tsp. salt
- ¼ tsp. baking soda
- Dash pepper
- 1 large egg, room temperature
- ⅓ cup sour cream
- ¼ cup 2% milk
- 1 Tbsp. canola oil
- 1 can (8¾ oz.) whole kernel corn, drained
- ½ to 1 jalapeno pepper, seeded and minced

HONEY BUTTER

- ¼ cup butter, softened
- 2 Tbsp. honey

CORN MUFFIN TIPS

How can you make these muffins spicier? Use an extra jalapeno or leave the seeds and membranes in the jalapeno. Or mix in ⅛ tsp. cayenne pepper.

What are some variations? Swap the fresh jalapeno for canned, or add minced chipotle pepper in adobo (this will tint the batter slightly). For milder muffins, use sweet bell pepper. You could also mix in cheddar cheese or pepper jack cheese.

1. Preheat oven to 400°. In a small bowl, combine first 7 ingredients. In another bowl, combine egg, sour cream, milk and oil. Stir into the dry ingredients just until moistened. Stir in corn and jalapeno.

2. Coat muffin cups with cooking spray; fill two-thirds full with batter. Bake until a toothpick inserted in the center comes out clean, 14-16 minutes. In a small bowl, combine butter and honey. Serve with warm muffins.

NOTE Wear disposable gloves when cutting hot peppers; the oils can burn skin. Avoid touching your face.

1 MUFFIN 175 cal., 7g fat (3g sat. fat), 40mg chol., 277mg sod., 24g carb. (9g sugars, 1g fiber), 4g pro.

EVERYTHING BREAD

I love to make bread from scratch, and this has become one of our tried-and-true favorites to serve with any meal, casual or formal.
—Traci Wynne, Denver, PA

PREP: 45 MIN. + RISING • **BAKE:** 25 MIN. • **MAKES:** 1 LOAF (25 PIECES)

- 1 pkg. (¼ oz.) active dry yeast
- ¾ cup warm water (110° to 115°)
- 1 cup warm 2% milk (110° to 115°)
- ¼ cup butter, softened
- 2 Tbsp. sugar
- 1 large egg yolk, room temperature
- 1½ tsp. salt
- 4 to 4½ cups all-purpose flour
- 1 large egg white
- 2 tsp. water
- 1 tsp. coarse sea salt or kosher salt
- 1 tsp. dried minced onion
- 1 tsp. each sesame, caraway and poppy seeds

1. In a large bowl, dissolve yeast in warm water. Add milk, butter, sugar, egg yolk, salt and 2 cups flour. Beat on medium speed for 3 minutes. Stir in enough remaining flour to form a firm dough.

2. Turn onto a floured surface; knead until smooth and elastic, 6-8 minutes. Place in a greased bowl, turning once to grease top. Cover and let rise until doubled, about 1 hour.

3. Punch dough down. Turn onto a lightly floured surface; divide dough into thirds. Shape each into a 20-in. rope. Place the ropes on a large greased baking sheet and braid; pinch ends to seal and tuck under. Cover and let rise until doubled, about 45 minutes.

4. Preheat the oven to 375°. Combine egg white and water; brush over dough. Combine salt, onion and seeds; sprinkle over bread. Bake 22-28 minutes or until golden brown. Remove from pan to a wire rack to cool.

1 PIECE 102 cal., 2g fat (1g sat. fat), 14mg chol., 237mg sod., 17g carb. (2g sugars, 1g fiber), 3g pro.

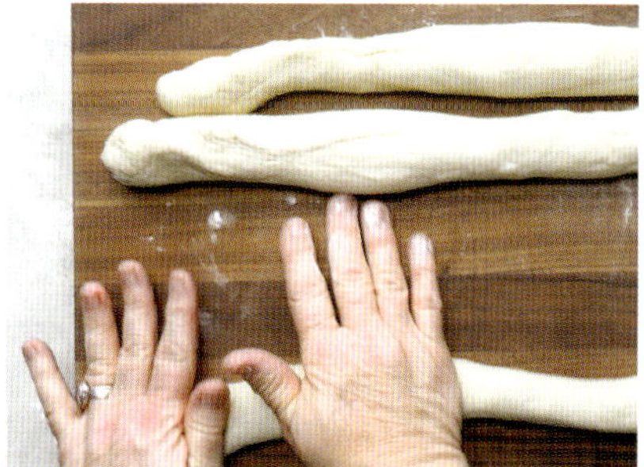

NEW ORLEANS BEIGNETS

These sweet French doughnuts, inspired by the ones found at Cafe du Monde in New Orleans, are square instead of round and have no hole in the middle. They're a traditional part of breakfast in New Orleans.
—Beth Dawson, Jackson, LA

PREP: 25 MIN. + CHILLING • **COOK:** 5 MIN./BATCH • **MAKES:** 4 DOZEN

- 1 pkg. (¼ oz.) active dry yeast
- ¼ cup warm water (110° to 115°)
- 1 cup evaporated milk
- ½ cup canola oil
- ¼ cup sugar
- 1 large egg
- 4¼ to 4¾ cups self-rising flour
- Oil for deep-fat frying
- Confectioners' sugar

1. In a large bowl, dissolve the yeast in warm water. Add milk, oil, sugar, egg and 2 cups flour. Beat until smooth. Stir in enough remaining flour to form a soft dough (the dough will be sticky). Do not knead. Cover and refrigerate overnight.

2. Punch down dough. Turn onto a floured surface; roll into a 16x12-in. rectangle. Cut into 2-in. squares.

3. In an electric skillet, heat 1 in. oil to 375°. Fry squares in batches until golden brown on both sides. Drain on paper towels. Roll warm beignets in confectioners' sugar.

NOTE As an alternative for each cup of the self-rising flour, place 1½ tsp. baking powder and ½ tsp. salt in a measuring cup. Add all-purpose flour to measure 1 cup.

1 BEIGNET 108 cal., 5g fat (1g sat. fat), 6mg chol., 146mg sod., 14g carb. (5g sugars, 0 fiber), 2g pro.

HONEY WHOLE WHEAT ROLLS

There's nothing quite like a warm yeast roll fresh from the oven.
I bake these rolls often, especially when I'm making soup or stew.
—Celecia Stoup, Hobart, OK

PREP: 20 MIN. + RISING • **BAKE:** 20 MIN. • **MAKES:** 15 ROLLS

- 2 pkg. (¼ oz. each) active dry yeast
- 1 cup warm water (110° to 115°)
- ¼ cup butter, melted
- ¼ cup honey
- 1 large egg, room temperature
- ¾ cup whole wheat flour
- ½ cup old-fashioned oats
- 1 tsp. salt
- 2½ to 3 cups all-purpose flour
- Additional melted butter, optional

READER REVIEW

"These rolls are fabulous! I did knead the dough by hand quite a bit longer, about 20 minutes. Also, I replaced the water with whole milk. These were fluffy, lightly sweet and full of flavor and texture!"

—NICOLE806, TASTEOFHOME.COM

1. In a small bowl, dissolve yeast in warm water. In a large bowl, combine melted butter, honey, egg, whole wheat flour, oats, salt, yeast mixture and 1 cup all-purpose flour; beat on medium speed until smooth. Stir in enough remaining flour to form a soft dough.

2. Turn dough onto a floured surface; knead 6-8 minutes or until smooth and elastic. Place in a greased bowl, turning once to grease top. Cover and let rise in a warm place until doubled, about 1 hour.

3. Punch down dough; shape into 15 balls. Place in a greased 13x9-in. pan. Cover dough with a kitchen towel; let rise in a warm place 45 minutes or until doubled. Preheat oven to 375°.

4. Bake for 20 minutes or until golden brown. If desired, brush with additional butter. Serve warm.

1 ROLL 151 cal., 4g fat (2g sat. fat), 21mg chol., 188mg sod., 25g carb. (5g sugars, 2g fiber), 4g pro.

SWISS BEER BREAD

This recipe is a family favorite because it isn't greasy like most other cheese breads I have tried. It will not last long!
—Debi Wallace, Chestertown, NY

PREP: 15 MIN. • **BAKE:** 50 MIN. + COOLING • **MAKES:** 1 LOAF (12 PIECES)

- 4 oz. Jarlsberg or Swiss cheese
- 3 cups all-purpose flour
- 3 Tbsp. sugar
- 3 tsp. baking powder
- 1½ tsp. salt
- ½ tsp. pepper
- 1 bottle (12 oz.) beer or nonalcoholic beer
- 2 Tbsp. butter, melted

1. Preheat oven to 375°. Divide cheese in half. Cut half into ¼-in. cubes; shred the remaining cheese. In a large bowl, combine next 5 ingredients. Stir beer into the dry ingredients just until moistened. Fold in cubed and shredded cheese.

2. Transfer to a greased 8x4-in. loaf pan. Drizzle with butter. Bake until a toothpick inserted in the center comes out clean, 50-60 minutes. Cool for 10 minutes before removing from pan to a wire rack.

1 PIECE 182 cal., 5g fat (3g sat. fat), 11mg chol., 453mg sod., 28g carb. (4g sugars, 1g fiber), 6g pro.

NOTES

MORNING GLORY

Do you know the muffin plan? Start with one brilliant base, add your fave flavors, then pop 'em in the oven to make your breakfast blossom.

ALL-STAR MUFFIN MIX

In a large bowl, whisk 8 cups **all-purpose flour**, 3 cups **sugar**, 3 Tbsp. **baking powder**, 2 tsp. **salt**, 2 tsp. **ground cinnamon** and 2 tsp. **ground nutmeg** until well blended. Store in airtight containers in a cool, dry place or in the freezer up to 6 months. **Makes: 4 batches**.

To make plain muffins: Preheat oven to 400°. Whisk together 1 large room temperature **egg**, 1 cup **2% milk** and ½ cup **melted butter**. Add 1 batch (2¾ cups) **muffin mix** and stir just until moistened. Fill paper-lined muffin cups three-fourths full. Bake until a toothpick inserted in the center comes out clean, 18-21 minutes. Cool 5 minutes before removing the muffins from pan to a wire rack. **Makes: 1 dozen**.

—NANCY MACKEY, MADISON, OH

BLUEBERRY MUFFINS

Fold 1 cup **fresh or frozen blueberries** into prepared batter.

BANANA MUFFINS

Add 1 cup **mashed ripe bananas** to the egg mixture.

CRANBERRY-PECAN MUFFINS

Toss 1 cup chopped **fresh or frozen cranberries**, ½ cup **chopped pecans** and 3 Tbsp. **sugar** with the muffin mix before adding it to the egg mixture.

RHUBARB-ORANGE MUFFINS

Add ⅓ cup **orange marmalade** to the egg mixture; fold ¾ cup **diced fresh or frozen rhubarb** into prepared batter.

CAPPUCCINO MUFFINS

Toss 1 cup **miniature semisweet chocolate chips** and 2 tsp. **instant coffee granules** with the muffin mix before adding it to the egg mixture.

CARROT-RAISIN MUFFINS

Toss ¾ cup **shredded carrots** and ⅓ cup **golden raisins** with the muffin mix before adding it to the egg mixture.

APRICOT-CHERRY MUFFINS

Toss ½ cup each **chopped dried apricots** and **dried cherries** with the muffin mix before adding it to the egg mixture.

ZUCCHINI-PINEAPPLE MUFFINS

Add ½ cup **drained pineapple tidbits** to egg mixture; fold ½ cup **shredded zucchini** into prepared batter.

APPLE-CHEESE MUFFINS

Toss ½ cup each **shredded peeled apple** and **shredded Colby-Monterey Jack cheese** with the muffin mix before adding it to the egg mixture.

RASPBERRY MUFFINS

Fold 1 cup **fresh or frozen raspberries** into prepared batter. Sprinkle tops of muffins with sugar before baking.

FIG-PISTACHIO MUFFINS

Toss 1 cup **chopped dried figs** and ⅓ cup **chopped pistachios** with the muffin mix before adding it to the egg mixture.

CHOCOLATE CHIP PUMPKIN BREAD

A touch of cinnamon helps blend the flavors in this tender pumpkin chocolate chip bread. And since the recipe makes two loaves, you can send one to a bake sale and keep one at home for your family to enjoy.
—Lora Stanley, Bennington, KS

PREP: 15 MIN. • **BAKE:** 1 HOUR + COOLING • **MAKES:** 2 LOAVES (12 PIECES EACH)

3 cups all-purpose flour
2 tsp. ground cinnamon
1 tsp. salt
1 tsp. baking soda
4 large eggs, room temperature
2 cups sugar
2 cups canned pumpkin
1½ cups canola oil
1½ cups semisweet chocolate chips

1. In a large bowl, combine the flour, ground cinnamon, salt and baking soda. In another large bowl, beat eggs, sugar, pumpkin and oil. Stir into dry ingredients just until moistened. Fold in chocolate chips.

2. Pour into 2 greased 8x4-in. loaf pans. Bake at 350° for 60-70 minutes or until a toothpick inserted in the center comes out clean. Cool for 10 minutes before removing from pans to wire racks.

1 PIECE 315 cal., 18g fat (3g sat. fat), 31mg chol., 165mg sod., 37g carb. (23g sugars, 2g fiber), 3g pro.

APPLE FRITTERS

This is an old southern recipe. When we got home from a trip through the South years ago, I found the recipe among the brochures I brought back. I have been making these fritters ever since.
—John Robbins, Springdale, PA

TAKES: 20 MIN. • **MAKES:** 2 SERVINGS

- 1 cup cake flour
- 1 Tbsp. sugar
- ¾ tsp. baking powder
- ¼ tsp. salt
- 1 large egg, room temperature
- ⅓ cup 2% milk
- 4 tsp. butter, melted
- 1 Tbsp. orange juice
- 2 tsp. grated orange zest
- ¼ tsp. vanilla extract
- ¾ cup chopped peeled tart apple
- Oil for frying
- Confectioners' sugar

APPLE FRITTER TIPS

What are some variations of these fritters? A dash of cinnamon goes a long way if you want to add more flavor to your apple fritters. You can also leave out the orange zest or replace the orange juice with an equal amount of milk or maple syrup.

How do you make sure each apple fritter is consistent? Avoid mixing the batter between frying batches of fritters. You can keep the size of the fritters roughly the same by using a tablespoon or small scoop to drop the batter into the oil. Be sure not to crowd the pan. This will keep the temperature of the oil consistent for all of the batches, ensuring you have crisp and fluffy fritters.

1. In a large bowl, combine flour, sugar, baking powder and salt. In another bowl, combine egg, milk, butter, orange juice, zest and vanilla. Add to dry ingredients just until moistened. Fold in apple.

2. In an electric skillet or deep-fat fryer, heat ¼ in. oil to 375°. Drop the batter by rounded tablespoonfuls into oil. Fry until golden brown on both sides. Drain on paper towels. Dust with confectioners' sugar. Serve warm.

1 SERVING 533 cal., 24g fat (3g sat. fat), 97mg chol., 530mg sod., 69g carb. (13g sugars, 2g fiber), 10g pro.

EASY SLOW-COOKER CINNAMON ROLLS

I love how these scrumptious treats make use of my slow cooker, and they are so easy! I can just walk away and come back to perfectly cooked cinnamon rolls ready for the taking!
—Nina Ward, New Port Richey, FL

PREP: 30 MIN. + STANDING • **COOK:** 2 HOURS • **MAKES:** 1 DOZEN

- 1 pkg. (¼ oz.) quick-rise yeast
- ¼ cup sugar, divided
- ¼ cup warm water (110° to 115°)
- ½ cup warm 2% milk (110° to 115°)
- 3 Tbsp. butter, softened
- 1 large egg, room temperature, lightly beaten
- 1 tsp. salt
- 2½ to 3 cups all-purpose flour

FILLING
- ¼ cup packed brown sugar
- 1 Tbsp. ground cinnamon
- 3 Tbsp. butter, softened
- Optional: Cream Cheese Frosting (recipe at right) and toasted chopped pecans

1. Place a piece of parchment in a 3½-qt. rectangular slow cooker, letting the ends extend up the sides; spritz the paper with cooking spray. In a small bowl, dissolve yeast and 1 tsp. sugar in warm water. In a large bowl, combine milk, remaining sugar, butter, egg, salt, yeast mixture and 2 cups flour; beat on medium speed until smooth. Stir in enough remaining flour to form a soft dough (dough will be sticky). Turn dough onto a floured surface; knead until smooth and elastic, 6-8 minutes. Let stand 10 minutes.

2. For filling, combine brown sugar and cinnamon. Punch down the dough. Turn onto a lightly floured surface; roll into a 16x10-in. rectangle. Spread butter within ½ in. of edges; sprinkle with brown sugar mixture. Roll up jelly-roll style, starting with a long side; pinch seam to seal. Cut into 12 slices. Place rolls side by side, cut side down, into slow cooker.

3. Cover slow cooker with a double layer of white paper towels; place lid securely over towels. Cook, covered, on high until rolls are set and edges begin to brown, about 2 hours. To avoid scorching, rotate slow cooker insert a half turn midway through cooking, lifting carefully with oven mitts. Using parchment, lift rolls from the slow cooker; cool slightly. If desired, top with cream cheese frosting and pecans.

1 CINNAMON ROLL 195 cal., 7g fat (4g sat. fat), 32mg chol., 255mg sod., 30g carb. (9g sugars, 1g fiber), 4g pro.

CREAM CHEESE FROSTING

Beat 4 oz. **softened cream cheese**, ¼ cup of **softened butter** and 1 tsp. **vanilla extract** until fluffy. Gradually beat in 1¾-2 cups **confectioners' sugar** to achieve desired consistency.

BAKING POWDER DROP BISCUITS

One day I had company coming and realized I had run out of biscuit mix. I'd never made biscuits from scratch before, but I decided to give this recipe a try. Now this is the only way I make them!
—Sharon Evans, Clear Lake, IA

TAKES: 20 MIN. • **MAKES:** 1 DOZEN

- 2 cups all-purpose flour
- 2 Tbsp. sugar
- 4 tsp. baking powder
- ½ tsp. cream of tartar
- ½ tsp. salt
- ½ cup shortening
- ⅔ cup 2% milk
- 1 large egg, room temperature

NOTES

1. Preheat oven to 450°. In a large bowl, combine the first 5 ingredients. Cut in shortening until mixture resembles coarse crumbs. In a small bowl, whisk milk and egg. Stir into crumb mixture just until moistened.

2. Drop by ¼ cupfuls 2 in. apart onto an ungreased baking sheet. Bake until golden brown, 10-12 minutes. Serve warm.

1 BISCUIT 170 cal., 9g fat (2g sat. fat), 17mg chol., 271mg sod., 19g carb. (3g sugars, 1g fiber), 3g pro.

DUTCH OVEN RAISIN WALNUT BREAD

On a cold day, nothing is better than a warm, crusty bread filled with raisins and walnuts.
—Catherine Ward, Mequon, WI

PREP: 15 MIN. + RISING • **BAKE:** 50 MIN. + COOLING • **MAKES:** 1 LOAF (32 PIECES)

- 6 to 7 cups (125 grams per cup) all-purpose flour
- ¼ cup sugar
- 2 tsp. active dry yeast
- 2 tsp. ground cinnamon
- 2 tsp. salt
- 1 cup raisins
- 1 cup chopped walnuts
- 3 cups cool water (70° to 75°)

DUTCH OVEN BREAD TIPS

This is a soft, no-knead dough that should be baked immediately after shaping. Preheating the Dutch oven and placing the bread quickly inside are the keys to success.

1. In a large bowl, whisk 6 cups flour, sugar, yeast, cinnamon and salt. Stir in the raisins and walnuts; add water and enough remaining flour to form a moist, shaggy dough. Do not knead. Cover and let rise in a cool place until doubled, 7-8 hours.

2. Preheat oven to 450°; place a Dutch oven with lid on the center rack and heat for at least 30 minutes. Once Dutch oven is heated, turn dough onto a generously floured surface. Using a metal scraper or spatula, quickly shape into a round loaf. Gently place on top of a piece of parchment.

3. Using a sharp knife, make a ¼-in.-deep slash across top of loaf. Using the parchment, immediately lower loaf into heated Dutch oven. Cover and bake for 30 minutes. Uncover and bake until the loaf is deep golden brown and sounds hollow when tapped, 20-30 minutes longer, partially covering if the bread is browning too much. Remove loaf from the Dutch oven and cool completely on wire rack.

1 PIECE 130 cal., 3g fat (0 sat. fat), 0 chol., 149mg sod., 24g carb. (4g sugars, 1g fiber), 3g pro.

how to cook ...

FAVORITE SIDES

EASY REFRIGERATOR PICKLES, PAGE 120

SUCCOTASH

You can't get more southern than succotash. This recipe comes from my mother, who was a fantastic cook. This dish made her famous, at least with everyone who ever tasted it.
—*Rosa Boone, Mobile, AL*

PREP: 1¾ HOURS • **COOK:** 1 HOUR • **MAKES:** 16 SERVINGS

- 1 smoked ham hock (about 1½ lbs.)
- 1 can (28 oz.) diced tomatoes, undrained
- 1½ cups frozen lima beans, thawed
- 1 pkg. (10 oz.) crowder peas, thawed, or 1 can (15½ oz.) black-eyed peas, drained
- 1 pkg. (10 oz.) frozen corn, thawed
- 1 medium green pepper, chopped
- 1 medium onion, chopped
- ⅓ cup ketchup
- 1½ tsp. salt
- 1½ tsp. dried basil
- 1 tsp. rubbed sage
- 1 tsp. paprika
- ½ tsp. pepper
- 1 bay leaf
- 1 cup sliced fresh or frozen okra
- Optional: Snipped fresh dill and chives

1. Place ham hock in a Dutch oven or large saucepan, add enough water to come halfway up side of the ham hock; cover and simmer about 1½ hours or until tender. Remove ham bone from Dutch oven, reserving 1 cup cooking liquid; let stand until cool enough to handle. Remove meat from bone and return to pan, along with reserved cooking liquid. Discard the bone and remaining broth or save for another use.

2. Add the tomatoes, beans, peas, corn, green pepper, onion, ketchup and seasonings. Simmer, uncovered, for 45 minutes. Add the okra; simmer, uncovered, 15 minutes or until tender. Discard bay leaf before serving. Garnish with dill and chives if desired.

¾ CUP 79 cal., 0 fat (0 sat. fat), 2mg chol., 442mg sod., 16g carb. (5g sugars, 3g fiber), 4g pro. **DIABETIC EXCHANGES** 1 starch.

SUCCOTASH TIPS

What is succotash? Succotash is a classic American dish bursting with color and flavor. It typically features sweet corn and tender lima beans, with add-ins like bell peppers, onions and tomatoes. Many versions include fresh herbs, spices or smoky touches like bacon or ham.

How can you make succotash your own? Customize this recipe by mixing in your favorite veggies or proteins. Try black beans, zucchini or summer squash for variety. Add thyme for earthiness, cayenne for spice or skip the ham hock to make it vegetarian. In that case, you could add smoked paprika or hickory salt to ensure your meatless dish still has a rich, smoky flavor.

What do you serve with succotash? Succotash pairs perfectly with crispy fried chicken, tangy pulled pork or grilled salmon. For a true southern spread, serve it with buttery corn, braised greens or warm, fluffy biscuits.

EASY REFRIGERATOR PICKLES

This easy recipe is a great way to use cucumbers and onions from the garden. Here in upstate New York, we often have an abundance of cucumbers.
—Catherine Seibold, Elma, NY

PREP: 20 MIN. + CHILLING • **MAKES:** 6 CUPS

- 6 cups thinly sliced cucumbers
- 2 cups thinly sliced onions
- 1½ cups sugar
- 1½ cups cider vinegar
- ½ tsp. salt
- ½ tsp. mustard seed
- ½ tsp. celery seed
- ½ tsp. ground turmeric
- ½ tsp. ground cloves

Place cucumbers and onions in a large bowl; set aside. Combine the remaining ingredients in a saucepan; bring to a boil. Cook and stir just until sugar is dissolved. Pour over cucumber mixture; cool. Cover tightly; refrigerate for at least 24 hours before serving.

¼ CUP 35 cal., 0 fat (0 sat. fat), 0 chol., 175mg sod., 8g carb. (7g sugars, 0 fiber), 0 pro.

NEVER-FAIL SCALLOPED POTATOES

Take the chill off any blustery day with something special to accompany meaty entrees. These creamy homemade scalloped potatoes are sure to be a favorite.
—Agnes Ward, Stratford, ON

PREP: 25 MIN. • **BAKE:** 1 HOUR • **MAKES:** 6 SERVINGS

- 2 Tbsp. butter
- 3 Tbsp. all-purpose flour
- 1 tsp. salt
- ¼ tsp. pepper
- 1½ cups fat-free milk
- ½ cup shredded reduced-fat cheddar cheese
- 2 lbs. potatoes, peeled and thinly sliced (about 4 cups)
- 1 cup thinly sliced onions, divided

READER REVIEW

"These potatoes are so easy and everybody loves them. I like to throw them under the broiler for the last couple of minutes to brown up the top."

—SHANNONDOBOS126, TASTEOFHOME.COM

1. Preheat the oven to 350°. In a small saucepan, melt butter; stir in the flour, salt and pepper until smooth. Gradually whisk in milk. Bring to a boil, stirring constantly; cook and stir for 2 minutes or until thickened. Remove from heat; stir in cheese until melted.

2. Coat an 8-in. square baking dish with cooking spray. Place half the potatoes in dish; layer with ½ cup onion and half cheese sauce. Repeat layers.

3. Bake, covered, 50 minutes. Uncover; bake 10-15 minutes longer or until bubbly and potatoes are tender.

¾ CUP 215 cal., 6g fat (4g sat. fat), 18mg chol., 523mg sod., 32g carb. (5g sugars, 3g fiber), 8g pro. **DIABETIC EXCHANGES** 2 starch, 1 fat.

EGGPLANT FRIES

My kids love this snack—and I like that it's healthy. Coated with Italian seasoning, Parmesan cheese and garlic salt, these veggie sticks are broiled, not fried, so there's no guilt when you crunch into them.
—Mary Murphy, Atwater, CA

TAKES: 20 MIN. • **MAKES:** 6 SERVINGS

- 2 large eggs
- ½ cup grated Parmesan cheese
- ½ cup toasted wheat germ
- 1 tsp. Italian seasoning
- ¾ tsp. garlic salt
- 1 medium eggplant (about 1¼ lbs.)
- Cooking spray
- 1 cup meatless pasta sauce, warmed

1. Preheat the broiler. In a shallow bowl, whisk together eggs. In another shallow bowl, mix cheese, wheat germ and seasonings.

2. Trim ends of eggplant; cut eggplant lengthwise into ½-in.-thick slices. Cut slices lengthwise into ½-in. strips. Dip eggplant in eggs, then coat with cheese mixture. Place on a baking sheet coated with cooking spray.

3. Spritz the eggplant with additional cooking spray. Broil 4 in. from the heat for 3 minutes. Turn the eggplant; spritz with additional cooking spray. Broil for 1-2 minutes or until golden brown. Serve immediately with pasta sauce.

1 SERVING 135 cal., 5g fat (2g sat. fat), 68mg chol., 577mg sod., 15g carb. (6g sugars, 4g fiber), 9g pro. **DIABETIC EXCHANGES** 1 vegetable, 1 medium-fat meat, ½ starch.

HUSH PUPPIES

A fish dinner isn't complete without a side of hush puppies, and my mom is well known for this recipe. It's the best!
—Mary McGuire, Graham, NC

TAKES: 25 MIN. • **MAKES:** 2 DOZEN

- 1 cup yellow cornmeal
- ¼ cup all-purpose flour
- 1½ tsp. baking powder
- ½ tsp. salt
- 1 large egg, room temperature, lightly beaten
- ¾ cup 2% milk
- 1 small onion, finely chopped
- Oil for deep-fat frying

1. In a large bowl, combine cornmeal, flour, baking powder and salt. Whisk egg, milk and onion; add to dry ingredients just until combined.

2. In a Dutch oven or an electric skillet, heat oil to 365°. Drop the batter by tablespoonfuls into oil. Fry until golden brown, 2-2½ minutes. Drain on paper towels. Serve warm.

1 HUSH PUPPY 55 cal., 3g fat (0 sat. fat), 9mg chol., 86mg sod., 7g carb. (1g sugars, 0 fiber), 1g pro.

BEST FRYING OIL

Peanut or vegetable oils are best for deep-frying. Both oils have a higher smoke point, allowing them to be heated to a high temperature before they start to break down.

FOUR-CHEESE MAC & CHEESE

Experience a heavenly blend of cheeses perfectly combined in this classic comfort food. Macaroni is enveloped in a velvety cheese sauce that combines the sharpness of aged cheddar, the nuttiness of Gruyere, the creamy indulgence of fontina and the salty punch of Parmesan.
—Taste of Home *Test Kitchen*

PREP: 15 MIN. • **COOK:** 30 MIN. • **MAKES:** 12 SERVINGS

- 1 lb. uncooked elbow macaroni
- ¼ cup butter
- ¼ cup all-purpose flour
- 2 cups whole milk
- 1 cup shredded sharp cheddar cheese
- 1 cup shredded Gruyere cheese
- ½ cup shredded fontina cheese
- 1 tsp. salt
- ½ tsp. pepper
- ¼ tsp. ground mustard
- ½ cup shredded Parmesan cheese

1. Preheat oven to 400°. Cook macaroni according to package directions. Drain; set aside.

2. In a large sauce pot, melt butter over medium heat. Whisk in the flour until smooth. Gradually add milk; cook, 3-4 minutes or until thickened, whisking occasionally. Stir in cheddar, Gruyere and fontina cheeses, salt, pepper and mustard until cheese has melted. Stir in cooked macaroni.

3. Transfer mixture to a greased 13x9-in. baking dish. Sprinkle with Parmesan. Bake until cheese is bubbly and edges are golden brown, 15-20 minutes.

⅔ CUP 311 cal., 14g fat (8g sat. fat), 41mg chol., 465mg sod., 32g carb. (3g sugars, 1g fiber), 14g pro.

NOTES

5i

ZUCCHINI LATKES

Here's a delicious twist on the potato latkes traditionally served during Hanukkah. My husband and our children really enjoy the zucchini version. I serve these fried pancakes with sour cream, cottage cheese and applesauce, plus a salad on the side.
—Chava Zaitschek, Milwaukee, WI

PREP: 30 MIN. • **COOK:** 5 MIN./BATCH • **MAKES:** 8 SERVINGS

- 3 medium zucchini, shredded (about 4½ cups)
- 1 tsp. salt, divided
- 2 eggs, beaten
- 1 small onion, grated
- ¼ cup matzo meal or dry bread crumbs
- ⅛ tsp. pepper
- Oil for frying
- Sour cream, optional

1. In a large bowl, toss shredded zucchini and ½ tsp. salt; let stand for 10 minutes. Squeeze zucchini dry. Stir in eggs, onion, matzo meal, pepper and remaining salt.

2. In a large skillet, heat oil over medium heat. Drop the batter by tablespoonfuls into oil; press lightly to flatten. Fry until golden brown, 2 minutes on each side. Serve with sour cream if desired.

2 LATKES 218 cal., 21g fat (2g sat. fat), 47mg chol., 319mg sod., 6g carb. (2g sugars, 1g fiber), 3g pro.

PARMESAN RISOTTO

Risotto is a creamy Italian rice dish. In this version, the rice is briefly sauteed, then slowly cooked in wine and seasonings. Watch for that magic moment when the risotto transforms from just rice in liquid to creamy, tender deliciousness.
—Taste of Home *Test Kitchen*

PREP: 15 MIN. • **COOK:** 30 MIN. • **MAKES:** 12 SERVINGS

- 8 cups chicken broth
- ½ cup finely chopped onion
- ¼ cup olive oil
- 3 cups arborio rice
- 2 garlic cloves, minced
- 1 cup dry white wine or water
- ½ cup shredded Parmesan cheese
- ¼ tsp. salt
- ¼ tsp. pepper
- 3 Tbsp. minced fresh parsley

1. In a saucepan, heat broth and keep warm. In a Dutch oven, saute onion in oil until tender. Add rice and garlic; cook and stir for 2-3 minutes. Reduce heat; stir in wine. Cook and stir until all liquid is absorbed.

2. Add heated broth, ½ cup at a time, stirring constantly and allowing liquid to absorb between additions. Cook just until risotto is creamy and rice is almost tender, about 20 minutes. Add remaining ingredients; cook and stir until heated through. Serve immediately.

¾ CUP 260 cal., 6g fat (1g sat. fat), 2mg chol., 728mg sod., 41g carb. (1g sugars, 1g fiber), 6g pro.

SAUSAGE MUSHROOM RISOTTO Reduce olive oil to 2 Tbsp. In a large skillet, cook 1 lb. bulk Italian sausage over medium heat until meat is no longer pink; drain. Set aside and keep warm. Add onion, oil and ½ lb. quartered fresh mushrooms to skillet and cook until tender. Proceed as directed.

ASPARAGUS RISOTTO Trim 1 lb. asparagus and cut into 2-in. pieces. Place asparagus in a large saucepan; add ½ in. water. Bring to a boil. Reduce heat; cover and simmer for 3 minutes or until crisp-tender. Drain and set aside. Stir into risotto just before serving.

OVEN FRIES

I jazz up my fries with paprika and garlic powder. Something about the combination of spices packs a punch. The leftovers are even good cold!
—Heather Byers, Pittsburgh, PA

PREP: 10 MIN. • **BAKE:** 40 MIN. • **MAKES:** 4 SERVINGS

- 4 medium potatoes
- 1 Tbsp. olive oil
- 2½ tsp. paprika
- ¾ tsp. salt
- ¾ tsp. garlic powder

OVEN FRY TIPS

How do you make baked french fries crispy? For crispy oven fries, use high heat and a good coating of oil. This seals in moisture, creating a crisp exterior and creamy interior. Yukon Gold potatoes are a great choice for their naturally tender texture.

Are baked french fries healthy? Baking fries is healthier than frying since you can control the fat content and salt. For a lighter version, skip the salt and amp up the herbs and spices. To add a nutrient boost, swap in sweet potatoes for some or all of the regular ones.

What's the best way to enjoy french fries? Elevate your fries with fun toppings! Turn them into poutine, load them up with chili and cheese, or get creative with different sauces, dressings and seasonings.

1. Preheat oven to 400°. Cut each potato into 12 wedges. In a large bowl, combine oil, paprika, salt and garlic powder. Add potatoes; toss to coat.

2. Transfer to a greased 15x10x1-in. baking pan. Bake for 40-45 minutes or until tender, turning once.

12 PIECES 200 cal., 4g fat (1g sat. fat), 0 chol., 457mg sod., 38g carb. (2g sugars, 5g fiber), 5g pro.

CAJUN OVEN FRIES Omit paprika, salt and garlic powder. Combine oil with 2-3 tsp. Cajun seasoning.

CHILI OVEN FRIES Omit paprika. Combine oil with salt, garlic powder and 1 Tbsp. chili powder.

HERBED OVEN FRIES Omit paprika and garlic powder. Combine oil with salt, ⅓ cup grated Parmesan, 4 tsp. dried basil and ¾ tsp. pepper.

CREAMY COLESLAW

For me, this is the best coleslaw recipe because a package of shredded cabbage and carrots really cuts down on prep time. It's perfect for potlucks or to serve to your family on a busy weeknight.
—Renee Endress, Galva, IL

TAKES: 10 MIN. • **MAKES:** 6 SERVINGS

- 1 pkg. (14 oz.) coleslaw mix
- ¾ cup mayonnaise
- ⅓ cup sour cream
- ¼ cup sugar
- ¾ tsp. seasoned salt
- ½ tsp. ground mustard
- ¼ tsp. celery salt

Place coleslaw mix in a large bowl. In a small bowl, combine remaining ingredients; stir until blended. Pour over coleslaw mix and toss to coat. Refrigerate until serving.

¾ CUP 256 cal., 23g fat (5g sat. fat), 19mg chol., 398mg sod., 13g carb. (11g sugars, 2g fiber), 1g pro.

CHEESY CHEDDAR BROCCOLI CASSEROLE

Even people who don't like broccoli beg me to make this comforting recipe. It's similar to a classic green bean casserole, but the melted cheddar cheese just puts it over the top.
—Elaine Hubbard, Pocono Lake, PA

PREP: 15 MIN. • **BAKE:** 35 MIN. • **MAKES:** 8 SERVINGS

- 1 can (10¾ oz.) condensed cream of mushroom soup, undiluted
- 1 cup sour cream
- 1½ cups shredded sharp cheddar cheese, divided
- 1 can (6 oz.) french-fried onions, divided
- 2 pkg. (16 oz. each) frozen broccoli florets, thawed

1. Preheat the oven to 325°. In a large saucepan, combine soup, sour cream, 1 cup cheese and 1¼ cups onions; heat through over medium heat, stirring until blended, 4-5 minutes. Stir in broccoli. Transfer to a greased 2-qt. baking dish.

2. Bake, uncovered, 25-30 minutes or until bubbly. Sprinkle with remaining cheese and onions. Bake until cheese is melted, 10-15 minutes.

¾ CUP 359 cal., 26g fat (11g sat. fat), 30mg chol., 641mg sod., 19g carb. (4g sugars, 3g fiber), 8g pro.

NOTES

GRANDMA'S SAUSAGE DRESSING

Every family seems to have its own favorite dressing recipe that becomes a tradition, and this is ours. It came from Grandma, who passed it down to my mother. Now our children have carried it into their kitchens. This is truly a good old-fashioned recipe for tasty sausage!
—Norma Howland, Joliet, IL

PREP: 20 MIN. • **BAKE:** 40 MIN. • **MAKES:** 6 CUPS

- 1 lb. bulk pork sausage
- 2 cups chopped celery
- 1 cup chopped onion
- 1 cup 2% milk
- 7 cups coarse dry bread cubes
- 2 large eggs, lightly beaten
- 2 Tbsp. minced fresh parsley
- ½ tsp. salt or salt to taste
- ¼ tsp. pepper

1. Preheat the oven to 350°. In a large skillet over medium heat, cook and crumble sausage until no longer pink, 6-7 minutes. Drain sausage, reserving 2 tsp. drippings; set sausage aside. In same skillet, cook and stir celery and onion in the reserved drippings over medium heat until celery is crisp-tender and onions are translucent, 3-4 minutes.

2. Meanwhile, in a small saucepan, heat milk over medium heat until bubbles form around side of pan. In a large bowl, combine sausage, celery mixture, milk, bread cubes, eggs, parsley, salt and pepper.

3. Transfer to a greased 2-qt. baking dish. Cover and bake 40 minutes or until lightly browned. If desired, sprinkle with additional parsley just before serving.

½ CUP 352 cal., 12g fat (4g sat. fat), 52mg chol., 826mg sod., 48g carb. (3g sugars, 2g fiber), 12g pro.

EVERYTHING MASHED POTATO CASSEROLE

Here is a great dish for the holidays or to take to a covered dish event. If I need to keep it warm for a long time, I sometimes place the mixture into a slow cooker and then add the sour cream, bacon, cheese and chives.
—Pamela Shank, Parkersburg, WV

PREP: 30 MIN. • **BAKE:** 15 MIN. • **MAKES:** 12 SERVINGS

- 3 lbs. potatoes (about 9 medium), peeled and quartered
- 1 pkg. (8 oz.) cream cheese, cubed
- ½ cup butter, cubed
- ½ cup whole milk
- ¼ tsp. salt
- ¼ tsp. pepper
- 2 cups sour cream
- 2 cups shredded cheddar cheese
- 3 bacon strips, cooked and crumbled
- 1 Tbsp. minced chives

1. Place potatoes in a large saucepan and cover with water. Bring to a boil. Reduce heat; cover and simmer for 15-20 minutes or until tender. Drain.

2. In a large bowl, mash potatoes. Beat in cream cheese, butter, milk, salt and pepper until fluffy. Transfer to a greased 3-qt. baking dish. Spread sour cream over top.

3. Bake casserole, uncovered, at 350° for 10 minutes. Sprinkle with cheddar cheese, bacon and chives. Bake until heated through and cheese is melted, about 5 minutes longer.

¾ CUP 433 cal., 33g fat (22g sat. fat), 114mg chol., 340mg sod., 20g carb. (4g sugars, 1g fiber), 10g pro.

CUCUMBER SHELL SALAD

Ranch dressing is the mild coating for this pleasant pasta salad, alive with the fresh flavors of crunchy cucumber, onion and green peas. Someone always seems to want the recipe!
—Paula Ishii, Ralston, NE

PREP: 20 MIN. + CHILLING • **MAKES:** 16 SERVINGS

- 1 pkg. (16 oz.) medium pasta shells
- 1 pkg. (16 oz.) frozen peas, thawed
- 1 medium cucumber, halved and sliced
- 1 small red onion, chopped
- 1 cup ranch salad dressing

Cook pasta according to the package directions; drain and rinse in cold water. In a large bowl, combine pasta, peas, cucumber and red onion. Add dressing; toss to coat. Cover and refrigerate for at least 2 hours before serving.

¾ CUP 187 cal., 7g fat (1g sat. fat), 2mg chol., 177mg sod., 26g carb. (3g sugars, 3g fiber), 5g pro.

PICK A PASTA SALAD

Start with a shape. Toss with mix-ins. Add dressing and flavorful accents. It's the simplest, most delicious equation that adds up to potluck perfection.

PASTA		MIX-INS		DRESSING		ACCENTS
ASIAN NOODLE Whole-wheat spaghetti	+	Cubed chicken, coleslaw mix, mandarin oranges	+	Sesame-ginger vinaigrette	+	Chow mein noodles
CALIFORNIA WALDORF Orecchiette	+	Smoked turkey, apples, celery, strawberries	+	2-1 ratio of plain yogurt and mayo	+	Walnuts, Dijon mustard
GARDEN RANCH Tricolor rotini	+	Broccoli, cucumbers, tomatoes	+	Ranch dressing	+	Crumbled bacon
TACO BEEF Rotini	+	Taco meat, cheddar, tomatoes, peppers	+	Catalina dressing	+	Tortilla chips, black olives
CLASSIC MAC Macaroni	+	Ham, cheddar, peas, green onions	+	Mayo thinned with vinegar	+	Pickle relish
TORTELLINI TIME Cheese tortellini	+	Broccoli, red peppers	+	Red wine vinaigrette	+	Prosciutto, green olives
UNDER THE SEA Shells	+	Imitation crab, peas	+	Mayonnaise	+	Dill
SPINACH BOW TIES Farfalle	+	Baby spinach, yellow pepper, dried apricots	+	Balsamic vinaigrette	+	Sliced almonds

RED POTATO & EGG SALAD

This flavorful salad with egg is the perfect side for summer cookouts. The red potatoes really dress it up.
—Margaret (Peggy) Blomquist, Newfield, NY

PREP: 40 MIN. + CHILLING • **MAKES:** 17 SERVINGS

- 5 lbs. medium red potatoes, halved
- 5 hard-boiled large eggs, chopped
- 1 celery rib, finely chopped
- ½ medium onion, finely chopped
- 1½ cups mayonnaise
- ¼ cup sweet pickle relish
- 3 Tbsp. sugar
- 2 Tbsp. dried parsley flakes
- 2 tsp. prepared mustard
- 1 tsp. salt
- 1 tsp. cider vinegar
- ⅛ tsp. pepper

1. Place potatoes in a large kettle; cover with water. Bring to a boil. Reduce heat; cook, covered, 15-20 minutes or until tender. Drain and cool. Cut potatoes into ¾-in. cubes.

2. In a large bowl, combine potatoes, eggs, celery and onion. In a small bowl, combine remaining ingredients. Pour over potato mixture and stir gently to coat. Cover and refrigerate for 6 hours or overnight.

¾ CUP 276 cal., 17g fat (3g sat. fat), 69mg chol., 309mg sod., 25g carb. (5g sugars, 2g fiber), 5g pro.

POTATO SALAD TIPS

Should you peel the potatoes for potato salad? No need to peel red potatoes—their thin skins are tender and add color and nutrition. Just give them a good scrubbing to remove any residue.

Is it better to boil red potatoes whole or cut up? Boiling cut potatoes speeds up cooking, but whole potatoes work too. Cut them to save time and get evenly cooked pieces.

How long will potato salad last in the fridge? Stored in a covered container, potato salad stays fresh for 3-5 days. Making it ahead also lets the flavors blend beautifully!

Can you boil eggs with the potatoes for red potato salad? Yes! Add eggs to the pot when the potatoes have about 9 minutes left to cook. This way, you can save time and dishes.

MICROWAVE RICE PILAF

This speedy side complements almost any main dish. It's just the right amount for my husband and me but is also easy to double for a larger group.
—Norma Jean Koelmel, Shattuc, IL

TAKES: 30 MIN. • **MAKES:** 2 SERVINGS

- ¼ cup each chopped onion, celery and green pepper
- 1 Tbsp. butter
- ½ cup hot water
- 1 jar (4½ oz.) sliced mushrooms, drained
- ⅓ cup uncooked instant rice
- 1½ tsp. chicken bouillon granules

NOTES

1. In a 1-qt. microwave-safe dish, combine onion, celery, green pepper and butter. Microwave, uncovered, on high for 2-4 minutes or until vegetables are crisp-tender.

2. Stir in remaining ingredients. Cook on high for 7-10 minutes or until rice is tender.

1 CUP 145 cal., 6g fat (4g sat. fat), 16mg chol., 960mg sod., 20g carb. (3g sugars, 3g fiber), 3g pro.

COWBOY CALICO BEANS

This is a tradition at the table when my girlfriends and I go up north for a girls' weekend. The husbands and kids are left at home, but the slow cooker comes with us!

—Julie Butsch, Hartland, WI

PREP: 30 MIN. • **COOK:** 4 HOURS • **MAKES:** 8 SERVINGS

- 1 lb. lean ground beef (90% lean)
- 1 large sweet onion, chopped
- ½ cup packed brown sugar
- ¼ cup ketchup
- 3 Tbsp. cider vinegar
- 2 Tbsp. yellow mustard
- 1 can (16 oz.) butter beans, drained
- 1 can (16 oz.) kidney beans, rinsed and drained
- 1 can (15 oz.) pork and beans
- 1 can (15¼ oz.) lima beans, rinsed and drained

1. In a large skillet, cook beef and onion over medium heat until meat is no longer pink, breaking meat into crumbles; drain.

2. Transfer meat to a 3-qt. slow cooker. Combine brown sugar, ketchup, vinegar and mustard; add to meat mixture. Stir in beans. Cover and cook on low until heated through, 4-5 hours.

¾ CUP 340 cal., 5g fat (2g sat. fat), 35mg chol., 691mg sod., 54g carb. (23g sugars, 12g fiber), 21g pro.

how to cook ...

MEAT

T-BONE STEAKS WITH HERB BUTTER, PAGE 152

PARMESAN PORK TENDERLOIN

I am of Danish descent and love all things pork, both old recipes and new. Here's a dish I came up with myself.
—John Hansen, Marstons Mills, MA

PREP: 25 MIN. • **COOK:** 25 MIN. • **MAKES:** 2 SERVINGS

- 1 pork tenderloin (¾ lb.)
- 6 Tbsp. grated Parmesan cheese
- 1 small sweet onion, sliced and separated into rings
- 1½ cups sliced fresh mushrooms
- 1 garlic clove, minced
- 2 tsp. butter, divided
- 2 tsp. olive oil, divided
- ¼ cup reduced-sodium beef broth
- 2 Tbsp. port wine or additional beef broth
- ⅛ tsp. salt, optional
- ⅛ tsp. each dried basil, thyme and rosemary, crushed
- Dash pepper
- ½ tsp. cornstarch
- 3 Tbsp. water

1. Cut pork into ½-in. slices; flatten to ⅛-in. thickness. Coat with Parmesan cheese; set aside.

2. In a large skillet, saute onion rings, mushrooms and garlic in 1 tsp. butter and 1 tsp. oil until tender; remove and keep warm. In same skillet, cook pork in remaining 1 tsp. butter and 1 tsp. oil in batches over medium heat until the juices run clear, about 2 minutes on each side. Remove and keep warm.

3. Add broth to pan, scraping to loosen browned bits. Stir in wine or additional broth; add seasonings. Bring to a boil. Reduce heat; simmer, uncovered, for 5 minutes. Combine cornstarch and water until smooth; stir into pan. Bring to a boil; cook and stir until thickened, about 2 minutes. Serve with pork and onion mixture.

1 SERVING 388 cal., 19g fat (8g sat. fat), 118mg chol., 472mg sod., 11g carb. (6g sugars, 2g fiber), 43g pro.

NOTES

5i

HOLIDAY HAM

Ham makes appearances at all of our holiday dinners. I also like to use whole pineapple rings and maraschino cherries.
—Betty Butler, Union Bridge, MD

PREP: 10 MIN. • **BAKE:** 1½ HOURS • **MAKES:** 20 SERVINGS

- 1 can (20 oz.) sliced pineapple
- 1 spiral-sliced fully cooked bone-in ham (8 to 10 lbs.)
- ⅔ cup maraschino cherries
- 1½ cups packed brown sugar
- ½ tsp. seasoned salt

1. Drain pineapple, reserving juice. Place ham on a rack in a shallow roasting pan. Secure pineapple and cherries to ham with toothpicks. Combine brown sugar and seasoned salt; rub over ham. Gently pour pineapple juice over ham.

2. Bake ham, uncovered, at 325° until a thermometer reads 140°, 1½-2 hours. Baste frequently with brown sugar mixture.

4 OZ. HAM 241 cal., 5g fat (2g sat. fat), 80mg chol., 1000mg sod., 23g carb. (22g sugars, 0 fiber), 27g pro.

CHINESE-STYLE RIBS

When I was working two jobs, slow cooking was my way of life. Sometimes I had more than one slow cooker going at a time to help me feed my family delicious home-cooked meals. It's nice to walk in after a hard day's work and have dinner ready. I hope you agree these ribs are quick, easy and delicious—enjoy them with friends and family!
—Paula Marchesi, Lenhartsville, PA

PREP: 20 MIN. • **COOK:** 6 HOURS • **MAKES:** 6 SERVINGS

- 3 lbs. boneless country-style pork ribs
- 6 green onions, cut into 1-in. pieces
- 1 can (8 oz.) sliced water chestnuts, drained
- ¾ cup hoisin sauce
- 3 Tbsp. soy sauce
- 2 Tbsp. sherry or chicken stock
- 5 garlic cloves, minced
- 1 Tbsp. minced fresh gingerroot
- 1 Tbsp. light corn syrup
- 1 Tbsp. orange marmalade
- 1 tsp. pumpkin pie spice
- ½ tsp. crushed red pepper flakes
- 2 Tbsp. cornstarch
- 2 Tbsp. water
- Hot cooked rice
- Additional sliced green onions, optional

DID YOU KNOW?

Hoisin sauce is a thick, sweet and somewhat spicy condiment popular in Chinese cooking. It's often made with fermented soybeans (miso), garlic, spices and sweet ingredients such as plums or sweet potatoes.

1. Place pork, green onions and water chestnuts in a 5-qt slow cooker. Mix hoisin sauce, soy sauce, sherry, garlic, ginger, corn syrup, marmalade, pie spice and pepper flakes in a bowl. Pour over pork. Cook, covered, on low until meat is tender, 6-8 hours.

2. Remove to a serving platter; keep warm. Skim fat from cooking juices; transfer to a small saucepan. Bring to a boil. Mix cornstarch and 2 Tbsp. water until smooth. Gradually stir mixture into saucepan. Bring to a boil; cook and stir until thickened, about 2 minutes. Serve sauce with the ribs, rice and, if desired, additional green onions.

1 SERVING 498 cal., 22g fat (8g sat. fat), 132mg chol., 1115mg sod., 29g carb. (15g sugars, 2g fiber), 42g pro.

EGG ROLL NOODLE BOWL

We love Asian egg rolls, but they can be challenging to make. Simplify everything with this deconstructed egg roll made on the stovetop and served in a bowl.
—Courtney Stultz, Weir, KS

TAKES: 30 MIN. • **MAKES:** 4 SERVINGS

1 Tbsp. sesame oil
½ lb. ground pork
1 Tbsp. soy sauce
1 tsp. ground ginger
½ tsp. salt
¼ tsp. ground turmeric
¼ tsp. pepper
6 cups shredded cabbage (about 1 small head)
2 large carrots, shredded (about 2 cups)
4 oz. rice noodles
3 green onions, thinly sliced
Additional soy sauce, optional

1. In a large cast-iron or other heavy skillet, heat oil over medium-high heat; cook and crumble pork for 4-6 minutes or until browned. Stir in soy sauce and seasonings. Add cabbage and carrots; cook until vegetables are tender, stirring occasionally, 4-6 minutes longer.

2. Cook noodles according to package directions; drain and immediately add to pork mixture, tossing to combine. Sprinkle with green onions. If desired, serve with additional soy sauce.

1½ CUPS 302 cal., 12g fat (4g sat. fat), 38mg chol., 652mg sod., 33g carb. (2g sugars, 4g fiber), 14g pro. **DIABETIC EXCHANGES** 2 medium-fat meat, 2 vegetable, 1½ starch, ½ fat.

VARIATION IDEAS

• **Use other veggies.** Swap in bell peppers, mushrooms or another veggie for the carrots and cabbage.

• **Top it with an egg.** We love adding a poached or over-easy egg on top of these egg roll noodles.

• **Make a meatless version.** Cube and brown firm tofu in step 1 instead of using pork. Remove from pan and stir into finished dish at the end.

COMPANY POT ROAST

The aroma of this roast slowly cooking in the oven is absolutely mouthwatering. It gives the home such a cozy, warm feeling, even on the chilliest winter days.
—Anita Osborne, Thomasburg, ON

PREP: 20 MIN. • **BAKE:** 2¾ HOURS • **MAKES:** 6 SERVINGS

- 1 boneless beef chuck roast (3 to 4 lbs.)
- 2 Tbsp. olive oil
- 1 cup sherry or beef broth
- ½ cup reduced-sodium soy sauce
- ¼ cup sugar
- 2 tsp. beef bouillon granules
- 1 cinnamon stick (3 in.)
- 8 medium carrots, cut into 2-in. pieces
- 6 medium potatoes, peeled and cut into 1½-in. pieces
- 1 medium onion, sliced
- 2 Tbsp. cornstarch
- 2 Tbsp. cold water

READER REVIEW

"One of the best roasts I have ever made in the oven. Very tender and delicious."

—GROUSEMAN, TASTEOFHOME.COM

1. Brown the roast in oil in an oven-safe Dutch oven on all sides; drain. Combine sherry, soy sauce, sugar, bouillon and cinnamon stick; pour over roast.

2. Cover and bake at 325° until the meat and vegetables are tender, 2¾-3¼ hours, adding the carrots, potatoes and onion during last 30 minutes of cooking.

3. Remove roast and vegetables to a serving platter; keep warm. Combine cornstarch and water until smooth. Stir into pan. Bring to a boil; cook and stir until thickened, about 2 minutes. Serve with roast and vegetables.

6 OZ. COOKED MEAT WITH 2 CUPS VEGETABLES AND ¼ CUP GRAVY 713 cal., 26g fat (9g sat. fat), 148mg chol., 1437mg sod., 56g carb. (17g sugars, 5g fiber), 49g pro.

ROOT BEER PULLED PORK SANDWICHES

My tasty recipe is sure to please a crowd! People say they love the subtle heat and hint of sweetness in these saucy sandwiches. Try serving them with coleslaw and pickles.
—Karen Currie, Kirkwood, MO

PREP: 30 MIN. • **COOK:** 9½ HOURS • **MAKES:** 8 SERVINGS

- 2 lbs. boneless pork sirloin roast
- 1 medium onion, sliced
- 2 Tbsp. dried minced garlic
- 3 cups root beer, divided
- 1 bottle (12 oz.) chili sauce
- ⅛ tsp. hot pepper sauce
- 8 kaiser rolls, split

1. Place roast in a 3-qt. slow cooker. Add onion, garlic and 1 cup root beer. Cover and cook on low for 9-10 hours or until meat is tender.

2. In a small saucepan, combine chili sauce, hot pepper sauce and remaining root beer. Bring to a boil. Reduce heat; simmer, uncovered, for 20-25 minutes or until thickened.

3. Remove meat from slow cooker; cool slightly. Discard cooking juices. Shred the pork with 2 forks and return to slow cooker. Stir in barbecue sauce. Cover and cook on low for 30 minutes or until heated through. Serve on rolls.

1 SANDWICH 424 cal., 9g fat (3g sat. fat), 68mg chol., 1066mg sod., 57g carb. (22g sugars, 2g fiber), 29g pro.

CHEESEBURGER MEAT LOAF

I created this meat loaf one day when I wanted to make cheeseburgers, but it was too chilly to grill outside. I've served it numerous times since then, and it never fails to get rave reviews. Even your most finicky eater will enjoy this.
—Paula Sullivan, Barker, NY

PREP: 20 MIN. • **BAKE:** 50 MIN. + STANDING • **MAKES:** 6 SERVINGS

- ½ cup ketchup, divided
- 1 large egg
- ¼ cup dry bread crumbs
- 1 tsp. onion powder
- 1 lb. lean ground beef (90% lean)
- 2 tsp. prepared mustard
- 2 tsp. dill pickle relish
- 6 slices American cheese, divided

1. In a bowl, combine ¼ cup ketchup, egg, bread crumbs and onion powder. Crumble beef over mixture and mix well. On a large piece of waxed paper, pat beef mixture into a 10x6-in. rectangle. Spread remaining ketchup over meat to within ½ in. of long sides and 1½ in. of short sides. Top with mustard and relish.

2. Place 4 cheese slices on top. Roll up loaf, jelly-roll style, starting with a short side and pulling away the waxed paper while rolling. Seal seams and ends well. Place meat loaf, seam side down, in a greased 11x7-in. baking pan.

3. Bake meat loaf at 350° for 45 minutes or until the meat is no longer pink and a thermometer reads 160°. Cut remaining cheese slices in half diagonally; place on top of loaf. Return to oven for 5 minutes or until the cheese is melted. Let stand 10 minutes before slicing.

1 PIECE 243 cal., 12g fat (6g sat. fat), 93mg chol., 595mg sod., 12g carb. (7g sugars, 0 fiber), 20g pro.

T-BONE STEAKS WITH HERB BUTTER

Whip up a delicious compound butter to add decadence to an already incredible cut of beef. Infused with garlic and Italian herbs, the T-bone is topped with butter and perfectly grilled to impress any steak fan.
—Taste of Home *Test Kitchen*

PREP: 15 MIN. + MARINATING • **GRILL:** 10 MIN. + STANDING • **MAKES:** 2 SERVINGS

HERB BUTTER

- 2 Tbsp. butter, softened
- 1 Tbsp. minced fresh parsley
- 1 garlic clove, minced
- ½ tsp. Italian seasoning

STEAKS

- 2 Tbsp. olive oil
- ½ tsp. salt
- ½ tsp. pepper
- ½ tsp. garlic powder
- 2 beef T-bone steaks (¾ lb. each)

1. In a bowl, combine the herb butter ingredients; stir until combined. Cover and refrigerate until serving.

2. In a shallow dish, combine the oil, salt, pepper and garlic powder. Coat steaks with oil mixture. Let stand at room temperature for 30 minutes, turning once.

3. Grill, covered, over medium-high heat until meat reaches the desired doneness (for medium-rare, a thermometer should read 135°; medium, 140°; medium-well, 145°), 4-6 minutes on each side. Remove steaks from the grill; top each steak with 1 Tbsp. herb butter. Let steaks stand for 5 minutes before serving.

1 STEAK 565 cal., 41g fat (15g sat. fat), 129mg chol., 810mg sod., 2g carb. (0 sugars, 0 fiber), 47g pro.

SPICE-RUBBED LAMB CHOPS

One of my favorite meals to eat anytime is lamb chops! My girls, Hanna and Amani, love watching me make my delicious chops, but they love eating them even more.
—Nareman Dietz, Beverly Hills, MI

PREP: 15 MIN. + CHILLING • **BAKE:** 5 MIN. • **MAKES:** 2 SERVINGS

- 2 tsp. lemon juice
- 2 tsp. Worcestershire sauce
- 1½ tsp. pepper
- 1¼ tsp. ground cumin
- 1¼ tsp. curry powder
- 1 garlic clove, minced
- ½ tsp. sea salt
- ½ tsp. onion powder
- ½ tsp. crushed red pepper flakes
- 4 lamb rib chops
- 1 Tbsp. olive oil

1. Mix first 9 ingredients; spread over chops. Refrigerate, covered, overnight.

2. Preheat oven to 450°. In an ovenproof skillet, heat the oil over medium-high heat; brown chops, 2 minutes per side. Transfer chops to the oven; roast until desired doneness (for medium-rare, a thermometer should read 135°; medium, 140°), 3-4 minutes.

2 LAMB CHOPS 290 cal., 17g fat (4g sat. fat), 90mg chol., 620mg sod., 5g carb. (1g sugars, 2g fiber), 29g pro. **DIABETIC EXCHANGES** 4 lean meat, 1½ fat.

CAROLINA-STYLE PORK BARBECUE

I am originally from North Carolina and this recipe is a favorite. My husband swears my authentic Carolina 'cue is the best barbecue he's ever eaten!
—Kathryn Ransom Williams, Sparks, NV

PREP: 30 MIN. • **COOK:** 6 HOURS • **MAKES:** 14 SERVINGS

- 1 boneless pork shoulder butt roast (4 to 5 lbs.)
- 2 Tbsp. brown sugar
- 2 tsp. salt
- 1 tsp. paprika
- ½ tsp. pepper
- 2 medium onions, quartered
- ¾ cup cider vinegar
- 4 tsp. Worcestershire sauce
- 1 Tbsp. sugar
- 1 Tbsp. crushed red pepper flakes
- 1 tsp. garlic salt
- 1 tsp. ground mustard
- ½ tsp. cayenne pepper
- 14 hamburger buns, split
- 1¾ lbs. deli coleslaw

READER REVIEW

"This is very, very good! After removing the pork from the cooking juices, I poured the juices and onions into a kettle. I reduced the juices by half, which concentrated the wonderful flavors. After shredding the meat, I strained the mixture into the meat. The next day, it was even better."

—FHQUILTING, TASTEOFHOME.COM

1. Cut roast into quarters. Mix brown sugar, salt, paprika and pepper; rub over meat. Place meat and onions in a 5-qt. slow cooker.

2. In a small bowl, whisk cider vinegar, Worcestershire sauce, sugar, pepper flakes, garlic salt, mustard and cayenne; pour over roast. Cook, covered, on low for 6-8 hours or until meat is tender.

3. Remove roast; cool slightly. Reserve 1½ cups of cooking juices; discard the remaining juices. Skim fat from reserved juices. Shred pork with 2 forks. Return pork and reserved juices to slow cooker; heat through. Serve pork on buns with coleslaw.

1 SANDWICH 453 cal., 22g fat (6g sat. fat), 85mg chol., 889mg sod., 35g carb. (14g sugars, 3g fiber), 27g pro.

TACO MAC

Pork sausage, taco seasoning and taco sauce add plenty of zip to easy macaroni and cheese. This zesty dish is just as yummy the next day.
—JoLynn Fribley, Nokomis, IL

TAKES: 30 MIN. • **MAKES:** 6 SERVINGS

- 1 pkg. (24 oz.) shells and cheese dinner mix
- ½ lb. bulk pork sausage, cooked and drained
- ⅓ cup taco sauce
- 1 Tbsp. taco seasoning
- 4 cups shredded lettuce
- 2 medium tomatoes, chopped
- Shredded cheddar cheese, optional

Prepare the shells and cheese mix according to package directions. Stir in sausage, taco sauce and seasoning; cook and stir until heated through. Top with lettuce, tomatoes and, if desired, cheddar cheese.

FREEZE OPTION Freeze cooled pasta mixture in freezer containers. To use, partially thaw in refrigerator overnight. Heat through in a saucepan, stirring occasionally; add milk if necessary. Garnish as directed.

1 SERVING 465 cal., 20g fat (11g sat. fat), 54mg chol., 1413mg sod., 51g carb. (7g sugars, 2g fiber), 20g pro.

SWEET-AND-SOUR PORK WITH PINEAPPLE

After my sister moved away to university, I used to visit her on weekends. She often made this wonderful and tangy pork dish. Now, every time I make it for my family, it reminds me of those special visits. Everyone who tries it loves it.
—Cherry Williams, St. Albert, AB

TAKES: 25 MIN. • **MAKES:** 4 SERVINGS

- 1 can (14 oz.) pineapple tidbits
- 2 Tbsp. cornstarch
- 2 Tbsp. brown sugar
- ¾ tsp. salt
- ¼ tsp. ground ginger
- ¼ tsp. pepper
- ⅓ cup water
- ⅓ cup ketchup
- 2 Tbsp. white vinegar
- 2 Tbsp. reduced-sodium soy sauce
- 1 lb. pork tenderloin, cut into 1½ x ¼-in. strips
- 1 medium onion, chopped
- 2 Tbsp. canola oil
- 1 green pepper, cut into thin strips
- Hot cooked rice
- Sesame seeds, optional

READER REVIEW

"Very tasty and simple to make. I happened to have a fresh, sweet pineapple on hand, so I used that. Will definitely make it again!"

—WIKERSHINE, TASTEOFHOME.COM

1. Drain pineapple, reserving the juice; set aside. In a bowl, combine cornstarch, brown sugar, salt, ginger and pepper. Stir in water, ketchup, vinegar, soy sauce and reserved juice until smooth.

2. In a large skillet or wok, stir-fry pork and onion in oil for 4-8 minutes or until tender. Stir pineapple juice mixture; add to skillet. Bring to a boil; cook and stir for 1-2 minutes or until thickened.

3. Add the green pepper and pineapple. Reduce heat; cover and cook until pepper is tender, about 5 minutes. Serve with rice and, if desired, sesame seeds.

1 SERVING 333 cal., 11g fat (2g sat. fat), 63mg chol., 1190mg sod., 35g carb. (24g sugars, 2g fiber), 25g pro.

BANH MI BABY BACK RIBS

This creative entree has all the flavors of the beloved Vietnamese sandwich—sans bread. Sprinkle the pork with roasted peanuts and sesame seeds, in addition to the other garnishes, for a fun crunch.
—Bonnie Geavaras-Bootz, Chandler, AZ

PREP: 3 HOURS • **GRILL:** 15 MIN. • **MAKES:** 4 SERVINGS

4 lbs. pork baby back ribs
2 whole garlic bulbs
1 large navel orange, quartered
1 cup Korean barbecue sauce, divided
¾ cup rice vinegar
½ cup sugar
⅓ cup water
½ cup shredded carrots
½ cup shredded daikon radish
½ cup thinly sliced green onions
Toppings: Thinly sliced cucumber, sliced fresh jalapeno pepper, cilantro leaves and lime wedges

1. Preheat the oven to 325°. Place ribs in a large roasting pan. Remove papery outer skin from garlic bulbs, but do not peel or separate cloves. Cut off top of garlic bulbs, exposing individual garlic cloves; add to roasting pan. Add orange; cover pan with heavy-duty foil and seal tightly. Bake until tender, 2-2½ hours, brushing with ½ cup barbecue sauce halfway through cooking.

2. Meanwhile, in a small saucepan, combine vinegar, sugar and water. Bring the mixture to a boil over high heat; cook until sugar is dissolved, about 2 minutes. Let cool completely. Place carrots, radish and green onions in a bowl; add vinegar mixture. Refrigerate until serving.

3. Prepare the grill for medium direct heat. Carefully remove the ribs from roasting pan; discard garlic and orange. Place ribs on grill rack; brush with some of the remaining ½ cup barbecue sauce. Grill, covered, over medium heat until browned, 15-20 minutes, turning and brushing occasionally with sauce. Cut into serving-size portions. Serve ribs with pickled vegetables, toppings and remaining sauce.

1 SERVING 718 cal., 50g fat (16g sat. fat), 163mg chol., 1499mg sod., 23g carb. (17g sugars, 1g fiber), 45g pro.

NOTES

BURGERS ON THE STOVE

You don't need a grill to create these juicy, tender burgers. This recipe uses the stovetop to create restaurant-quality burgers that just might be the best you've ever had!
—Lindsay Mattison, Hillsboro, OR

TAKES: 25 MIN. • **MAKES:** 4 SERVINGS

- 1 1/3 lbs. ground beef
- 3 Tbsp. butter, softened, divided
- 4 hamburger buns, split
- 1 tsp. kosher salt
- Optional: Cheese, lettuce, tomato, red onion, mayonnaise, ketchup and mustard

1. Shape beef into four 1-in.-thick patties. Using your thumb, press a ½-in. hole in center of each patty. Refrigerate patties until cooking.

2. Meanwhile, spread 2 Tbsp. butter over the cut sides of buns. In a large cast-iron skillet over medium-high heat, toast the buns, cut sides down, in batches; remove to serving plates. Wipe skillet clean. Sprinkle chilled patties with salt.

3. In the same skillet, melt remaining 1 Tbsp. butter over medium-high heat. Add chilled, seasoned patties. Cook until a thermometer reads 160°, 4-5 minutes per side. Serve on toasted buns with toppings as desired.

1 BURGER 472 cal., 28g fat (13g sat. fat), 116mg chol., 849mg sod., 22g carb. (3g sugars, 1g fiber), 31g pro.

RED WINE FILET MIGNON

Although this filet is such a simple recipe, you can feel confident serving it to your guests. The rich sauce adds a touch of elegance. Just add a veggie and rolls.
—Jauneen Hosking, Waterford, WI

TAKES: 20 MIN. • **MAKES:** 2 SERVINGS

- 2 beef tenderloin steaks (8 oz. each)
- 3 Tbsp. butter, divided
- 1 Tbsp. olive oil
- 1 cup merlot
- 2 Tbsp. heavy whipping cream
- ⅛ tsp. salt

READER REVIEW

"I didn't have merlot, so I used a red blend. I also added sauteed mushrooms to the sauce. These steaks were delicious. Good recipe!
—LOISCOOKS, TASTEOFHOME.COM

1. In a small skillet, cook steaks in 1 Tbsp. butter and oil over medium heat until meat reaches the desired doneness (for medium-rare, a thermometer should read 135°; medium, 140°; medium-well, 145°), 4-6 minutes on each side. Remove and keep warm.

2. In the same skillet, add wine, stirring to loosen browned bits from pan. Bring to a boil; cook until liquid is reduced to ¼ cup. Add cream, salt and remaining butter; bring to a boil. Cook and stir until slightly thickened and butter is melted, 1-2 minutes. Serve with steaks.

1 STEAK WITH 2 TBSP. SAUCE 690 cal., 43g fat (20g sat. fat), 165mg chol., 279mg sod., 4g carb. (1g sugars, 0 fiber), 49g pro.

COLD WEATHER BRAISED BEEF

This braised beef recipe is so convenient. I like to prep it on Saturday, pop it into the fridge overnight and then bake it on Sunday while spending time with family. The aroma of the beef while it's cooking will make your mouth water.
—Vicki Christiansen, Elkhorn, WI

PREP: 35 MIN. • **BAKE:** 2½ HOURS • **MAKES:** 8 SERVINGS

- 3 Tbsp. butter
- 1 lb. sliced fresh mushrooms
- 3 medium onions, halved and thinly sliced
- 2 garlic cloves, minced
- 2 lbs. boneless beef chuck roast, cut into 1-in. cubes
- 2½ cups water, divided
- 2 cups beef broth
- ½ cup dry red wine
- 3 Tbsp. reduced-sodium soy sauce
- 3 Tbsp. cornstarch
- ½ tsp. salt
- ½ tsp. coarsely ground pepper
- Hot cooked mashed potatoes or noodles

1. Preheat the oven to 325°. In a large skillet, melt butter over medium heat. Add mushrooms and onions; cook and stir until softened, 5-7 minutes. Add garlic; cook and stir 1 minute longer. Spoon mixture into a greased 13x9-in. baking dish, leaving drippings in skillet.

2. In same skillet over medium heat, brown beef in batches, adding more butter if necessary. Spoon browned beef over mushroom mixture in the baking dish.

3. Add 2 cups water, broth, wine and soy sauce to skillet; increase heat to medium-high. Cook 1 minute, stirring to loosen browned bits from pan. In a small bowl, mix cornstarch and the remaining ½ cup water until smooth. Gradually whisk into broth mixture. Bring to a boil, stirring constantly; cook and stir until slightly thickened, 1-2 minutes. Stir in salt and pepper. Pour over beef in baking dish.

4. Cover and bake until beef is almost tender, about 2 hours. Uncover and bake until beef is tender, 30-35 minutes. Serve over mashed potatoes or noodles.

TO MAKE AHEAD Prepare the recipe as directed through step 3. Instead of baking, cover and refrigerate for up to 2 days. Remove from the refrigerator 30 minutes before baking. Bake as directed.

1 CUP 284 cal., 15g fat (7g sat. fat), 85mg chol., 656mg sod., 10g carb. (3g sugars, 1g fiber), 25g pro.

NOTES

MINI MEAT LOAF SHEET-PAN MEAL

I grew up with this meat loaf recipe, but I adapted it to mini meat loaves so that it would bake quicker. The sauce topping is always a hit. I added the potatoes and asparagus to make the meal easier.
—Deanne Johnson, Reading, PA

PREP: 35 MIN. • **BAKE:** 40 MIN. • **MAKES:** 6 SERVINGS

- 2 large eggs, lightly beaten
- 1 cup tomato juice
- ¾ cup quick-cooking oats
- ¼ cup finely chopped onion
- ½ tsp. salt
- 1½ lbs. lean ground beef (90% lean)
- ¼ cup ketchup
- 3 Tbsp. brown sugar
- 1 tsp. prepared mustard
- ¼ tsp. ground nutmeg
- 3 large potatoes, peeled and cut into ½-in. pieces
- 3 Tbsp. olive oil, divided
- ½ tsp. garlic salt, divided
- ¼ tsp. pepper, divided
- 1 lb. fresh asparagus, trimmed and halved

1. Preheat the oven to 425°. In a large bowl, combine eggs, tomato juice, oats, onion and salt. Add the beef; mix lightly but thoroughly. Shape into six 4x2½-in. loaves; place on a sheet pan or in a large shallow roasting pan. Combine ketchup, brown sugar, mustard and nutmeg; brush over loaves.

2. Combine potatoes with 2 Tbsp. oil, ¼ tsp. garlic salt and ⅛ tsp. pepper; toss to coat. Add to the pan in a single layer. Bake loaves and potatoes 25 minutes.

3. Combine asparagus with remaining 1 Tbsp. oil, ¼ tsp. garlic salt and ⅛ tsp. pepper; toss to coat. Add to pan. Bake until a thermometer inserted into meat loaves reads 160° and the vegetables are tender, 15-20 minutes. Let stand 5 minutes before serving.

1 MEAT LOAF WITH 1¼ CUPS VEGETABLES
460 cal., 19g fat (5g sat. fat), 133mg chol., 690mg sod., 45g carb. (13g sugars, 3g fiber), 29g pro.

BREADED PORK CHOPS

These traditional pork chops have a wonderful home-cooked flavor, just like the ones Mom used to make. The breading makes them crispy outside and tender and juicy inside. Why not treat your family to them tonight?
—Deborah Amrine, Fort Myers, FL

TAKES: 20 MIN. • **MAKES:** 6 SERVINGS

- 1 large egg, lightly beaten
- ½ cup 2% milk
- 1½ cups crushed saltine crackers
- 6 boneless pork loin chops (1 in. thick)
- ¼ cup canola oil

1. In a shallow bowl, combine egg and milk. Place cracker crumbs in another shallow bowl. Dip each pork chop into the egg mixture, then coat with cracker crumbs, patting to make a thick coating.

2. In a large skillet, cook pork chops in oil for 4-5 minutes on each side or until a thermometer reads 145°. Let meat stand for 5 minutes before serving.

1 PORK CHOP 405 cal., 22g fat (5g sat. fat), 115mg chol., 233mg sod., 14g carb. (1g sugars, 0 fiber), 36g pro.

PORK CHOP BREADING TIPS

To help the breading adhere, pat the pork dry with paper towels before dipping it into the egg mixture. Also ensure proper oil temperature. To test, drop a piece of breading into the oil. The oil is ready if the breading immediately starts to bubble and float to the top.

CARNE ADOVADA SOPES

I call this "dude food"—my husband and son would eat this weekly if they could. The tender shredded pork is great on top.
—Johnna Johnson, Scottsdale, AZ

PREP: 25 MIN. + MARINATING • **COOK:** 2 HOURS • **MAKES:** 12 SERVINGS

- 3 cups chicken broth, divided
- ¾ cup chili powder
- 2 Tbsp. red wine vinegar
- 1 Tbsp. chopped fresh cilantro
- 1 Tbsp. honey
- 2 tsp. ground cumin
- 2 tsp. dried oregano
- 1 tsp. salt
- 1 tsp. ground cinnamon
- 1 boneless pork shoulder butt roast (3 to 4 lbs.), cut into ¾-in. cubes
- 5 Tbsp. canola oil, divided
- 2 large onions, chopped
- 6 garlic cloves, minced
- 1 can (10 oz.) diced tomatoes and green chiles, undrained

SOPES

- 3 cups masa harina
- ½ tsp. salt
- 2 cups water
- 3 Tbsp. canola oil
- Optional toppings: Hot refried beans, shredded lettuce, chopped tomatoes, shredded cheddar cheese, guacamole and/or sour cream

1. In a large shallow dish, combine 1 cup of broth, chili powder, vinegar, cilantro, honey and seasonings. Add pork; turn to coat. Refrigerate 4 hours or overnight.

2. In an ovenproof Dutch oven, brown pork in 4 Tbsp. oil in batches. Remove and keep warm. In the same pan, saute onions in remaining oil until tender. Add garlic; cook 2 minutes longer.

3. Return pork to pan; add remaining broth and tomatoes. Bring to a boil. Cover and bake at 350° until the meat is tender, 1½-1¾ hours. With a slotted spoon, remove meat to a large bowl. Skim fat from cooking liquid. Bring to a boil over high heat; cook until slightly thickened and reduced to about 2 cups, stirring occasionally. Return meat to pan; set aside and keep warm.

4. For sopes, in a large bowl, combine the masa harina and salt; stir in 2 cups water. Knead the dough until smooth, adding additional water, 1 tsp. at a time, if necessary. Divide into 12 portions, about ¼ cup each. Roll each to form a ball; flatten to 4-in. patty. Cover.

5. Heat a large ungreased skillet over medium heat until hot. Cook sopes in batches until lightly browned, about 1 minute on each side. Remove from the pan. Immediately pinch edges to form a ½-in. rim; set aside.

6. To serve, in the same skillet over medium-high heat, cook sopes in hot oil in batches until golden brown and slightly crisp, 15-30 seconds on each side. Drain on paper towels. Using a slotted spoon, place pork on sopes; serve with toppings of your choice.

1 SOPE WITH ½ CUP PORK MIXTURE
423 cal., 23g fat (5g sat. fat), 68mg chol., 787mg sod., 32g carb. (4g sugars, 6g fiber), 24g pro.

PORK & RAMEN STIR-FRY

I put a bit of a spin on a typical stir-fry that you'd normally serve over rice. Ramen noodles are quick to substitute for the expected rice, and I find that bagged coleslaw mix gives the dish a good crisp-tender bite along with some fresh broccoli.
—*Barbara Pletzke, Herndon, VA*

TAKES: 30 MIN. • **MAKES:** 4 SERVINGS

- ¼ cup reduced-sodium soy sauce
- 2 Tbsp. ketchup
- 2 Tbsp. Worcestershire sauce
- 2 tsp. sugar
- ¼ tsp. crushed red pepper flakes
- 3 tsp. canola oil, divided
- 1 lb. boneless pork loin chops, cut into ½-in. strips
- 1 cup fresh broccoli florets
- 4 cups coleslaw mix
- 1 can (8 oz.) bamboo shoots, drained
- 4 garlic cloves, minced
- 2 pkg. (3 oz. each) ramen noodles

RAMEN STIR-FRY TIPS

• Pork loin is a lean cut that cooks very quickly. To maintain tender meat, be sure not to overcook it.

• Make your shopping list even shorter by swapping broccoli slaw for the coleslaw mix and broccoli florets!

• Instead of pork, use boneless skinless chicken breasts, beef sirloin steak or cubed tofu as other tasty and lean protein sources.

1. In a small bowl, whisk the first 5 ingredients until blended. In a large skillet, heat 2 tsp. oil over medium-high heat. Add pork; stir-fry 2-3 minutes or until no longer pink. Remove from pan.

2. In the same pan, stir-fry broccoli in remaining oil 3 minutes. Add coleslaw mix, bamboo shoots and garlic; stir-fry 3-4 minutes longer or until broccoli is crisp-tender. Stir in soy sauce mixture and pork; heat through.

3. Meanwhile, cook noodles according to package directions, discarding or saving seasoning packets for another use. Drain noodles; add to pork mixture and toss to combine.

1¾ CUPS 354 cal., 14g fat (5g sat. fat), 44mg chol., 794mg sod., 32g carb. (6g sugars, 3g fiber), 23g pro.

FRENCH MEAT & VEGETABLE PIE

Some time ago, a co-worker brought a meat pie to lunch. The aroma was familiar—after one taste, I was amazed to discover it was the same pie my grandmother used to serve when I was a youngster! My co-worker shared the recipe, and I have been enjoying it ever since.
—Rita Winterberger, Huson, MT

PREP: 20 MIN. • **BAKE:** 30 MIN. • **MAKES:** 8 SERVINGS

- 2 Tbsp. canola oil
- 1 large onion, thinly sliced
- 1 lb. ground beef
- 1 lb. ground pork
- 1 cup mashed potatoes (with added milk and butter)
- 1 can (8 oz.) mixed vegetables, drained
- 2 tsp. ground allspice
- 1 tsp. salt
- ¼ tsp. pepper
- Dough for double crust pie
- 1 large egg, lightly beaten, optional

1. Preheat the oven to 375°. In a skillet, heat oil over medium heat. Saute onion until tender, 1-2 minutes. Remove and set aside. In same skillet, brown beef and pork together until no longer pink, breaking the meat into crumbles; drain. Combine onion, meat, mashed potatoes, vegetables and seasonings.

2. On a lightly floured surface, roll half dough to a ⅛-in.-thick circle; transfer to a 9-in. pie plate. Trim the dough even with the rim. Roll remaining dough to a ⅛-in.-thick circle. Fill bottom crust with meat mixture. Place top crust over filling; trim, seal and flute edge. Cut slits in top. If desired, brush with egg.

3. Bake for 30-35 minutes or until crust is golden brown.

DOUGH FOR DOUBLE-CRUST PIE
Combine 2½ cups all-purpose flour and ½ tsp. salt; cut in 1 cup cold butter until crumbly. Gradually add ⅓-⅔ cup ice water, tossing with a fork until dough holds together when pressed. Divide dough in half. Shape each into a disk; wrap and refrigerate 1 hour.

1 SERVING 531 cal., 32g fat (12g sat. fat), 103mg chol., 724mg sod., 35g carb. (4g sugars, 1g fiber), 25g pro.

SLOW-COOKER SPAGHETTI & MEATBALLS

I've been cooking for 50 years, and this dish is still one that guests request frequently. It is my No. 1 standby recipe and also makes amazing meatball sandwiches. The sauce works for any type of pasta.
—Jane Whittaker, Pensacola, FL

PREP: 50 MIN. • **COOK:** 5 HOURS • **MAKES:** 12 SERVINGS

- 1 cup seasoned bread crumbs
- 2 Tbsp. grated Parmesan and Romano cheese blend
- 1 tsp. pepper
- ½ tsp. salt
- 2 large eggs, lightly beaten
- 2 lbs. ground beef

SAUCE

- 1 large onion, finely chopped
- 1 medium green pepper, finely chopped
- 3 cans (15 oz. each) tomato sauce
- 2 cans (14½ oz. each) diced tomatoes, undrained
- 1 can (6 oz.) tomato paste
- 6 garlic cloves, minced
- 2 bay leaves
- 1 tsp. each dried basil, oregano and parsley flakes
- 1 tsp. salt
- ½ tsp. pepper
- ¼ tsp. crushed red pepper flakes
- Hot cooked spaghetti

1. In a large bowl, mix the bread crumbs, cheese, pepper and salt; stir in eggs. Add beef; mix lightly but thoroughly. Shape into 1½-in. balls. In a large skillet, brown the meatballs in batches over medium heat; drain.

2. Place first 5 sauce ingredients in a 6-qt. slow cooker; stir in garlic and seasonings. Add meatballs, stirring gently to coat. Cook, covered, on low for 5-6 hours or until meatballs are cooked through.

3. Discard bay leaves. Serve meatballs and sauce with spaghetti.

ABOUT 3 MEATBALLS WITH ¾ CUP SAUCE
250 cal., 11g fat (4g sat. fat), 79mg chol., 1116mg sod., 20g carb. (7g sugars, 4g fiber), 20g pro.

SPAGHETTI & MEATBALL TIPS

What should you serve with spaghetti and meatballs? Spaghetti and meatballs pair nicely with a simple, crisp Italian salad or crusty, cheesy garlic bread fresh out of the oven.

Can you overcook meatballs in a slow cooker? Generally, slow cookers cook low and slow, so meatballs are less likely to overcook than if you were to quickly bake them in the oven. The longer you leave meatballs in a slow cooker, however, you do risk them becoming tougher and a bit chewier. For the best results, stick to the amount of time suggested in the recipe for perfect, tender meatballs cooked just right.

SHREDDED ITALIAN BEEF

This is one of my all-time favorite slow-cooker recipes! It is packed with delicious flavors and delivers 29 grams of protein per serving—a wonderful way to meet your daily needs!
—Jami Hilker, Harrison, AR

PREP: 15 MIN. • **COOK:** 8 HOURS • **MAKES:** 8 SERVINGS

- 1 beef sirloin tip roast (2 lbs.)
- 1 can (14½ oz.) diced tomatoes, undrained
- 1 medium green pepper, chopped
- ½ cup water
- 1 Tbsp. sesame seeds
- 1½ tsp. garlic powder
- 1 tsp. fennel seed, crushed
- ½ tsp. salt
- ½ tsp. pepper
- 8 kaiser rolls, split

1. Place roast in a 3-qt. slow cooker. In a small bowl, combine tomatoes, green pepper, water and seasonings; pour over roast. Cover; cook on low for 8-9 hours or until meat is tender.

2. Remove the roast; cool slightly. Skim fat from cooking juices; shred beef and return to the slow cooker. Serve on rolls.

1 SANDWICH 333 cal., 8g fat (2g sat. fat), 72mg chol., 573mg sod., 34g carb. (3g sugars, 3g fiber), 29g pro. **DIABETIC EXCHANGES** 3 lean meat, 2 starch.

STOVETOP ITALIAN BEEF ON ROLLS
Place the roast in a Dutch oven. Pour tomato mixture over the top. Bring to a boil. Reduce heat; cover and simmer for 1½-2 hours or until the meat is very tender. Proceed as directed.

SPICY ITALIAN BEEF Add 1 chopped jalapeno pepper or ½ tsp. crushed red pepper along with the other seasoning to the slow cooker.

SLOW-COOKER BABY BACK RIBS

These smoky ribs are so tender that they fall off the bone, and the spice blend makes your house smell like a dream.
—Taste of Home *Test Kitchen*

PREP: 15 MIN. • **COOK:** 5 HOURS • **MAKES:** 6 SERVINGS

- 2 Tbsp. brown sugar
- 1 tsp. salt
- 1 tsp. garlic powder
- 1 tsp. smoked paprika
- ½ tsp. onion powder
- ½ tsp. pepper
- 3 lbs. pork baby back ribs
- ½ cup water
- 1 cup barbecue sauce

1. In a small bowl, combine the first 6 ingredients. Cut ribs into serving-size pieces; rub with the seasoning mixture. Place water in a 6-qt. slow cooker; add ribs. Cook, covered, on low until meat is tender, 5-6 hours.

2. Preheat broiler. Transfer ribs, bone side down, to a foil-lined 15x10x1-in. baking pan; brush with sauce. Broil 4-5 in. from the heat until browned, 2-3 minutes. If desired, serve with additional sauce.

1 SERVING 382 cal., 21g fat (8g sat. fat), 81mg chol., 952mg sod., 24g carb. (20g sugars, 1g fiber), 23g pro.

BASIC PIZZA CRUST

I like to double this recipe and keep one baked crust in the freezer for a quick snack or meal later.
—Beverly Anderson, Sinclairville, NY

PREP: 10 MIN. + STANDING • **BAKE:** 25 MIN. • **MAKES:** 1 PIZZA CRUST (ABOUT 1 LB.)

1 pkg. (¼ oz.) active dry yeast
1 cup warm water (110° to 115°)
2 Tbsp. canola oil
1 tsp. sugar
¼ tsp. salt
2½ to 2¾ cups all-purpose flour
Cornmeal
Pizza toppings of your choice

5 TIPS FOR PIZZA CRUST PERFECTION

Making your own pizza crust is far easier than you might think. Just keep these secrets in mind.

- Make sure to use the type of yeast called for in the pizza crust recipe.
- Use a thermometer to check the temperature of the water. If it's too cool, it won't activate the yeast; if it's too hot, it may kill the yeast.
- Don't use too much flour. Start with the minimum amount and add more only until the dough reaches the desired consistency indicated in the recipe.
- Use just enough flour on your work surface to keep the dough from sticking when you're kneading it.
- Continue kneading until the dough is no longer sticky, has a smooth, satiny texture and springs back when pressed with your fingers.

1. In a large bowl, dissolve yeast in warm water. Add oil, sugar, salt and 1½ cups flour. Beat until smooth. Stir in enough remaining flour to form a firm dough. Turn onto a floured surface; cover and let rest for 10 minutes.

2. Roll into a 13-in. circle. Grease a 12-in. pizza pan and sprinkle with cornmeal. Transfer dough to prepared pan, building up edge slightly. Do not let rise. Bake at 425° until browned, 12-15 minutes. Add toppings; bake for 10-15 minutes longer.

⅙ OF CRUST 236 cal., 5g fat (1g sat. fat), 0 chol., 100mg sod., 41g carb. (2g sugars, 2g fiber), 6g pro.

POSH PIES

Think outside the (pizza) box with these tempting topping ideas.

Red-Sauce Pizzas:

HOG WILD
Italian sausage, bacon, Canadian bacon, shredded mozzarella, fresh oregano

VEGGIE
Mushrooms, onion, mini pepper rings, basil, shredded mozzarella

White-Sauce Pizzas:

GENOVESE
Salami, marinated artichoke hearts, red onion, shredded mozzarella, Parmesan

PROSCIUTTO FIG
Prosciutto, fresh quartered figs, arugula, olive oil, shredded mozzarella

Other Pizzas:

BEST-O PESTO
Pesto, roasted cherry tomatoes, basil, fresh mozzarella, pepper flakes

CALIFORNIA
BBQ sauce, diced chicken, red onion, jalapenos, shredded Colby-Jack, Fontina

ALOHA BURGERS

I love hamburgers and pineapple, so it just seemed natural for me to combine them. My family often requests these unique sandwiches. It's a nice change of pace from the same old boring burger.
—Joi McKim-Jones, Waikoloa, HI

TAKES: 30 MIN. • **MAKES:** 4 SERVINGS

- 1 can (8 oz.) sliced pineapple
- ¾ cup reduced-sodium teriyaki sauce
- 1 lb. ground beef
- 1 large sweet onion, sliced
- 1 Tbsp. butter
- 4 sesame seed or onion buns, split and toasted
- 4 lettuce leaves
- 4 slices Swiss cheese
- 4 bacon strips, cooked

1. Drain the pineapple juice into a small bowl; add teriyaki sauce. Place 3 Tbsp. in a shallow dish. Add pineapple slices; turn to coat and set aside.

2. Shape beef into 4 patties; place in an 8-in. square baking dish. Pour remaining teriyaki sauce mixture over the patties; marinate for 5-10 minutes, turning once.

3. Remove patties from the marinade; discard marinade. Grill, covered, over medium heat or broil 4 in. from the heat for 6-9 minutes on each side or until a thermometer reads 160°. Meanwhile, in a small skillet, saute onion in butter until tender, about 5 minutes; set aside.

4. Remove pineapple from marinade; discard marinade. Place pineapple on grill or under broiler to heat through. Layer bottom buns with lettuce and onion. Top with the burgers, cheese, pineapple and bacon. Replace tops.

1 BURGER 513 cal., 25g fat (11g sat. fat), 96mg chol., 716mg sod., 39g carb. (17g sugars, 3g fiber), 33g pro.

EASY GROUND BEEF TACO SALAD

Every time I have to bring a dish to a party, friends ask for my taco salad. Even players on my son's football team ask for it.
—Lori Buntrock, Wisconsin Rapids, WI

TAKES: 30 MIN. • **MAKES:** 6 SERVINGS

- 1 lb. ground beef
- 1 envelope reduced-sodium taco seasoning
- ¾ cup water
- 1 medium head iceberg lettuce, torn (about 8 cups)
- 2 cups shredded cheddar cheese
- 2 cups broken nacho-flavored tortilla chips
- ¼ cup Catalina salad dressing
- Optional toppings: Diced tomatoes, black beans, cubed avocado, salsa or pico de gallo

1. In a large skillet, cook the beef over medium heat 6-8 minutes or until no longer pink, breaking into crumbles; drain. Stir in the taco seasoning and water; bring to a boil. Reduce heat; simmer, uncovered, 4-6 minutes or until thickened, stirring occasionally. Cool slightly.

2. In a large bowl, toss lettuce with cheese. Top with beef mixture and chips; drizzle with dressing and toss to combine. Serve immediately with toppings as desired.

1⅔ CUPS 416 cal., 27g fat (12g sat. fat), 86mg chol., 830mg sod., 19g carb. (7g sugars, 2g fiber), 25g pro.

GONE-ALL-DAY GOULASH

With this recipe, you can put in a full day's work, run some errands and still get dinner on the table in no time. Make it extra special by serving the meat sauce over spaetzle.
—Cyndy Gerken, Naples, FL

PREP: 25 MIN. • **COOK:** 8½ HOURS • **MAKES:** 4 SERVINGS

- 2 lbs. beef stew meat
- 2 Tbsp. olive oil
- 1 can (14½ oz.) beef broth
- 1 large onion, chopped
- ½ cup ketchup
- 2 Tbsp. Worcestershire sauce
- 1 Tbsp. brown sugar
- 1 Tbsp. paprika
- ½ tsp. ground mustard
- 2 Tbsp. all-purpose flour
- ¼ cup water
- Hot cooked egg noodles or spaetzle

1. In a large skillet, brown beef in oil; drain. Transfer to a 3-qt. slow cooker. Combine the broth, onion, ketchup, Worcestershire sauce, brown sugar, paprika and mustard. Pour over beef. Cover and cook on low for 8-10 hours or until meat is tender.

2. In a small bowl, combine flour and water until smooth. Gradually stir into beef mixture. Cover and cook on high 30 minutes longer or until thickened. Serve with noodles.

1 CUP 478 cal., 23g fat (7g sat. fat), 141mg chol., 1021mg sod., 20g carb. (14g sugars, 1g fiber), 45g pro.

NOTES

APPLE-STUFFED PORK CHOPS

Usually, pork chops are paired with applesauce. This delicious entree has been on my menu for many years and piles apples into the pork chops instead.
—Paula Disterhaupt, Bakersfield, CA

PREP: 15 MIN. • **BAKE:** 1 HOUR • **MAKES:** 6 SERVINGS

- 1 Tbsp. chopped onion
- ¼ cup butter
- 3 cups soft bread cubes
- 2 cups finely chopped apples
- ¼ cup finely chopped celery
- 2 tsp. minced fresh parsley
- ¾ tsp. salt, divided
- 6 bone-in pork loin chops (1½ in. thick and 7 oz. each)
- ⅛ tsp. pepper
- 1 Tbsp. vegetable oil

1. In a small skillet, saute onion in butter until tender. Remove from heat; add the bread cubes, apples, celery, parsley and ¼ tsp. salt.

2. Cut a pocket in each chop by making a horizontal cut through meat almost to the bone. Sprinkle inside and outside with pepper and remaining salt. Spoon stuffing loosely into pockets.

3. In a large skillet, brown chops on both sides in oil. Place in an ungreased large baking pan. Cover and bake at 350° for 30 minutes. Uncover; bake 30 minutes longer or until a thermometer reads 145°. Let the meat stand for 5 minutes before serving.

NOTE To make soft bread crumbs, tear bread into pieces and place in a food processor or blender. Cover and pulse until crumbs form. One slice of bread yields ½-¾ cup crumbs.

1 SERVING 364 cal., 19g fat (8g sat. fat), 107mg chol., 534mg sod., 15g carb. (6g sugars, 2g fiber), 32g pro.

how to cook ... POULTRY

CRISPY FRIED CHICKEN, PAGE 223

COCONUT CURRY CHICKEN

My husband and I love this yummy dish! It's easy to prepare in the slow cooker, and it tastes just like a meal you'd have at your favorite Indian or Thai restaurant.
—Andi Kauffman, Beavercreek, OR

PREP: 20 MIN. • **COOK:** 5 HOURS • **MAKES:** 4 SERVINGS

- 2 medium potatoes, peeled and cubed
- 1 small onion, chopped
- 2 tsp. canola oil
- 1 lb. boneless skinless chicken breast halves
- 1 cup light coconut milk
- 4 tsp. curry powder
- 1 garlic clove, minced
- 1 tsp. reduced-sodium chicken bouillon granules
- ¼ tsp. salt
- ¼ tsp. pepper
- 2 cups hot cooked rice
- Optional: Cilantro, shredded coconut, chopped peanuts and thinly sliced red chiles

1. Place potatoes and onion in a 3- or 4-qt. slow cooker. In a large nonstick skillet, heat oil over medium heat; add chicken. Cook until lightly browned, 3-5 minutes, turning once. Transfer to slow cooker.

2. In a small bowl, combine coconut milk, curry powder, garlic, bouillon, salt and pepper; pour over chicken. Cover and cook on low for 5-6 hours or until the meat is tender. Remove chicken to cutting board. Cut into slices.

3. Serve chicken and sauce with rice. If desired, top with cilantro, coconut, peanuts and chiles.

1 SERVING 371 cal., 10g fat (4g sat. fat), 63mg chol., 265mg sod., 42g carb. (3g sugars, 3g fiber), 27g pro. **DIABETIC EXCHANGES** 3 starch, 3 lean meat, 1½ fat.

NOTES

PESTO-TURKEY LAYERED LOAF

This great sandwich is easy to make and travels well to picnics and potlucks. Use any meat, veggies and cheese you like.
—Marion Sundberg, Yorba Linda, CA

PREP: 20 MIN. • **BAKE:** 25 MIN. + STANDING • **MAKES:** 6 SERVINGS

- 1 loaf (1 lb.) French bread
- 1 cup prepared pesto
- 1 lb. thinly sliced deli turkey
- ½ lb. provolone cheese, thinly sliced
- 2 small zucchini, thinly sliced
- 2 medium tomatoes, thinly sliced
- 1 medium red onion, thinly sliced

1. Preheat oven to 350°. Cut top fourth off loaf of bread. Hollow out the bottom, leaving a ½-in. shell. (Discard removed bread or save for another use.) Spread pesto on the inside of top and bottom of bread. Set top aside.

2. Inside hollowed-out loaf, layer turkey, cheese, zucchini, tomatoes and onion. Press layers together. Replace bread top and wrap tightly in foil.

3. Place on a baking sheet. Bake until heated through, 25-30 minutes. Let stand 10 minutes before cutting.

1 PIECE 544 cal., 30g fat (11g sat. fat), 67mg chol., 1828mg sod., 41g carb. (7g sugars, 3g fiber), 29g pro.

SESAME CHICKEN STIR-FRY

When our children were little, my husband frequently worked late. This eye-catching stir-fry was a satisfying alternative to a big dinner for me and the kids.

—Michelle McWilliams, Fort Lupton, CO

TAKES: 30 MIN. • **MAKES:** 1 SERVING

- 1 boneless skinless chicken breast half, cut into 1½-in. pieces
- 2 tsp. canola oil
- 7 snow peas
- 1 cup fresh broccoli florets
- ⅓ cup julienned sweet red pepper
- 3 medium fresh mushrooms, sliced
- ¾ cup sliced onion
- 1 Tbsp. cornstarch
- 1 tsp. sugar
- ½ cup cold water
- 3 to 4 Tbsp. soy sauce
- Hot cooked rice
- 1 tsp. sesame seeds, toasted
- Thinly julienned green onions, optional

1. In a large skillet or wok, stir-fry the chicken in oil for until juices run clear, 6-8 minutes. Remove chicken and set aside. In the same skillet, stir-fry peas, broccoli and red pepper for 2-3 minutes. Add mushrooms and onion; stir-fry for 3-4 minutes.

2. Combine cornstarch and sugar; stir in water and soy sauce until smooth. Add to the pan. Bring to a boil; cook and stir until thickened, 1-2 minutes. Return chicken to pan; cook until mixture is heated through and vegetables are tender. Serve over rice. Sprinkle with sesame seeds and, if desired, green onions.

1 SERVING 398 cal., 14g fat (2g sat. fat), 63mg chol., 2858mg sod., 33g carb. (16g sugars, 7g fiber), 36g pro.

EASY CHICKEN ALFREDO

This classic Alfredo sauce is almost as easy as opening up a jar but tastes so much better. Paired with a quickly sauteed chicken breast, dinner can be on the table in less than 30 minutes.
—Taste of Home *Test Kitchen*

TAKES: 20 MIN. • **MAKES:** 4 SERVINGS

- 8 oz. uncooked fettuccine
- 2 boneless skinless chicken breasts
- ½ tsp. salt, divided
- ¼ tsp. pepper, divided
- 2 tsp. olive oil
- 6 Tbsp. butter, cubed
- 2 cups heavy whipping cream
- ¾ cup grated Parmesan cheese, divided
- ½ cup grated Romano cheese
- ⅛ tsp. ground nutmeg
- 2 large egg yolks, lightly beaten
- Minced fresh parsley, optional

READER REVIEW

"Good! I subbed 2% milk for the heavy cream and was concerned the sauce wouldn't thicken properly, but it did!"
—TAMMYCOOKBLOGSBOOKS, TASTEOFHOME.COM

1. Cook fettuccine according to package directions. Meanwhile, sprinkle chicken with ¼ tsp. salt and ⅛ tsp. pepper. In a large skillet, cook chicken in oil over medium heat for 8-10 minutes or until a thermometer reads 165°, turning once. Remove and let stand at least 5 minutes.

2. In the same skillet, melt butter over medium-low heat. Stir in cream, ½ cup Parmesan cheese, Romano cheese, nutmeg and remaining ¼ tsp. salt and ⅛ tsp. pepper.

3. In a small bowl, whisk egg yolks; stir in a small amount of hot cream mixture into egg yolks. Return all to pan, stirring constantly. Cook and stir over medium-low heat until the sauce has thickened slightly and a thermometer reads 160°.

4. Drain fettuccine; serve with Alfredo sauce, sliced chicken and remaining ¼ cup Parmesan cheese. If desired, garnish with parsley.

1 SERVING 998 cal., 77g fat (46g sat. fat), 326mg chol., 1015mg sod., 45g carb. (5g sugars, 2g fiber), 36g pro.

BUFFALO CHICKEN SALAD

This cool-yet-spicy salad is a staple at our house. Sometimes we cook the chicken on the grill, then sprinkle the hot sauce over it with the dressing, because you've gotta have that kick!
—Cori Cooper, Boise, ID

TAKES: 25 MIN. • **MAKES:** 4 SERVINGS

- 1 Tbsp. olive oil
- 1 lb. boneless skinless chicken breasts, cut into ¾-in. cubes
- 2 Tbsp. Louisiana-style hot sauce
- ¼ tsp. salt
- ¼ tsp. pepper
- 1 bunch romaine, chopped (about 8 cups)
- 2 celery ribs, chopped
- 1 cup shredded carrots
- ½ cup fat-free ranch salad dressing

1. In a large skillet, heat oil over medium-high heat. In batches, saute chicken until no longer pink, 3-4 minutes; remove to a bowl. Stir in hot sauce, salt and pepper.

2. On a platter, combine romaine, celery and carrots. Top with chicken. Serve with salad dressing.

1 SERVING 229 cal., 7g fat (1g sat. fat), 63mg chol., 644mg sod., 16g carb. (4g sugars, 3g fiber), 25g pro. **DIABETIC EXCHANGES** 3 lean meat, 1 starch, 1 vegetable, ½ fat.

CHICKEN PAPRIKASH

My mom learned to make this tender chicken dish when she volunteered to help prepare the dinners served at her church. It's my favorite main dish, and the gravy, seasoned with paprika, sour cream and onions, is the best.
—Pamela Eaton, Monclova, OH

PREP: 20 MIN. • **BAKE:** 1 HOUR • **MAKES:** 6 SERVINGS

- ¼ cup butter, cubed
- 1 large onion, chopped
- 1 broiler/fryer chicken (4 to 5 lbs.), cut up
- 2 Tbsp. paprika
- 1 tsp. salt
- ½ tsp. pepper
- 1½ cups water
- 2 Tbsp. cornstarch
- 2 Tbsp. cold water
- 1 cup sour cream

PAPRIKASH TIPS

What can I serve with Chicken Paprikash? This traditional Hungarian dish is delicious alongside vegetables, potatoes or rice. For an authentic option, pair it with spaetzle dumplings or buttery egg noodles.

Can I use different cuts of chicken for this recipe? Traditionally, a cut-up whole chicken is used in this dish. You can substitute all thighs, bone-in breasts or drumsticks for the whole chicken—or even use boneless skinless chicken breasts. (If using boneless meat, decrease the cook time considerably.)

How should I store leftovers of this recipe? Cool, then refrigerate in a covered container for 3–4 days or freeze in an airtight container for up to 2 months.

1. Preheat the oven to 350°. In a large skillet, heat butter over medium-high heat. Add the onion; cook and stir until tender. Sprinkle chicken with paprika, salt and pepper; place in an ungreased roasting pan. Spoon the onion mixture over chicken. Add water. Bake, covered, 1 hour or until chicken juices run clear.

2. Remove chicken and keep warm. Pour drippings and the loosened browned bits from roasting pan into a saucepan. Skim fat. In a small bowl, mix cornstarch and 2 Tbsp. cold water until smooth. Stir into the pan juices with onion. Bring to a boil; cook and stir until thickened, 1-2 minutes. Remove from heat. Stir in sour cream. Serve with chicken.

1 SERVING 379 cal., 23g fat (12g sat. fat), 145mg chol., 552mg sod., 7g carb. (3g sugars, 1g fiber), 34g pro.

CITRUS-HERB ROAST CHICKEN

This dish is one of my all-time favorites. The flavorful, juicy chicken combines with the aromas of spring in fresh herbs, lemon and onions to form the perfect one-pot meal. I make the gravy right in the pan.
—Megan Fordyce, Fairchance, PA

PREP: 25 MIN. • **BAKE:** 2 HOURS + STANDING • **MAKES:** 8 SERVINGS

- 6 garlic cloves
- 1 roasting chicken (6 to 7 lbs.)
- 3 lbs. baby red potatoes, halved
- 6 medium carrots, halved lengthwise and cut into 1-in. pieces
- 4 fresh thyme sprigs
- 4 fresh dill sprigs
- 2 fresh rosemary sprigs
- 1 medium lemon
- 1 small navel orange
- 1 tsp. salt
- ½ tsp. pepper
- 3 cups chicken broth, warmed
- 6 green onions, cut into 2-in. pieces

1. Preheat oven to 350°. Peel and cut garlic into quarters. Place chicken on a cutting board. Tuck wings under chicken. With a sharp paring knife, cut 24 small slits in breasts, drumsticks and thighs. Insert garlic in slits. Tie drumsticks together.

2. Place potatoes and carrots in a shallow roasting pan; top with herbs. Place the chicken, breast side up, over vegetables and herbs. Cut lemon and orange in half; gently squeeze juices over chicken and vegetables. Place the squeezed fruits inside chicken cavity. Sprinkle chicken with salt and pepper. Pour broth around chicken.

3. Roast chicken for 2-2½ hours or until a thermometer inserted in the thickest part of thigh reads 170°-175°. Sprinkle green onions over vegetables during the last 20 minutes. (Cover loosely with foil if chicken browns too quickly.)

4. Remove chicken from oven; tent with foil. Let stand 15 minutes before carving. Discard herbs. If desired, skim fat and thicken pan drippings for gravy. Serve gravy with chicken and vegetables.

7 OZ. COOKED CHICKEN WITH 1¼ CUPS VEGETABLES 561 cal., 24g fat (7g sat. fat), 136mg chol., 826mg sod., 39g carb. (5g sugars, 5g fiber), 47g pro.

CHICKEN STRAWBERRY SPINACH SALAD

This pretty salad topped with grilled chicken, strawberries and almonds features a delectably sweet poppy seed dressing. Made in moments, this dish is a refreshing lunch or light supper.
—Ginger Ellsworth, Caldwell, ID

TAKES: 30 MIN. • **MAKES:** 2 SERVINGS

- ¾ lb. boneless skinless chicken breasts, cut into strips
- ¼ cup reduced-sodium chicken broth
- ¼ cup poppy seed salad dressing, divided
- 2 cups fresh baby spinach
- 1 cup torn romaine
- 1 cup sliced fresh strawberries
- ¼ cup sliced almonds, toasted

1. Place chicken on a double thickness of heavy-duty foil (about 18x15 in.). Combine broth and 1 Tbsp. salad dressing; spoon over chicken. Fold edges of foil around chicken mixture, leaving center open. Grill, covered, over medium heat until chicken is no longer pink, 10-12 minutes.

2. In a large salad bowl, combine the spinach, romaine and strawberries. Add chicken and the remaining poppy seed dressing; toss to coat. Sprinkle with toasted almonds.

2 CUPS 438 cal., 22g fat (3g sat. fat), 104mg chol., 386mg sod., 18g carb. (11g sugars, 5g fiber), 39g pro.

CHICKEN CLUB PIZZA

Pizza topped with lettuce, tomatoes and dressing? You're in for a treat! Vegetables give the cheesy crust a cool and welcoming crunch.
—Debbie Reid, Clearwater, FL

TAKES: 25 MIN. • **MAKES:** 8 SERVINGS

- 1 prebaked 12-in. pizza crust
- 4 oz. cream cheese, softened
- 1 shallot, minced
- 2 cups shredded rotisserie chicken
- 1½ cups shredded Monterey Jack cheese
- 1 cup shredded sharp cheddar cheese
- 8 slices ready-to-serve fully cooked bacon, cut into 1-in. pieces
- ¼ cup sour cream
- 3 Tbsp. 2% milk
- 2 tsp. ranch salad dressing mix
- 1 cup shredded lettuce
- 1 plum tomato, seeded and chopped

1. Place the crust on an ungreased pizza pan. Combine cream cheese and shallot; spread over crust. Top with chicken, cheeses and bacon.

2. Bake at 425° until the edge is lightly browned and the cheeses are melted, 12-15 minutes .

3. Meanwhile, in a small bowl, combine the sour cream, milk and dressing mix. Sprinkle lettuce and tomato over pizza; drizzle with dressing.

1 PIECE 444 cal., 25g fat (13g sat. fat), 84mg chol., 939mg sod., 26g carb. (1g sugars, 0 fiber), 28g pro.

READER REVIEW

"Great use of leftover chicken. I'm always trying to find ways to rebrand due to the leftover snobs in my household, and this fits the bill."

—JUSTMBETH, TASTEOFHOME.COM

PARMESAN CHICKEN SANDWICHES

Coat chicken breasts with seasoned bread crumbs and smother in marinara sauce. Serve on a hoagie, and they're a real treat!

—Sue Bosek, Whittier, CA

TAKES: 25 MIN. • **MAKES:** 2 SERVINGS

- ½ cup all-purpose flour
- 1 large egg, lightly beaten
- ¾ cup seasoned bread crumbs
- 3 Tbsp. grated Parmesan cheese
- 2 boneless skinless chicken breast halves (5 oz. each)
- ⅛ tsp. salt
- ⅛ tsp. pepper
- 2 Tbsp. olive oil
- 2 Italian rolls, split
- 2 slices provolone cheese
- ⅓ cup marinara or other meatless pasta sauce, warmed

1. Place the flour and egg in separate shallow bowls. In another bowl, toss bread crumbs with Parmesan cheese.

2. Pound chicken with a meat mallet to ½-in. thickness; sprinkle with salt and pepper. Dip chicken in flour to coat both sides; shake off excess. Dip in egg, then in crumb mixture.

3. In a large skillet, heat oil over medium heat. Add chicken; cook until coating is golden brown and chicken is no longer pink, 4-5 minutes per side. Serve in rolls with provolone cheese and sauce.

1 SANDWICH 669 cal., 32g fat (10g sat. fat), 198mg chol., 1124mg sod., 45g carb. (3g sugars, 3g fiber), 48g pro.

SOURDOUGH CHICKEN CLUBS Prepare chicken as directed. Spread 4 slices of sourdough bread with mayonnaise if desired; top 2 slices with a lettuce leaf, a slice of Swiss cheese, tomato slice, 1 cooked bacon strip, cut in half; and the chicken breast. Top with remaining toast.

CHICKEN FINGER TACOS FOR TWO

Using chicken fingers in this recipe makes for the perfectly sized taco and also cuts down on prep time. I like to pair it with Spanish rice and refried beans for a complete meal for two.
—Kathy Williams, Layton, UT

TAKES: 20 MIN. • **MAKES:** 2 SERVINGS

1 large egg, lightly beaten
½ cup seasoned bread crumbs
¼ tsp. salt
⅛ tsp. pepper
4 chicken tenderloins
1 Tbsp. canola oil
4 corn tortillas (6 in.), warmed
½ cup shredded cheddar cheese
Optional: Salsa, sour cream, guacamole, chopped tomatoes, shredded lettuce and fresh cilantro leaves

1. Place egg in a shallow bowl. In another shallow bowl, combine bread crumbs, salt and pepper. Dip chicken in egg, then roll in bread crumb mixture.

2. In a large skillet over medium heat, cook chicken in oil for 4-5 minutes on each side or until juices run clear. Serve on tortillas with cheese and optional toppings as desired.

2 TACOS 414 cal., 17g fat (5g sat. fat), 110mg chol., 725mg sod., 34g carb. (2g sugars, 4g fiber), 31g pro.

MONTEREY CHICKEN

It's easy to turn regular chicken into a dish to savor with barbecue sauce, crisp bacon and melted cheese. It gets even better with a sprinkling of fresh tomato and green onion.
—Linda Coleman, Cedar Rapids, IA

TAKES: 25 MIN. • **MAKES:** 4 SERVINGS

- 4 bacon strips
- 4 boneless skinless chicken breast halves (4 oz. each)
- 1 Tbsp. butter
- ½ cup barbecue sauce
- 3 green onions, chopped
- 1 medium tomato, chopped
- 1 cup shredded cheddar cheese

READER REVIEW

"This was so easy and tasty too! I loved all the flavors together and think the green onions set it all off perfectly. I will make this repeatedly!"
—BEVS511, TASTEOFHOME.COM

1. Cut bacon strips in half widthwise. In a large skillet, cook bacon over medium heat until cooked but not crisp. Remove to paper towels to drain.

2. Drain drippings from the skillet; cook the chicken in butter over medium heat for 5-6 minutes on each side or until a thermometer reads 170°.

3. Top each chicken breast with sauce, green onions, tomato and 2 bacon pieces; sprinkle with cheese. Cover and cook for 5 minutes or until cheese is melted.

1 SERVING 318 cal., 17g fat (10g sat. fat), 107mg chol., 680mg sod., 8g carb. (5g sugars, 1g fiber), 32g pro.

CHICKEN & DUMPLINGS

After a very long week, I needed some comfort food, so I made this meal on a whim. Cayenne pepper gives it a little kick and rotisserie chicken drastically cuts the prep time, so we don't have to wait long for dinner to be ready.
—Jessica Rehs, Cuyahoga Falls, OH

PREP: 25 MIN. • **COOK:** 35 MIN. • **MAKES:** 6 SERVINGS

- 6 cups reduced-sodium chicken broth
- 3 bay leaves
- 5 fresh thyme sprigs
- 4 garlic cloves, peeled
- 1 tsp. crushed red pepper flakes
- 1 cup chopped carrots
- 1 cup chopped celery
- 3 Tbsp. olive oil
- 2 Tbsp. butter
- 3 garlic cloves, minced
- 2 Tbsp. all-purpose flour
- 1 cup frozen peas
- 1 rotisserie chicken, shredded
- ¼ cup heavy whipping cream

DUMPLINGS

- 2 cups all-purpose flour
- 1 Tbsp. baking powder
- 1 tsp. salt
- 1 tsp. cayenne pepper
- 1 cup buttermilk
- 2 large eggs, lightly beaten
- ¼ cup minced chives

1. In a large saucepan, combine the first 5 ingredients. Bring to a boil. Reduce the heat; simmer, uncovered, for 30 minutes. Strain and set aside. Discard bay leaves before serving.

2. In a Dutch oven, saute carrots and celery in oil and butter until tender. Add minced garlic; cook 1 minute longer. Stir in flour until blended; gradually add the prepared broth. Bring to a boil; cook for 2 minutes or until thickened, stirring frequently.

3. Add peas; return to a boil. Cook for 3-5 minutes or until peas are tender. Stir in chicken and cream; heat through.

4. For dumplings, combine flour, baking powder, salt and cayenne in a large bowl. In another bowl, combine buttermilk and eggs; stir into the dry ingredients just until moistened.

5. Drop by tablespoonfuls onto the simmering chicken mixture. Cover and simmer for 15-20 minutes or until a toothpick inserted in a dumpling comes out clean. Garnish with chives before serving.

NOTE Substitute 1 Tbsp. white vinegar or lemon juice plus enough milk to measure 1 cup for each cup of buttermilk. Stir, then let stand for 5 minutes. Or use 1 cup plain yogurt or 1¾ tsp. cream of tartar plus 1 cup milk.

1 SERVING 576 cal., 24g fat (9g sat. fat), 189mg chol., 1398mg sod., 44g carb. (7g sugars, 3g fiber), 44g pro.

SPANISH-STYLE PAELLA

If you enjoy cooking ethnic foods, this hearty rice dish is wonderful. It's brimming with generous chunks of sausage, shrimp and veggies.
—Taste of Home *Test Kitchen*

PREP: 10 MIN. • **COOK:** 35 MIN. • **MAKES:** 8 SERVINGS

- ¾ lb. boneless skinless chicken breasts, cubed
- ½ lb. Spanish chorizo links, sliced
- 1 Tbsp. olive oil
- 1 garlic clove, minced
- 1 cup uncooked short grain rice
- 1 cup chopped onion
- 1½ cups chicken broth
- 1 can (14½ oz.) stewed tomatoes, undrained
- ½ tsp. paprika
- ¼ tsp. ground cayenne pepper
- ¼ tsp. salt
- 10 strands saffron, crushed, or ⅛ tsp. ground saffron
- ½ lb. uncooked shrimp (31-40 per lb.), peeled and deveined
- ½ cup sweet red pepper strips
- ½ cup green pepper strips
- ½ cup frozen peas
- Optional: Minced fresh parsley and lemon wedges

1. In a large saucepan or skillet over medium-high heat, cook chicken and sausage in oil for 5 minutes or until the sausage is lightly browned and chicken is no longer pink, stirring frequently. Add garlic; cook 1 minute longer. Drain if necessary.

2. Stir in rice and onion. Cook until onion is tender and the rice is lightly browned, stirring frequently. Add broth, tomatoes, paprika, cayenne, salt and saffron. Bring to a boil. Reduce heat to low; cover and cook for 10 minutes.

3. Stir in shrimp, peppers and peas. Cover and cook 10 minutes longer or until rice is tender, shrimp turn pink and liquid is absorbed. Top with fresh parsley and lemon wedges if desired.

1 CUP 237 cal., 7g fat (2g sat. fat), 62mg chol., 543mg sod., 27g carb. (5g sugars, 2g fiber), 16g pro.

DID YOU KNOW?

Green peppers are the unripened versions of red, yellow or orange peppers. They are cheaper than colored peppers because farmers can pick them right away instead of waiting for them to ripen. Colored peppers add more sweetness to a dish. Green peppers actually taste a little "green"—as in, not ripe.

QUICK & EASY TURKEY SLOPPY JOES

When we were first married, I found this simple recipe and adjusted it to suit our tastes. The fresh bell pepper and red onion give it a wonderful flavor.
—Kallee Twiner, Maryville, TN

TAKES: 30 MIN. • **MAKES:** 8 SERVINGS

- 1 lb. lean ground turkey
- 1 large red onion, chopped
- 1 large green pepper, chopped
- 1 can (8 oz.) tomato sauce
- ½ cup barbecue sauce
- 1 tsp. dried oregano
- 1 tsp. ground cumin
- 1 tsp. chili powder
- ¼ tsp. salt
- 8 hamburger buns, split

1. In a large skillet, cook turkey, onion and green pepper over medium heat for 6-8 minutes or until turkey is no longer pink and vegetables are tender, breaking up turkey into crumbles.

2. Stir in tomato sauce, barbecue sauce and seasonings. Bring to a boil. Reduce heat; simmer, uncovered, for 10 minutes to allow the flavors to blend, stirring occasionally. Serve on buns.

1 SANDWICH 251 cal., 6g fat (2g sat. fat), 39mg chol., 629mg sod., 32g carb. (10g sugars, 2g fiber), 16g pro. **DIABETIC EXCHANGES** 2 lean meat, 1½ starch, 1 vegetable.

JUICY ROAST TURKEY

I can't wait to serve this juicy turkey at Thanksgiving—so I make it several times a year. The aroma that wafts through the house during baking is almost as mouthwatering as the turkey dinner itself.
—Terrie Herman, North Myrtle Beach, SC

PREP: 20 MIN. + CHILLING • **BAKE:** 3½ HOURS + STANDING • **MAKES:** 12 SERVINGS

¼ cup ground mustard
2 Tbsp. Worcestershire sauce
2 Tbsp. olive oil
½ tsp. white vinegar
1 tsp. salt
⅛ tsp. pepper
1 turkey (10 to 12 lbs.)
1 medium onion, quartered
2 celery ribs, quartered lengthwise
Fresh parsley sprigs
2 bacon strips
¼ cup butter, softened
2 cups chicken broth
1 cup water

1. In a small bowl, combine the first 6 ingredients. Brush over turkey. Place turkey on a platter. Cover and refrigerate for at least 1 hour or overnight.

2. Preheat oven to 325°. Place turkey on a rack in a shallow roasting pan, breast side up. Add onion, celery and parsley to turkey cavity. Tuck wings under turkey; tie drumsticks together. Arrange bacon over top of turkey breast. Spread butter over turkey. Pour broth and 1 cup water into pan.

3. Bake, uncovered, 3½-4 hours or until a thermometer inserted in the thickest part of thigh reads 170°-175°, basting occasionally. Remove turkey from oven. If desired, remove and discard the bacon. Tent with foil; let stand 20 minutes before carving. If desired, skim fat and thicken pan drippings for gravy. Serve with turkey.

8 OZ. COOKED TURKEY 535 cal., 29g fat (9g sat. fat), 219mg chol., 594mg sod., 2g carb. (1g sugars, 0 fiber), 62g pro.

NOTES

5i

SIMPLE SALSA CHICKEN

My husband and I prefer our food a little spicier than our children like it, so one evening I baked plain chicken for the kids and created this dish for us. It's now a regular menu item at our house.
—Jan Cooper, Troy, AL

PREP: 10 MIN. • **BAKE:** 25 MIN. • **MAKES:** 2 SERVINGS

- 2 boneless skinless chicken breast halves (5 oz. each)
- ⅛ tsp. salt
- ⅓ cup salsa
- 2 Tbsp. taco sauce
- ⅓ cup shredded Mexican cheese blend
- Optional: Lime wedges and sliced avocado

CUSTOMIZE IT

- **Spice it up.** Add a teaspoon of your favorite hot sauce when blending the salsa and taco sauce for an extra kick.
- **Use chicken thighs.** Substitute chicken thighs for breasts without changing the recipe, but check the meat's temperature after about 15 minutes, as they may cook faster.
- **Skip the cheese.** The chicken is flavorful enough with just the sauce and salsa, so omit the cheese to reduce calories and fat.

1. Place chicken in a shallow 2-qt. baking dish coated with cooking spray. Sprinkle with salt. Combine salsa and taco sauce; drizzle over the chicken. Sprinkle with shredded cheese.

2. Cover and bake chicken at 350° for 25-30 minutes or until a thermometer reads 165°. If desired, serve with lime wedges and sliced avocado.

1 SERVING 226 cal., 7g fat (3g sat. fat), 92mg chol., 628mg sod., 3g carb. (2g sugars, 0 fiber), 34g pro. **DIABETIC EXCHANGES** 5 lean meat, 1 fat.

5i

GLAZED CORNISH HENS

If you're looking to add a touch of elegance to your dinner table, consider these Cornish game hens topped with a sweet apricot glaze.
—Taste of Home *Test Kitchen*

PREP: 10 MIN. • **BAKE:** 1 HOUR • **MAKES:** 4 SERVINGS

- 2 Cornish game hens (20 to 24 oz. each), split lengthwise
- ¼ tsp. salt
- ⅛ tsp. white pepper
- ⅓ cup apricot spreadable fruit
- 1 Tbsp. orange juice

1. Preheat oven to 350°. Place hens on a rack in a shallow roasting pan. Sprinkle with salt and pepper. Bake, uncovered, 30 minutes.

2. In a small bowl, combine spreadable fruit and orange juice. Spoon some of apricot mixture over hens. Bake until golden brown and the juices run clear, 30-35 minutes, basting several times with remaining apricot mixture. Let stand 5 minutes before serving.

½ HEN 402 cal., 24g fat (7g sat. fat), 175mg chol., 233mg sod., 14g carb. (11g sugars, 0 fiber), 30g pro.

FAVORITE CHICKEN POTPIE

Chock-full of chicken, potatoes, peas and corn, this autumn favorite makes two golden pies, so you can serve one at supper and save the other for a busy night. These chicken potpies are perfect for company or a potluck.
—*Karen Johnson, Bakersfield, CA*

PREP: 40 MIN. • **BAKE:** 35 MIN. + STANDING • **MAKES:** 2 POTPIES (8 SERVINGS EACH)

- 2 cups diced peeled potatoes
- 1¾ cups sliced carrots
- 1 cup butter, cubed
- ⅔ cup chopped onion
- 1 cup all-purpose flour
- 1¾ tsp. salt
- 1 tsp. dried thyme
- ¾ tsp. pepper
- 3 cups chicken broth
- 1½ cups whole milk
- 4 cups cubed cooked chicken
- 1 cup frozen peas
- 1 cup frozen corn
- 4 sheets refrigerated pie crust

1. Preheat oven to 425°. Place potatoes and carrots in a large saucepan; add water to cover. Bring to a boil. Reduce heat; cook, covered, 8-10 minutes or until crisp-tender; drain.

2. In a large skillet, heat butter over medium-high heat. Add onion; cook and stir until tender. Stir in flour and seasonings until blended. Gradually stir in broth and milk. Bring to a boil, stirring constantly; cook and stir for 2 minutes or until thickened.

3. In a large bowl, combine chicken, peas, corn and potato-carrot mixture. Stir in broth mixture.

4. Unroll a pie crust into each of two 9-in. pie plates; trim crusts even with rims of plates. Add chicken mixture. Unroll the remaining crusts; place over filling. Trim, seal and flute edges. Cut slits in tops.

5. Bake for 35-40 minutes or until crust is lightly browned. Let stand 15 minutes before cutting.

1 PIECE 475 cal., 28g fat (14g sat. fat), 74mg chol., 768mg sod., 41g carb. (5g sugars, 2g fiber), 15g pro.

BAKED CHICKEN & MUSHROOMS

I made up this dish years ago, and it still remains a family favorite. It's a fast and healthy weeknight meal, but the fresh mushrooms and sherry make it special enough for a weekend dinner party.
—Lise Prestine, South Bend, IN

PREP: 5 MIN. • **BAKE:** 30 MIN. • **MAKES:** 6 SERVINGS

- 6 boneless skinless chicken breast halves (4 oz. each)
- ¼ tsp. paprika
- ½ lb. fresh mushrooms, sliced
- 1 Tbsp. butter
- ½ cup sherry or chicken broth
- 3 green onions, chopped
- 1 garlic clove, minced
- ½ tsp. salt
- ⅛ tsp. pepper
- ¾ cup shredded part-skim mozzarella cheese

1. Arrange chicken in a 13x9-in. baking dish coated with cooking spray. Sprinkle with paprika. Bake, uncovered, at 350° for 15 minutes.

2. Meanwhile, in a large nonstick skillet, saute sliced mushrooms in butter for 5 minutes. Add sherry or broth, green onions, garlic, salt and pepper. Bring to a boil. Pour over chicken.

3. Bake until a thermometer reads 165°, 10-15 minutes longer. Top with cheese. Bake for 3-5 minutes or until the cheese is melted.

1 SERVING 215 cal., 8g fat (4g sat. fat), 77mg chol., 604mg sod., 6g carb. (2g sugars, 1g fiber), 28g pro. **DIABETIC EXCHANGES** 4 lean meat, ½ starch, ½ fat.

CHICKEN ENCHILADA BAKE

Good thing the recipe makes a lot, because your family won't want to stop eating this cheesy southwestern casserole. The green enchilada sauce brightens it right up.
—Melanie Burns, Pueblo West, CO

PREP: 20 MIN. • **BAKE:** 50 MIN. + STANDING • **MAKES:** 10 SERVINGS

4½ cups shredded rotisserie chicken
1 can (28 oz.) green enchilada sauce
1¼ cups sour cream
9 corn tortillas (6 in.), cut into 1½-in. pieces
4 cups shredded Monterey Jack cheese
Fresh minced parsley, optional

DID YOU KNOW?
A Monterey, California, businessman named David Jacks made Monterey Jack cheese popular in the late 1800s by shipping it to San Francisco and other areas of the U.S.

1. Preheat the oven to 375°. In a greased 13x9-in. baking dish, layer half of each of the following: chicken, enchilada sauce, sour cream, tortillas and cheese. Repeat layers.

2. Bake, covered, 40 minutes. Uncover; bake until bubbly, about 10 minutes longer. Let stand for 15 minutes before serving. If desired, sprinkle with parsley.

FREEZE OPTION Cover and freeze the unbaked casserole. To use, partially thaw in refrigerator overnight. Remove from refrigerator 30 minutes before baking. Preheat oven to 375°. Bake casserole as directed, increasing time as necessary to heat through and for a thermometer inserted in center to read 165°. If desired, sprinkle with parsley.

1 CUP 428 cal., 27g fat (14g sat. fat), 103mg chol., 709mg sod., 16g carb. (3g sugars, 1g fiber), 32g pro.

KOREAN FRIED CHICKEN

These Korean-style chicken wings have a shatteringly crisp crunch and a sweet and spicy sauce that makes them simply irresistible. Tossing the wings in a seasoned cornstarch mixture before frying gives them their signature flavor and texture.
—Ann Kim, Bremerton, WA

PREP: 30 MIN. • **COOK:** 10 MIN./BATCH • **MAKES:** ABOUT 3½ DOZEN

SAUCE

- 4 garlic cloves, minced
- ¼ cup honey
- ¼ cup packed brown sugar
- 2 Tbsp. reduced-sodium soy sauce
- 2 Tbsp. ketchup
- 1 Tbsp. gochujang (Korean red pepper paste)
- 1 Tbsp. sesame oil

CHICKEN

- 4½ lbs. chicken wings
- ½ tsp. salt
- ½ tsp. pepper
- 1 tsp. minced fresh gingerroot
- ¾ cup cornstarch
- Oil for deep-fat frying

GARNISH

- 1 tsp. sesame seeds, toasted
- 1 green onion, thinly sliced

1. In a large saucepan, combine sauce ingredients. Bring to a simmer; cook for 5-7 minutes, stirring frequently, until sauce thickens. Keep warm.

2. Separate the chicken wings into drumettes, flats and tips; discard tips. Place drumettes and flats in a large bowl; sprinkle with salt, pepper and ginger; mix well. Place cornstarch in a shallow bowl; roll the wings through cornstarch until coated. Set wings on a baking sheet.

3. Place a wire rack over a baking sheet lined with paper towels. Heat the oil in a Dutch oven to 350°. Working in batches, drop the wings in oil one by one, being careful not to splatter or crowd. Fry until lightly golden, 6-8 minutes. Remove wings with a slotted spoon; transfer to prepared wire rack. Let oil heat back up to 350° before frying the next batch.

4. Increase the fryer heat to 375°. Drop wings in oil 1 at a time; fry until medium-brown and crispy, 3-4 minutes. Use a slotted spoon to transfer wings back to prepared wire rack. Repeat with the remaining wings.

5. Brush sauce generously on one side of wings; flip and brush sauce on other side. Arrange wings on a serving platter. Garnish with toasted sesame seeds and green onion.

ABOUT 6 PIECES706 cal., 50g fat (8g sat. fat), 93mg chol., 553mg sod., 34g carb. (19g sugars, 0 fiber), 31g pro.

PIZZA ON THE GRILL

I make pizza at least once a week, and recruiting the grill for help is a wonderful way to switch things up. The barbecue flavor in this grilled pizza mingles with the cheese to create a delicious end result.

—Lisa Boettcher, Columbus, WI

PREP: 30 MIN. + RISING • **GRILL:** 10 MIN. • **MAKES:** 4 SERVINGS

- 1 pkg. (¼ oz.) active dry yeast
- 1 cup warm water (110° to 115°)
- 2 Tbsp. canola oil
- 2 tsp. sugar
- 1 tsp. baking soda
- 1 tsp. salt
- 2¾ to 3 cups all-purpose flour

TOPPINGS

- ½ to ¾ cup barbecue sauce
- 2 cups shredded Monterey Jack cheese
- 2 cups shredded or cubed cooked chicken
- ½ cup julienned green pepper

1. In a large bowl, dissolve yeast in water. Add the oil, sugar, baking soda, salt and 2 cups flour. Stir in enough remaining flour to form a soft dough.

2. Turn onto a floured surface; knead until smooth and elastic, 6-8 minutes. Cover and let rest for 10 minutes. On a floured surface, roll dough into a 13-in. circle. Transfer to a greased 12-in. pizza pan. Build up edge slightly.

3. Grill, covered, over medium heat for 5 minutes. Remove from grill. Spread barbecue sauce over crust. Sprinkle with cheese, chicken and green pepper. Grill, covered, 5-10 minutes longer or until crust is golden and the cheese is melted.

1 PIECE 757 cal., 31g fat (13g sat. fat), 113mg chol., 1525mg sod., 73g carb. (8g sugars, 3g fiber), 44g pro.

CHICKEN A LA KING

I've been making this thick and creamy chicken recipe for over 30 years. It's a wonderful way to create a quick lunch or dinner with leftover chicken.
—Ruth Lee, Troy, ON

TAKES: 25 MIN. • **MAKES:** 4 SERVINGS

- 4 individually frozen biscuits
- 1¾ cups sliced fresh mushrooms
- ¼ cup chopped onion
- ¼ cup chopped celery
- ⅓ cup butter, cubed
- ¼ cup all-purpose flour
- ⅛ to ¼ tsp. salt
- 1 cup chicken broth
- 1 cup whole milk
- 2 cups cubed cooked chicken
- 2 Tbsp. diced pimientos

1. Bake biscuits according to package directions. Meanwhile, in a large skillet, saute mushrooms, onion and celery in butter until crisp-tender. Stir in flour and salt until blended. Gradually stir in broth and milk. Bring to a boil; cook and stir for 2 minutes or until thickened.

2. Add chicken and pimientos; heat through. Serve with biscuits.

1 SERVING 551 cal., 34g fat (15g sat. fat), 110mg chol., 1185mg sod., 35g carb. (8g sugars, 2g fiber), 29g pro.

FAVORITE BARBECUED CHICKEN

Is there a better place than Texas to find a fantastic barbecue sauce? That's where this one is from—it's my father-in-law's own recipe. We have served this chicken at many family reunions and think it's the best!
—Bobbie Morgan, Woodstock, GA

PREP: 15 MIN. • **GRILL:** 40 MIN. • **MAKES:** 12 SERVINGS

- 2 broiler/fryer chickens (3 to 4 lbs. each), cut up
- Salt and pepper

BARBECUE SAUCE

- 2 Tbsp. canola oil
- 2 small onions, finely chopped
- 2 cups ketchup
- ¼ cup lemon juice
- 2 Tbsp. brown sugar
- 2 Tbsp. water
- 1 tsp. ground mustard
- ½ tsp. garlic powder
- ¼ tsp. pepper
- ⅛ tsp. salt
- ⅛ tsp. hot pepper sauce

1. Sprinkle chicken pieces with salt and pepper. Grill, skin side down, uncovered, on a greased rack over medium heat for 20 minutes.

2. Meanwhile, for barbecue sauce, in a small saucepan, heat oil over medium heat. Add onions; cook until tender. Stir in the remaining sauce ingredients and bring to a boil. Reduce the heat; simmer, uncovered, for 10 minutes.

3. Turn chicken; brush with barbecue sauce. Grill until a thermometer reads 165° when inserted in the breast and 170°-175° in thigh, 20-25 minutes longer, brushing frequently with sauce.

4 OZ. COOKED CHICKEN 370 cal., 19g fat (5g sat. fat), 104mg chol., 622mg sod., 15g carb. (14g sugars, 0 fiber), 33g pro.

NOTES

BEST CHICKEN KIEV

From holiday suppers to potlucks, this is one of my most-requested meals. Folks love the mildly seasoned chicken roll-ups.
—Karin Erickson, Burney, CA

PREP: 15 MIN. + FREEZING • **BAKE:** 35 MIN. • **MAKES:** 6 SERVINGS

- ¼ cup butter, softened
- 1 Tbsp. minced chives
- 1 garlic clove, minced
- 6 boneless skinless chicken breast halves (8 oz. each)
- ¾ cup crushed cornflakes
- 2 Tbsp. minced fresh parsley
- ½ tsp. paprika
- ⅓ cup buttermilk

1. In a small bowl, combine the butter, chives and garlic. Shape into a 3x2-in. rectangle. Cover and freeze until firm, about 30 minutes.

2. Flatten each chicken breast to ¼-in. thickness. Cut butter mixture into six 1-in. pieces; place 1 piece in the center of each chicken breast. Roll up chicken from a long side and tuck ends under. Secure with toothpicks.

3. In a shallow bowl, combine cornflakes, parsley and paprika. Place buttermilk in another shallow bowl. Dip chicken into buttermilk, then coat evenly with the cornflake mixture.

4. Preheat oven to 425°; place coated chicken in a greased 13x9-in. baking dish, seam side down. Bake, uncovered, for 35-40 minutes or until chicken reaches an internal temperature of 170°. Discard toothpicks.

NOTE Substitute 1 Tbsp. white vinegar or lemon juice plus enough milk to measure 1 cup for each cup of buttermilk. Stir, then let stand for 5 minutes. Or use 1 cup plain yogurt or 1¾ tsp. cream of tartar plus 1 cup milk.

1 SERVING 357 cal., 13g fat (6g sat. fat), 146mg chol., 281mg sod., 10g carb. (2g sugars, 0 fiber), 47g pro.

THAI CHICKEN PASTA

I try to buy fresh chicken when it's on sale. I cook a big batch in the slow cooker, then cut it up and package it in small amounts suitable for recipes like this. When I want it, I just need to pull it out of the freezer and let it thaw.
—Jeni Pittard, Statham, GA

TAKES: 25 MIN. • **MAKES:** 2 SERVINGS

- 3 oz. uncooked whole wheat linguine
- ½ cup salsa
- 2 Tbsp. reduced-fat creamy peanut butter
- 1 Tbsp. orange juice
- 1½ tsp. honey
- 1 tsp. reduced-sodium soy sauce
- 1 cup cubed cooked chicken breast
- 1 Tbsp. chopped unsalted peanuts
- 1 Tbsp. minced fresh cilantro

1. Cook linguine according to the package directions.

2. Meanwhile, in a microwave-safe dish, combine salsa, peanut butter, orange juice, honey and soy sauce. Cover and microwave on high for 1 minute; stir. Add chicken; heat through.

3. Drain linguine. Serve with the chicken mixture. Garnish with peanuts and fresh cilantro.

1 SERVING 409 cal., 10g fat (2g sat. fat), 54mg chol., 474mg sod., 46g carb. (10g sugars, 6g fiber), 33g pro.

LASAGNA DELIZIOSA

Everyone loves this lasagna. It's often served as a birthday treat for guests. I've lightened it up a lot from the original, but no one can tell the difference!
—Heather O'Neill, Troy, OH

PREP: 45 MIN. • **BAKE:** 50 MIN. + STANDING • **MAKES:** 12 SERVINGS

- 9 uncooked lasagna noodles
- 1 pkg. (19½ oz.) Italian turkey sausage links, casings removed
- ½ lb. lean ground beef (90% lean)
- 1 large onion, chopped
- 2 garlic cloves, minced
- 1 can (28 oz.) diced tomatoes, undrained
- 1 can (12 oz.) tomato paste
- ¼ cup water
- 2 tsp. sugar
- 1 tsp. dried basil
- ½ tsp. fennel seed
- ¼ tsp. pepper
- 1 large egg, lightly beaten
- 1 carton (15 oz.) reduced-fat ricotta cheese
- 1 Tbsp. minced fresh parsley
- ½ tsp. salt
- 2 cups shredded part-skim mozzarella cheese
- ¾ cup grated Parmesan cheese
- Torn fresh basil leaves, optional

1. Cook noodles according to package directions. Meanwhile, in a Dutch oven, cook and crumble sausage and beef with onion over medium heat until meat is no longer pink. Add garlic; cook 1 minute longer. Drain.

2. Stir in tomatoes, tomato paste, water, sugar, basil, fennel and pepper. Bring to a boil. Reduce heat; cover and simmer 15-20 minutes, stirring occasionally.

3. Meanwhile, preheat the oven to 375°. In a small bowl, combine egg, ricotta cheese, parsley and salt. Drain noodles and rinse in cold water. Spread 1 cup meat sauce into a 13x9-in. baking dish coated with cooking spray. Top with 3 noodles, 2 cups meat sauce, ⅔ cup ricotta mixture, ⅔ cup mozzarella and ¼ cup Parmesan cheese. Repeat layers twice.

4. Cover and bake 40 minutes. Uncover; bake 10-15 minutes longer or until bubbly. Let stand for 10 minutes before cutting. If desired, top with fresh basil leaves and sprinkle with additional Parmesan.

1 PIECE 323 cal., 12g fat (5g sat. fat), 79mg chol., 701mg sod., 28g carb. (11g sugars, 4g fiber), 25g pro. **DIABETIC EXCHANGES** 3 lean meat, 2 vegetable, 1 starch, 1 fat

READER REVIEW

"Absolutely amazing! I like it more than traditional lasagna."

—HUNTERJ2, TASTEOFHOME.COM

HERBED TURKEY BREAST

Like many of you, I always serve turkey for our family's Thanksgiving meal. But instead of roasting a whole bird, I opt for a turkey breast since most of us prefer white meat. The herb butter basting sauce keeps it so moist, and it's easy to carve.
—Ruby Williams, Bogalusa, LA

PREP: 10 MIN. • **BAKE:** 1½ HOURS + STANDING • **MAKES:** 12 SERVINGS

½ cup butter, cubed
¼ cup lemon juice
2 Tbsp. reduced-sodium soy sauce
2 Tbsp. finely chopped green onions
1 Tbsp. rubbed sage
1 tsp. dried thyme
1 tsp. dried marjoram
¼ tsp. pepper
1 bone-in turkey breast (5½ to 6 lbs.)

1. Preheat the oven to 325°. In a small saucepan, combine first 8 ingredients; bring to a boil. Remove from heat. Place turkey in a shallow roasting pan; drizzle with butter mixture.

2. Bake, uncovered, 1½-2 hours or until a thermometer reads 165°, basting every 30 minutes. Let stand for 10 minutes before carving.

5 OZ. COOKED TURKEY 291 cal., 11g fat (3g sat. fat), 112mg chol., 192mg sod., 1g carb. (0 sugars, 0 fiber), 44g pro.

NOTES

CRISPY FRIED CHICKEN

This fried chicken can be served hot or pulled out of the fridge the next day as leftovers. Either way, folks love it.
—Jeanne Schnitzler, Lima, MT

PREP: 15 MIN. • **COOK:** 15 MIN./BATCH • **MAKES:** 12 SERVINGS

- 4 cups all-purpose flour, divided
- 2 Tbsp. garlic salt
- 1 Tbsp. paprika
- 3 tsp. pepper, divided
- 2½ tsp. poultry seasoning
- 2 large eggs
- 1½ cups water
- 1 tsp. salt
- 2 broiler/fryer chickens (3½ to 4 lbs. each), cut up
- Oil for deep-fat frying

1. In a large shallow dish, combine 2⅔ cups flour, garlic salt, paprika, 2½ tsp. pepper and poultry seasoning. In another shallow dish, beat eggs and water; add salt and remaining 1⅓ cups flour and ½ tsp. pepper. Dip chicken in egg mixture, then place in flour mixture, a few pieces at a time. Turn to coat.

2. In a deep-fat fryer, heat oil to 375°. Fry chicken, several pieces at a time, until golden brown and juices run clear, 7-8 minutes on each side. Drain on paper towels.

5 OZ. COOKED CHICKEN 543 cal., 33g fat (7g sat. fat), 137mg chol., 798mg sod., 17g carb. (0 sugars, 1g fiber), 41g pro.

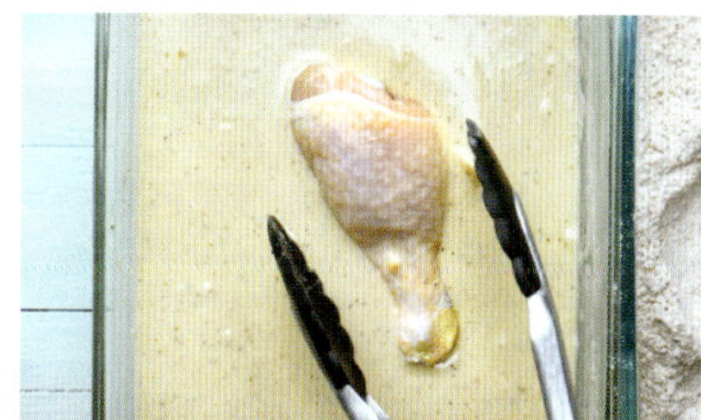

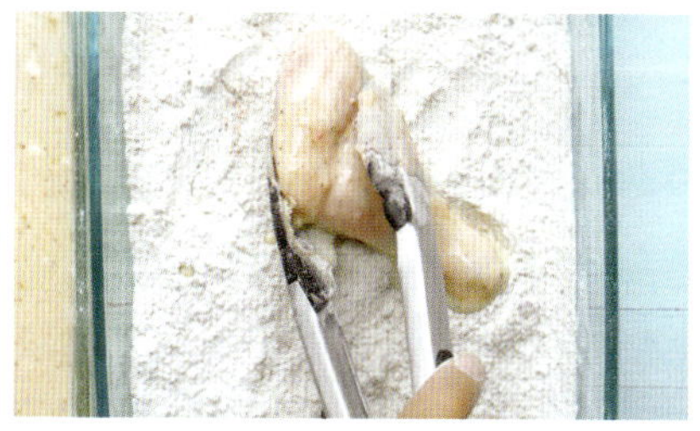

GREEK ROASTED CHICKEN & POTATOES

This meal is a nice one to serve to company or your family for Sunday dinner. All you need with this dish is a tossed salad and some crusty French bread.
—*Pella Visnick, Dallas, TX*

PREP: 15 MIN. • **BAKE:** 2 HOURS + STANDING • **MAKES:** 8 SERVINGS

- 1 roasting chicken (6 to 7 lbs.)
  Salt and pepper to taste
- 2 to 3 tsp. dried oregano, divided
- 4 baking potatoes, peeled and quartered
- ¼ cup butter, melted
- 3 Tbsp. lemon juice
- ¾ cup chicken broth

1. Preheat oven to 350°. Place chicken breast side up on a rack in a roasting pan. Sprinkle with salt and pepper and half oregano. Arrange potatoes around chicken; sprinkle with salt, pepper and remaining oregano. Pour butter and lemon juice over chicken and potatoes. Add chicken broth to pan.

2. Bake, uncovered, 2-2½ hours or until a thermometer inserted in the thigh reads 170°, basting frequently with pan drippings.

3. Remove chicken from oven; tent with foil. Let stand 15 minutes before carving. If desired, skim fat and thicken the pan drippings for gravy. Serve with chicken.

6 OZ. COOKED CHICKEN WITH 2 PIECES POTATO 530 cal., 30g fat (10g sat. fat), 150mg chol., 262mg sod., 19g carb. (1g sugars, 2g fiber), 45g pro.

ROSEMARY-LEMON ROAST CHICKEN
Brush the chicken with 1 Tbsp. olive oil. Combine 2 Tbsp. each grated lemon zest and minced fresh rosemary with 2 tsp. each salt and coarsely ground pepper; sprinkle over chicken and potatoes. Add broth to pan and bake as directed.

how to cook ...

SEAFOOD

SHRIMP PAD THAI, PAGE 232

FRIED WALLEYE WITH TARTAR SAUCE

I love to eat fish, especially walleye, and this is my favorite way to make it. The homemade tartar sauce promotes this meal to restaurant grade.
—Carolyn Turner, Reno, NV

PREP: 20 MIN. • **COOK:** 10 MIN./BATCH • **MAKES:** 6 SERVINGS (1¼ CUPS SAUCE)

- 1 cup mayonnaise
- ⅓ cup sweet pickle relish
- 4½ tsp. lemon juice
- ¼ tsp. salt
- ⅛ tsp. pepper

FISH

- 2 cups all-purpose flour
- 2 tsp. lemon-pepper seasoning
- 1 tsp. baking powder
- 1 tsp. garlic salt
- ½ tsp. dried parsley flakes
- 1½ cups ice water
- 2 Tbsp. canola oil
- Oil for deep-fat frying
- 2 lbs. walleye fillets, cut into 6 pieces
- Lemon wedges

1. In a small bowl, combine the first 5 ingredients; cover and refrigerate until serving.

2. For fish, in a shallow bowl, combine the flour, lemon pepper, baking powder, garlic salt and parsley flakes. Combine ice water and 2 Tbsp. oil; whisk into the dry ingredients just until smooth.

3. In an electric skillet or deep fryer, heat oil to 375°. Dip fillets in batter, turning to coat; allow excess batter to drip off. Fry fillets, a few at a time, until golden brown and the fish just begins to flake easily with a fork, 5-7 minutes on each side. Drain on paper towels. Serve with sauce and lemon.

4 OZ. COOKED FISH WITH 3 TBSP. SAUCE
754 cal., 55g fat (6g sat. fat), 143mg chol., 882mg sod., 30g carb. (4g sugars, 1g fiber), 32g pro.

NOTES

CREAMY TUNA-NOODLE CASSEROLE

When you need supper fast, this tuna casserole with peas, peppers and onions makes a super one-dish meal. Cooked chicken breast works well in place of the tuna.

—Edie DeSpain, Logan, UT

PREP: 20 MIN. • **BAKE:** 25 MIN. • **MAKES:** 6 SERVINGS

- 5 cups uncooked egg noodles
- 1 cup frozen peas
- 1 can (10¾ oz.) reduced-fat reduced-sodium condensed cream of mushroom soup, undiluted
- 1 cup fat-free sour cream
- ⅔ cup grated Parmesan cheese
- ⅓ cup 2% milk
- ¼ tsp. salt
- 2 cans (5 oz. each) light tuna in water, drained and flaked
- ¼ cup finely chopped onion
- ¼ cup finely chopped green pepper

TOPPING

- ½ cup soft bread crumbs
- 1 Tbsp. butter, melted

CREAMY TUNA-NOODLE CASSEROLE TIPS

What can I substitute for peas? You can swap in 1 cup frozen mixed vegetables or chopped broccoli.

Does tuna noodle casserole freeze well? Yes! Unbaked tuna casserole freezes beautifully. Double the recipe and save half for later. Thaw in the fridge for 24 hours. Then let stand at room temperature for 30 minutes before baking as usual.

How do you fix a dry casserole? Add moisture by warming ½ cup chicken or vegetable broth and drizzling it over the casserole. Cover with foil and let stand for 10 minutes.

1. Preheat oven to 350°. Cook noodles according to the package directions for al dente, adding peas during the last minute of cooking; drain.

2. Meanwhile, in a large bowl, combine soup, sour cream, cheese, milk and salt; stir in the tuna, onion and pepper. Add the noodles and peas; toss to combine.

3. Transfer to an 11x7-in. baking dish coated with cooking spray. In a small bowl, toss bread crumbs with melted butter; sprinkle over the top. Bake, uncovered, 25-30 minutes or until bubbly.

NOTE To make soft bread crumbs, tear bread into pieces and place in a food processor or blender. Cover and pulse until crumbs form. A single slice of bread yields ½-¾ cup crumbs.

1⅓ CUPS 340 cal., 8g fat (4g sat. fat), 63mg chol., 699mg sod., 41g carb. (7g sugars, 3g fiber), 25g pro. **DIABETIC EXCHANGES** 3 starch, 2 lean meat, ½ fat.

SENSATIONAL SPICED SALMON

A sweet and spicy rub gives this quick salmon entree fantastic flavor. Paired with a green veggie and rice, it's a delightful weeknight dinner that's special enough for company.
—Michele Doucette, Stephenville, NL

TAKES: 25 MIN. • **MAKES:** 4 SERVINGS

- 2 Tbsp. brown sugar
- 4 tsp. chili powder
- 2 tsp. grated lemon zest
- ¾ tsp. ground cumin
- ½ tsp. salt
- ¼ tsp. ground cinnamon
- 4 salmon fillets (4 oz. each)

Preheat oven to 350°. Combine the first 6 ingredients; rub over salmon. Place in an 11x7-in. baking dish coated with cooking spray. Bake, uncovered, until fish flakes easily with a fork, 15-20 minutes.

1 FILLET 244 cal., 13g fat (3g sat. fat), 67mg chol., 392mg sod., 9g carb. (7g sugars, 1g fiber), 23g pro. **DIABETIC EXCHANGES** 3 lean meat, ½ starch.

READER REVIEW

"My salmon eaters loved this! Sweet, a little spicy and well balanced. Very simple to put together and something we'll definitely enjoy again. Five stars!"

—DEBGLASS11, TASTEOFHOME.COM

SHRIMP PAD THAI

You can make this yummy Thai classic in no time. Find fish sauce and chili garlic sauce in the Asian foods aisle of your grocery store.
—Elise Ray, Shawnee, KS

TAKES: 30 MIN. • **MAKES:** 4 SERVINGS

- 4 oz. uncooked thick rice noodles
- ½ lb. uncooked shrimp (41-50 per lb.), peeled and deveined
- 2 tsp. canola oil
- 1 large onion, chopped
- 1 garlic clove, minced
- 1 large egg, lightly beaten
- 3 cups coleslaw mix
- 4 green onions, thinly sliced
- ⅓ cup rice vinegar
- ¼ cup sugar
- 3 Tbsp. reduced-sodium soy sauce
- 2 Tbsp. fish sauce or additional reduced-sodium soy sauce
- 2 to 3 tsp. chili garlic sauce
- 2 Tbsp. chopped salted peanuts
- Optional: Fresh cilantro leaves and chopped salted peanuts

1. Cook noodles according to package directions.

2. In a large nonstick skillet or wok, stir-fry shrimp in oil until shrimp turn pink; remove. Add onion and garlic to pan. Make a well in center of the onion mixture; add egg. Stir-fry 2-3 minutes or until egg is completely set.

3. Add the coleslaw mix, green onion, vinegar, sugar, soy sauce, fish sauce, chili garlic sauce and peanuts; heat through. Return shrimp to the pan and heat through. Drain noodles; toss with shrimp mixture. Garnish with cilantro and additional chopped salted peanuts.

1¼ CUPS 338 cal., 7g fat (1g sat. fat), 115mg chol., 1675mg sod., 52g carb. (23g sugars, 3g fiber), 17g pro.

SCALLOPS IN SAGE CREAM

I didn't want to hide the ocean freshness of the scallops I bought on the dock from a local fisherman, so I used simple ingredients to showcase them.
—Joan Churchill, Dover, NH

TAKES: 20 MIN. • **MAKES:** 4 SERVINGS

- 1½ lbs. sea scallops
- ¼ tsp. salt
- ⅛ tsp. pepper
- 3 Tbsp. olive oil, divided
- ½ cup chopped shallots
- ¾ cup heavy whipping cream
- 6 fresh sage leaves, thinly sliced
- Hot cooked pasta, optional

1. Sprinkle scallops with salt and pepper. In a large skillet, cook scallops in 2 Tbsp. oil until firm and opaque, 1½-2 minutes on each side. Remove and keep warm.

2. In the same skillet, saute shallots in remaining 1 Tbsp. oil until tender. Add cream; bring to a boil. Cook and stir for 30 seconds or until slightly thickened.

3. Return scallops to pan; heat through. Stir in sage. Serve with pasta if desired.

1 SERVING 408 cal., 28g fat (12g sat. fat), 117mg chol., 441mg sod., 9g carb. (1g sugars, 0 fiber), 30g pro.

READER REVIEW

"These are wonderful! I was careful to cook the scallops to 125^{0}-130^{0} so they would not be overcooked."

—JUSTMBETH, TASTEOFHOME.COM

ORANGE TILAPIA IN PARCHMENT

Sweet orange juice and spicy cayenne pepper give this no-fuss dish fabulous flavor. A bonus? Cleanup is a breeze!
—Tiffany Diebold, Nashville, TN

TAKES: 30 MIN. • **MAKES:** 4 SERVINGS

- ¼ cup orange juice
- 4 tsp. grated orange zest
- ¼ tsp. salt
- ¼ tsp. cayenne pepper
- ¼ tsp. pepper
- 4 tilapia fillets (6 oz. each)
- ½ cup julienned carrot
- ½ cup julienned zucchini

1. Preheat oven to 450°. In a small bowl, combine first 5 ingredients; set aside. Cut parchment or heavy-duty foil into four 18x12-in. lengths; place a fish fillet on each. Top with carrot and zucchini; drizzle with orange juice mixture.

2. Fold parchment over fish. Working from the bottom inside corner, fold up about ¾ in. of the paper and crimp both layers to seal. Repeat, folding edges up and crimping, until a half-moon shaped packet is formed. Repeat for remaining packets. Place on baking sheets.

3. Bake until fish flakes easily with a fork, 12-15 minutes. Open packets carefully to allow steam to escape.

1 PACKET 158 cal., 2g fat (1g sat. fat), 83mg chol., 220mg sod., 4g carb. (2g sugars, 1g fiber), 32g pro. **DIABETIC EXCHANGES** 5 lean meat.

CREAMY SEAFOOD-STUFFED SHELLS

Inspired by my love of pasta shells and seafood Alfredo, I created this dish that combines them both. Make it a meal with garlic bread and a green salad. Your friends will think they're eating at a five-star restaurant!
—Katie Sloan, Charlotte, NC

PREP: 40 MIN. • **BAKE:** 30 MIN. • **MAKES:** 8 SERVINGS

- 24 uncooked jumbo pasta shells
- ¼ cup finely chopped celery
- ¼ cup finely chopped green pepper
- ¼ cup finely chopped red onion
- 1 Tbsp. butter plus ¼ cup butter, divided
- 2 cans (6 oz. each) lump crabmeat, drained
- 8 oz. peeled and deveined cooked shrimp (41-50 per lb.), chopped
- ½ cup shredded part-skim mozzarella cheese
- 1½ tsp. seafood seasoning, divided
- ¼ tsp. pepper
- 1 large egg, lightly beaten
- ¼ cup mayonnaise
- 2 Tbsp. plus 4 cups 2% milk, divided
- ¼ cup all-purpose flour
- ¼ tsp. salt
- ¼ tsp. coarsely ground pepper
- 1½ cups grated Parmesan cheese
- Optional: Soft bread crumbs, toasted in butter and chopped fresh parsley

1. Cook pasta according to the package directions.

2. Meanwhile, in a small skillet, saute the celery, green pepper and onion in 1 Tbsp. butter until tender; set aside.

3. In a large bowl, combine crab, shrimp, mozzarella cheese, 1 tsp. seafood seasoning, pepper and celery mixture. In a small bowl, whisk egg, mayonnaise and 2 Tbsp. milk until smooth; stir into crab mixture.

4. Preheat oven to 350°. Drain and rinse pasta; stuff each shell with 1 rounded Tbsp. seafood mixture. Place in a greased 13x9-in. baking dish.

5. In a small saucepan, melt remaining ¼ cup butter over medium heat. Whisk in flour, salt and coarsely ground pepper; gradually whisk in remaining 4 cups milk. Bring to a boil; cook and stir 2 minutes or until thickened. Stir in the Parmesan cheese.

6. Pour over the stuffed shells. Sprinkle with the remaining seafood seasoning. Bake, uncovered, 30-35 minutes or until bubbly. If desired, top with toasted bread crumbs, chopped parsley and additional Parmesan cheese.

3 STUFFED SHELLS 448 cal., 23g fat (11g sat. fat), 148mg chol., 710mg sod., 31g carb. (7g sugars, 1g fiber), 29g pro.

SOUTHERN SHRIMP & GRITS

A southern specialty, sometimes called breakfast shrimp, this dish tastes great for brunch, dinner and when company's coming. It's down-home comfort food at its finest.
—Mandy Rivers, Lexington, SC

PREP: 15 MIN. • **COOK:** 20 MIN. • **MAKES:** 4 SERVINGS

- 2 cups reduced-sodium chicken broth
- 2 cups 2% milk
- ⅓ cup butter, cubed
- ¾ tsp. salt
- ½ tsp. pepper
- ¾ cup uncooked old-fashioned grits
- 1 cup shredded cheddar cheese

SHRIMP

- 8 thick-sliced bacon strips, chopped
- 1 lb. uncooked shrimp (31-40 per lb.), peeled and deveined
- 3 garlic cloves, minced
- 1 tsp. Cajun or blackened seasoning
- 4 green onions, chopped

1. In a large saucepan, bring broth, milk, butter, salt and pepper to a boil. Slowly stir in grits. Reduce heat. Cover and cook 15-20 minutes or until thickened, stirring occasionally. Stir in cheese until melted. Set aside and keep warm.

2. In a large skillet, cook bacon over medium heat until crisp. Remove to paper towels with a slotted spoon; drain, reserving 4 tsp. drippings in pan. Saute the shrimp, garlic and seasoning in drippings until the shrimp turn pink. Stir in bacon; heat through. Serve with grits and sprinkle with green onion.

1 CUP GRITS WITH ½ CUP SHRIMP MIXTURE 699 cal., 44g fat (22g sat. fat), 240mg chol., 1835mg sod., 36g carb. (7g sugars, 2g fiber), 41g pro.

AIR-FRYER FISH & CHIPS

Looking for easy air fryer recipes? Try these simple fish and chips. The fish fillets have a fuss-free coating that's healthier but just as crunchy and golden as the deep-fried kind. Simply seasoned, the crispy fries are perfect on the side.
—Janice Mitchell, Aurora, CO

PREP: 15 MIN. • **COOK:** 25 MIN. • **MAKES:** 2 SERVINGS

- 1 medium potato
- 1 Tbsp. olive oil
- ⅛ tsp. pepper
- ⅛ tsp. salt

FISH

- 3 Tbsp. all-purpose flour
- ⅛ tsp. pepper
- 1 large egg
- 2 Tbsp. water
- ⅓ cup crushed cornflakes
- 1½ tsp. grated Parmesan cheese
- Dash cayenne pepper
- ⅛ tsp. salt
- ½ lb. haddock or cod fillets
- Tartar sauce, optional

1. Preheat air fryer to 400°. Peel and cut potato lengthwise into ½-in.-thick slices; cut slices into ½-in.-thick sticks.

2. In a large bowl, toss potato with oil, pepper and salt. Place potato pieces in a single layer in air-fryer basket; cook until just tender, 5-10 minutes Toss the potatoes in the basket to redistribute; continue to cook until lightly browned and crisp, 5-10 minutes longer.

3. Meanwhile, in a shallow bowl, mix flour and pepper. In another shallow bowl, whisk egg with water. In a third bowl, toss cornflakes with cheese and cayenne. Sprinkle fish with th salt; dip in flour mixture to coat both sides and shake off excess. Dip in egg mixture, then in cornflake mixture, patting to help coating adhere.

4. Remove fries from the basket; keep warm. Place the fish in a single layer in air-fryer basket. Cook until the fish is lightly browned and just beginning to flake easily with a fork, turning halfway through cooking, 8-10 minutes. Do not overcook. Return fries to basket to heat through. Serve immediately. If desired, serve with tartar sauce.

NOTE Cook times vary dramatically among brands of air fryers. Refer to your air-fryer manual for general cook times and adjust if necessary.

1 SERVING 304 cal., 9g fat (2g sat. fat), 84mg chol., 503mg sod., 33g carb. (3g sugars, 1g fiber), 23g pro. **DIABETIC EXCHANGES** 3 lean meat, 2 starch, 1½ fat.

OVEN-ROASTED SALMON

When I'm starving after work, I want a fast meal with no-fail technique. Roasted salmon is super tender and has a delicate sweetness. It's also an easy wowza for company.
—Jeanne Ambrose, Des Moines, IA

TAKES: 20 MIN. • **MAKES:** 4 SERVINGS

- 1 center-cut salmon fillet (1½ lbs.)
- 1 Tbsp. olive oil
- ½ tsp. salt
- ¼ tsp. pepper

OVEN-ROASTED SALMON TIP

It's important to cook salmon the right way to prevent it from drying out. When the flesh flakes easily with a fork or when the internal temperature reaches 125°, you know the salmon is done.

1. Place a large cast-iron or other ovenproof skillet in a cold oven. Preheat oven to 450°. Meanwhile, brush salmon with the oil and sprinkle with the salt and pepper.

2. Carefully remove skillet from oven. Place the fish skin side down in skillet. Return to oven; bake uncovered, until salmon flakes easily and a thermometer reads 125°, 14-18 minutes. Cut salmon into 4 equal portions.

1 FILLET 295 cal., 19g fat (4g sat. fat), 85mg chol., 380mg sod., 0 carb. (0 sugars, 0 fiber), 29g pro. **DIABETIC EXCHANGES** 4 lean meat, ½ fat.

FLAVOR BOOSTS

This weeknight-reliable salmon is perfect with just salt and pepper. But it's easily customized with a slather of flavored butter or a sweet-spicy glaze. Choose your favorite and get ready for the "wows!"

GREMOLATA SALMON

Mix ¼ cup minced **fresh parsley**, 2 Tbsp. **olive oil**, 1 Tbsp. **lemon juice**, 1 minced **garlic clove**, 1 tsp. grated **lemon zest**, ½ tsp. **salt** and ¼ tsp. **pepper**. Spoon over roasted salmon.

ORANGE-DIJON GLAZED SALMON

Combine ½ cup **orange marmalade**, 1 Tbsp. **Dijon mustard**, ½ tsp. **garlic powder** and ⅛ tsp. **ground ginger**. Set aside about a third of the mixture; smooth the remainder over salmon before roasting. Spoon or brush reserved glaze over roasted salmon.

MAPLE-SOY GLAZED SALMON

Mix ¼ cup **maple syrup**, 2 Tbsp. **soy sauce**, 1 minced **green onion**, ½ tsp. grated **fresh ginger** and ¼ tsp. **red pepper flakes**. Spoon over the salmon before roasting.

POMEGRANATE & THYME BUTTERED SALMON

In a small saucepan, combine ½ cup **pomegranate juice**, ¼ cup **balsamic vinegar** and 1 minced **shallot**. Cook until liquid is reduced by half, about 10 minutes. Transfer to a small bowl; cool. Beat in ¼ cup softened **butter** and ¾ tsp. minced **fresh thyme**. Spoon over roasted salmon.

DILL & CAPER BUTTER SALMON

Mix ¼ cup softened **butter**, 1 Tbsp. minced **shallot**, 1 Tbsp. minced **fresh dill**, 1 tsp. **Dijon mustard** and 1 tsp. chopped **capers**. Spoon over roasted salmon.

PRETZEL-CRUSTED CATFISH

I'm not a big fish lover, so any concoction that has me enjoying fish is a keeper in my book. This combination of flavors works for me. It's awesome served with corn muffins, butter and honey!
—Kelly Williams, Forked River, NJ

TAKES: 30 MIN. • **MAKES:** 4 SERVINGS

- 4 catfish fillets (6 oz. each)
- ½ tsp. salt
- ½ tsp. pepper
- 2 large eggs
- ⅓ cup Dijon mustard
- 2 Tbsp. 2% milk
- ½ cup all-purpose flour
- 4 cups honey mustard miniature pretzels, coarsely crushed
- Oil for frying
- Lemon slices, optional

1. Sprinkle catfish with salt and pepper. Whisk the eggs, mustard and milk in a shallow bowl. Place flour and pretzels in separate shallow bowls. Coat fillets with flour, then dip in egg mixture and coat with pretzels.

2. Heat ¼ in. oil to 375° in an electric skillet. Fry fillets, a few at a time, until fish flakes easily with a fork, 3-4 minutes on each side. Drain on paper towels. Serve with lemon slices if desired.

1 FILLET 610 cal., 31g fat (4g sat. fat), 164mg chol., 1579mg sod., 44g carb. (2g sugars, 2g fiber), 33g pro.

LEMON-PARSLEY BAKED COD

After trying a few cod recipes, this was the first fish recipe that got two thumbs-ups from my picky meat-only eaters. The tangy lemon gives the cod some oomph.
—Trisha Kruse, Eagle, ID

TAKES: 30 MIN. • **MAKES:** 4 SERVINGS

- 3 Tbsp. lemon juice
- 3 Tbsp. butter, melted
- ¼ cup all-purpose flour
- ½ tsp. salt
- ¼ tsp. paprika
- ¼ tsp. lemon-pepper seasoning
- 4 cod fillets (6 oz. each)
- 2 Tbsp. minced fresh parsley
- 2 tsp. grated lemon zest

LONG-LASTING HERB BUNCH

To keep parsley fresh for up to a month, trim the stems and place the bunch in a tumbler with an inch of water. Be sure no leaves are in the water. Tie a produce bag around the tumbler to trap humidity; store it in the refrigerator. Each time you use the parsley, change the water and turn the bag inside out so any moisture built up inside can escape.

1. Preheat oven to 400°. In a shallow bowl, mix lemon juice and butter. In a separate shallow bowl, mix flour and seasonings. Dip fillets in lemon juice mixture, then in flour mixture to coat both sides; shake off excess.

2. Place in a 13x9-in. baking dish coated with cooking spray. Drizzle with the remaining lemon juice mixture. Bake 12-15 minutes or until fish just begins to flake easily with a fork. Mix parsley and lemon zest; sprinkle over fish.

1 FILLET 232 cal., 10g fat (6g sat. fat), 87mg chol., 477mg sod., 7g carb. (0 sugars, 0 fiber), 28g pro. **DIABETIC EXCHANGES** 4 lean meat, 2 fat, ½ starch.

HOISIN SHRIMP & BROCCOLI

Get out the chopsticks—this Asian-inspired dinner is our healthier alternative to takeout and is so easy to prepare. Sesame, ginger and soy sauce add a rich flavor that enhances the taste of fresh broccoli.
—Mary Kisinger, Calgary, AB

TAKES: 30 MIN. • **MAKES:** 4 SERVINGS

- 1 Tbsp. cornstarch
- ⅓ cup reduced-sodium chicken broth
- 4½ tsp. reduced-sodium soy sauce
- 4½ tsp. hoisin sauce
- 1 tsp. sesame oil
- 3 cups fresh broccoli florets
- 1 Tbsp. canola oil
- 4 green onions, chopped
- 3 garlic cloves, minced
- 1 tsp. minced fresh gingerroot
- 1 lb. uncooked medium shrimp, peeled and deveined
- 2 cups hot cooked rice
- Sesame seeds, toasted, optional

SHRIMP AND BROCCOLI STIR-FRY TIPS

What else can you put in shrimp and broccoli stir-fry? Every stir fry recipe starts with a basic formula: veggies + protein + sauce + a base (such as rice). From there, you can make virtually a brand-new stir-fry every time! In this dish, consider adding snow peas or sliced red pepper. You can also add some heat with sriracha or red pepper flakes.

What else can you serve with this stir-fry? Most stir-fry recipes are served with rice, but you can switch it up by using rice noodles or multigrain linguine as a base. This dish pairs well with egg rolls or crab rangoon.

1. In a small bowl, combine cornstarch and broth until smooth. Stir in the soy sauce, hoisin sauce and sesame oil; set aside.

2. In a large nonstick skillet or wok, stir-fry broccoli in oil until crisp-tender. Add the green onion, garlic and ginger; stir-fry until the vegetables are tender, 3-4 minutes. Add shrimp; stir-fry until shrimp turn pink, 4-5 minutes longer.

3. Stir cornstarch mixture and add to pan. Bring to a boil; cook and stir until thickened, about 2 minutes. Serve with rice. If desired, garnish with toasted sesame seeds.

1 SERVING 289 cal., 7g fat (1g sat. fat), 138mg chol., 524mg sod., 33g carb. (3g sugars, 2g fiber), 23g pro. **DIABETIC EXCHANGES** 3 lean meat, 1½ starch, 1 vegetable, 1 fat.

MINI SCALLOP CASSEROLES

Tiny and tender bay scallops take center stage in these miniature dishes. They're reminiscent of potpies, very creamy and packed with flavorful veggies in every bite.
—Vivian Manary, Nepean, ON

PREP: 30 MIN. • **BAKE:** 20 MIN. • **MAKES:** 4 SERVINGS

- 3 celery ribs, chopped
- 1 cup sliced fresh mushrooms
- 1 medium green pepper, chopped
- 1 small onion, chopped
- 2 Tbsp. butter
- ⅓ cup all-purpose flour
- ¼ tsp. salt
- ¼ tsp. pepper
- 2 cups fat-free milk
- 1 lb. bay scallops

TOPPING

- 1 cup soft bread crumbs
- 1 Tbsp. butter, melted
- ¼ cup shredded cheddar cheese

1. In a large skillet, saute the celery, mushrooms, green pepper and onion in butter until tender. Stir in flour, salt and pepper until blended; gradually add the milk. Bring to a boil; cook and stir 2 minutes or until thickened.

2. Reduce heat; add the scallops. Cook, stirring occasionally, 3-4 minutes or until scallops are firm and opaque.

3. Preheat oven to 350°. Divide mixture among four 10-oz. ramekins or custard cups. In a small bowl, combine crumbs and butter; sprinkle over scallop mixture.

4. Bake, uncovered, 15-20 minutes or until bubbly. Sprinkle with the cheese; bake 5 minutes longer or until cheese is melted.

1 SERVING 332 cal., 12g fat (7g sat. fat), 70mg chol., 588mg sod., 27g carb. (9g sugars, 2g fiber), 28g pro.

EASY CRAB CAKES

Ready-to-go crabmeat makes these delicate patties ideal for dinner when you are pressed for time. You can also form the crab mixture into four thick patties instead of eight cakes.
—Charlene Spelock, Apollo, PA

TAKES: 25 MIN. • **MAKES:** 4 SERVINGS

- 1 cup seasoned bread crumbs, divided
- 2 green onions, finely chopped
- ¼ cup finely chopped sweet red pepper
- 1 large egg, lightly beaten
- ¼ cup reduced-fat mayonnaise
- 1 Tbsp. lemon juice
- ½ tsp. garlic powder
- ⅛ tsp. cayenne pepper
- 2 cans (6 oz. each) crabmeat, drained, flaked and cartilage removed
- 1 Tbsp. butter

1. In a large bowl, combine ⅓ cup bread crumbs, green onion, red pepper, egg, mayonnaise, lemon juice, garlic powder and cayenne; fold in crab.

2. Place the remaining bread crumbs in a shallow bowl. Divide crab mixture into 8 portions; shape into 2-in. balls. Gently coat with bread crumbs and shape into ½-in.-thick patties.

3. In a large nonstick skillet, heat butter over medium-high heat. Add crab cakes; cook until golden brown, 3-4 minutes on each side.

2 CRAB CAKES 239 cal., 11g fat (3g sat. fat), 141mg chol., 657mg sod., 13g carb. (2g sugars, 1g fiber), 21g pro. **DIABETIC EXCHANGES** 3 lean meat, 2 fat, 1 starch.

KEEPING IN SHAPE

To keep crab cakes from falling apart, handle them gently while shaping and frying them. Pop the crab mixture in the fridge for 20-30 minutes to help it set up before shaping the crab cakes.

BLACKENED SHRIMP

With a nice amount of spice, this blackened shrimp makes for a great quick dinner. It's perfect served over rice.
—Taste of Home *Test Kitchen*

TAKES: 25 MIN. • **MAKES:** 4 SERVINGS

- 2 tsp. paprika
- 1 tsp. onion powder
- 1 tsp. garlic powder
- ½ tsp. salt
- ½ tsp. pepper
- ½ tsp. dried oregano
- ½ tsp. dried thyme
- ¼ tsp. cayenne pepper
- 1½ lbs. uncooked shrimp (26-30 per lb.), peeled and deveined
- 3 Tbsp. butter
- Lemon wedges

1. In a large bowl, combine the first 8 ingredients. Add shrimp; toss to coat.

2. In a large cast-iron or heavy-duty skillet, melt butter over medium heat. Add shrimp; cook and stir until shrimp turn pink and edges are browned. Serve with lemon wedges.

ABOUT 10 SHRIMP 230 cal., 11g fat (6g sat. fat), 230mg chol., 567mg sod., 3g carb. (0 sugars, 1g fiber), 28g pro.

NOTES

BUTTER PAT

LINGUINE WITH CLAM SAUCE

This impressive pasta looks and tastes so much like fancy restaurant fare that you'll want to serve it to guests. But the recipe is easy enough to prepare just about anytime.
—Carolee Snyder, Hartford City, IN

PREP: 20 MIN. • **COOK:** 15 MIN. • **MAKES:** 4 SERVINGS

- 1 can (10 oz.) whole baby clams
- 1 can (6½ oz.) minced clams
- ½ cup finely chopped onion
- ¼ cup olive oil
- ¼ cup butter
- ⅓ cup minced fresh parsley
- 4 garlic cloves, minced
- 2 Tbsp. cornstarch
- ½ cup white wine or chicken broth
- ¼ cup minced fresh basil or 4 tsp. dried basil
- Dash pepper
- Dash cayenne pepper
- Hot cooked linguine
- Shredded Parmesan cheese

1. Drain clams, reserving juice; set the clams and juice aside. In a large skillet, saute onion in oil and butter until tender. Add parsley and garlic; saute 2 minutes.

2. Add drained clams; saute 2 minutes longer.

3. Combine cornstarch and clam juice until smooth; stir into skillet with wine or broth. Bring to a boil; cook and stir 1-2 minutes or until thickened. Stir in basil, pepper and cayenne. Serve sauce over linguine; sprinkle with Parmesan cheese.

1⅔ CUPS 328 cal., 26g fat (9g sat. fat), 73mg chol., 521mg sod., 10g carb. (1g sugars, 1g fiber), 10g pro.

FIRECRACKER SHRIMP

These delightful grilled shrimp are coated in a sweet and spicy glaze. The marinade comes together in moments for sizzling shrimp skewers.
—Mary Tallman, Arbor Vitae, WI

TAKES: 20 MIN. • **MAKES:** 2½ DOZEN

- ½ cup apricot preserves
- 1 tsp. canola oil
- 1 tsp. soy sauce
- ½ tsp. crushed red pepper flakes
- 1 lb. uncooked shrimp (25-30 per lb.), peeled and deveined

READER REVIEW

"A wonderful way to have shrimp. It's just the right ratio of heat to sweetness. I like to have this dish on special nights when it's just my husband and I. It goes great with garlic biscuits. I have been making these shrimp for years and will continue."

—SOUTHERNCOOK37, TASTEOFHOME.COM

1. In a small bowl, combine the apricot preserves, oil, soy sauce and pepper flakes. Thread shrimp onto metal or soaked wooden skewers.

2. Grill, uncovered, over medium heat or broil 4 in. from the heat until shrimp turn pink, 2-3 minutes on each side, basting frequently with apricot mixture.

1 SHRIMP 27 cal., 0 fat (0 sat. fat), 18mg chol., 30mg sod., 4g carb. (2g sugars, 0 fiber), 3g pro.

how to cook ...

VEGETARIAN

VEGAN STIR-FRY, PAGE 269

BUFFALO TOFU WRAPS

My family loves the tofu filling in these wraps. For parties, we often serve it as a dip with tortilla chips or pita bread. It's easy to double the recipe if needed.
—Deanna Wolfe, Madison, SD

TAKES: 20 MIN. • **MAKES:** 6 SERVINGS

- 1 cup shredded dairy-free cheddar-flavored cheese
- ½ cup vegan mayonnaise
- ¼ cup finely chopped onion
- ¼ cup finely chopped celery
- 3 Tbsp. Louisiana-style hot sauce
- 1 Tbsp. lemon juice
- ½ tsp. garlic powder
- ¼ tsp. salt
- ¼ tsp. pepper
- 1 pkg. (16 oz.) extra-firm tofu, drained
- 6 spinach tortillas (8 in.), warmed
- 1½ cups fresh baby spinach

In a large bowl, combine the first 9 ingredients. Crumble tofu into bowl; mix well. Spoon about ½ cup of tofu mixture down center of each tortilla; top with spinach. Fold bottom and side of tortilla over filling and roll up.

1 WRAP 452 cal., 29g fat (7g sat. fat), 0 chol., 1066mg sod., 38g carb. (1g sugars, 2g fiber), 11g pro.

READER REVIEW

"I crumbled up the uncooked tofu as the recipe described and followed everything exactly, except that I used nonvegan cheese. Delicious and it's ready in just a few minutes."

—SHANNON535, TASTEOFHOME.COM

GENERAL TSO'S CAULIFLOWER

Cauliflower florets are deep-fried to a crispy, golden brown, then coated in a sauce with just the right amount of kick. This is a fun alternative to the classic chicken dish.
—Nick Iverson, Denver, CO

PREP: 25 MIN. • **COOK:** 20 MIN. • **MAKES:** 4 SERVINGS

Oil for deep-fat frying
½ cup all-purpose flour
½ cup cornstarch
1 tsp. salt
1 tsp. baking powder
¾ cup club soda
1 medium head cauliflower, cut into 1-in. florets (about 6 cups)

SAUCE

¼ cup orange juice
3 Tbsp. sugar
3 Tbsp. soy sauce
3 Tbsp. vegetable broth
2 Tbsp. rice vinegar
2 tsp. sesame oil
2 tsp. cornstarch
2 Tbsp. canola oil
2 to 6 dried pasilla or other hot chiles, chopped
3 green onions, white part minced, green part thinly sliced
3 garlic cloves, minced
1 tsp. grated fresh gingerroot
½ tsp. grated orange zest
4 cups hot cooked rice

1. In an electric skillet or a deep fryer, heat oil to 375°. Combine the flour, cornstarch, salt and baking powder. Stir in club soda just until blended (batter will be thin). Dip florets, a few at a time, into batter and fry for 8-10 minutes or until cauliflower is tender and coating is light brown. Drain on paper towels.

2. For sauce, whisk together the first 6 ingredients; whisk in cornstarch until smooth.

3. In a large saucepan, heat the oil over medium-high heat. Add chiles; cook and stir until fragrant, 1-2 minutes. Add white part of onions, garlic, ginger and zest; cook 1 minute or until fragrant. Stir soy sauce mixture; add to saucepan. Bring to a boil; cook and stir until thickened, 2-4 minutes.

4. Add cauliflower to sauce; toss to coat. Serve with cooked rice; sprinkle with thinly sliced green onions.

1 CUP WITH 1 CUP RICE 584 cal., 17g fat (2g sat. fat), 0 chol., 1628mg sod., 97g carb. (17g sugars, 5g fiber), 11g pro.

CUSTOMIZE THE SAUCE

To adjust the spice level in this dish, increase or decrease the amount of hot chiles used in the sauce. If you're really sensitive to heat, omit them entirely. For a make-ahead meal, prepare the sauce 1-3 days in advance and refrigerate it. Reheat it gently in a saucepan as you prepare the cauliflower.

VEGAN EGGPLANT PARMESAN

This vegan eggplant Parmesan is a lightened-up version of the classic comfort food dish. It's made with layers of roasted eggplant slices and plant-based cheese.
—Taste of Home *Test Kitchen*

PREP: 65 MIN. + STANDING • **BAKE:** 35 MIN. • **MAKES:** 12 SERVINGS

- 2 large eggplants, each cut into six ½-in. rounds
- 2 tsp. sea salt
- 1 cup unsweetened almond milk
- ½ cup all-purpose flour
- 3 cups panko bread crumbs
- 2 tsp. dried basil
- 1 tsp. Italian seasoning
- 1 tsp. dried oregano
- 1 jar (24 oz.) marinara sauce
- 3 cups shredded dairy-free mozzarella-flavored cheese
- 1 cup shredded dairy-free Parmesan-flavored cheese
- Optional: Hot cooked spaghetti and torn fresh basil

1. Place eggplant in a colander; sprinkle with salt. Let stand 30 minutes.

2. Preheat oven to 400°. Rinse eggplant slices; pat dry with paper towels. In a shallow bowl, combine almond milk and flour; combine bread crumbs, dried basil, Italian seasoning and oregano in another shallow bowl. Dip eggplant into milk mixture, then coat with the crumb mixture, patting to help adhere. Place slices on greased baking sheets. Bake for 35-40 minutes or until breading is golden brown, turning once.

3. In a greased 13x9-in. baking dish, layer half each of the eggplant, marinara and mozzarella. Repeat layers. Sprinkle with Parmesan cheese. Bake, uncovered, until the cheese is melted, 30-35 minutes. If desired, serve with spaghetti; top with fresh basil.

1 PIECE 242 cal., 10g fat (4g sat. fat), 1mg chol., 739mg sod., 32g carb. (6g sugars, 7g fiber), 5g pro. **DIABETIC EXCHANGES** 2 starch, 2 fat.

HEALTH TIP

To keep this recipe dairy free, be sure to use plain panko bread crumbs. Italian-style crumbs contain cheese.

VEGGIE NICOISE SALAD

More and more people in my workplace are becoming vegetarians. When we cook or eat together, the focus is on fresh produce. This salad combines some of our favorite ingredients in one dish. And with hard-boiled eggs and kidney beans, it also delivers enough protein to satisfy those who are skeptical of vegetarian fare.

—Elizabeth Kelley, Chicago, IL

PREP: 40 MIN. • **COOK:** 25 MIN. • **MAKES:** 8 SERVINGS

- ⅓ cup olive oil
- ¼ cup lemon juice
- 2 tsp. minced fresh oregano
- 2 tsp. minced fresh thyme
- 1 tsp. Dijon mustard
- 1 garlic clove, minced
- ¼ tsp. coarsely ground pepper
- ⅛ tsp. salt
- 1 can (16 oz.) kidney beans, rinsed and drained
- 1 small red onion, halved and thinly sliced
- 1 lb. small red potatoes (about 9), halved
- 1 lb. fresh asparagus, trimmed
- ½ lb. fresh green beans, trimmed
- 12 cups torn romaine (about 2 small bunches)
- 6 hard-boiled large eggs, quartered
- 1 jar (6½ oz.) marinated quartered artichoke hearts, drained
- ½ cup Nicoise or kalamata olives

1. For vinaigrette, whisk together the first 8 ingredients. In another bowl, toss the kidney beans and onion with 1 Tbsp. vinaigrette. Set aside bean mixture and remaining vinaigrette.

2. Place potatoes in a saucepan and cover with water. Bring to a boil. Reduce heat; simmer, covered, 10-15 minutes or until tender. Drain. While potatoes are warm, toss with 1 Tbsp. vinaigrette.

3. In a pot of boiling water, cook fresh asparagus for 2-4 minutes or just until crisp-tender. Remove with tongs and immediately drop into ice water. Drain and pat dry. In the same pot of boiling water, cook green beans until crisp-tender, 3-4 minutes. Remove beans; place in ice water. Drain and pat dry.

4. To serve, toss asparagus with 1 Tbsp. vinaigrette; toss green beans with 2 tsp. vinaigrette. Toss romaine with remaining vinaigrette; place on a platter. Arrange vegetables, kidney bean mixture, eggs, artichoke hearts and olives on top.

1 SERVING 329 cal., 19g fat (4g sat. fat), 140mg chol., 422mg sod., 28g carb. (6g sugars, 7g fiber), 12g pro. **DIABETIC EXCHANGES** 3 fat, 2 vegetable, 2 medium-fat meat, 1½ starch.

DID YOU KNOW?

Dijon, a town in eastern France's famous Burgundy wine-growing region, is the home of Dijon mustard. Mustard is commonly grown as a cover crop among grapevines. The plants attract beneficial insects and give nutrients back to the soil. And the scores of tiny mustard seeds mean the crop reseeds itself year after year. Dijon mustard is made with white wine instead of vinegar.

THE ULTIMATE GRILLED CHEESE

These ooey-gooey grilled cheese sandwiches, subtly seasoned with garlic, taste delightful for lunch with sliced apples. And they're really fast to whip up too. To save time, I soften the cream cheese in the microwave, then blend it with the rest of the ingredients in the same bowl. That makes cleanup a breeze.
—Kathy Norris, Streator, IL

TAKES: 15 MIN. • **MAKES:** 5 SERVINGS

- 3 oz. cream cheese, softened
- ¾ cup mayonnaise
- 1 cup shredded part-skim mozzarella cheese
- 1 cup shredded cheddar cheese
- ½ tsp. garlic powder
- ⅛ tsp. seasoned salt
- 10 slices Italian bread (½ in. thick)
- 2 Tbsp. butter, softened

1. In a large bowl, beat cream cheese and mayonnaise until smooth. Stir in cheeses, garlic powder and seasoned salt. Spread 5 bread slices with cheese mixture, about ⅓ cup on each. Top with remaining bread.

2. Butter the outsides of sandwiches. In a skillet over medium heat, toast sandwiches for 4-5 minutes on each side or until bread is lightly browned and cheese is melted.

1 SANDWICH 646 cal., 50g fat (18g sat. fat), 84mg chol., 885mg sod., 32g carb. (3g sugars, 2g fiber), 16g pro.

VEGGIE TACOS

These vegetarian tacos are stuffed with a blend of sauteed cabbage, peppers and black beans that is so filling you won't miss the meat. Top with avocado, cheese or a dollop of sour cream.
—Taste of Home *Test Kitchen*

TAKES: 30 MIN. • **MAKES:** 4 SERVINGS

- 2 Tbsp. canola oil
- 3 cups shredded cabbage
- 1 medium sweet red pepper, julienned
- 1 medium onion, halved and sliced
- 2 tsp. sugar
- 1 can (15 oz.) black beans, rinsed and drained
- 1 cup salsa
- 1 can (4 oz.) chopped green chiles
- 1 tsp. minced garlic
- 1 tsp. chili powder
- ¼ tsp. ground cumin
- 8 taco shells, warmed
- ½ cup shredded cheddar cheese
- 1 medium ripe avocado, peeled and sliced

1. In a large skillet, heat oil over medium-high heat; saute cabbage, pepper and onion until crisp-tender, about 5 minutes. Sprinkle with sugar.

2. Stir in the beans, salsa, green chiles, garlic, chili powder and cumin; bring to a boil. Reduce heat; simmer, covered, until flavors are blended, about 5 minutes.

3. Serve in taco shells. Top with cheese and avocado.

2 TACOS 430 cal., 22g fat (5g sat. fat), 14mg chol., 770mg sod., 47g carb. (8g sugars, 10g fiber), 12g pro.

READER REVIEW

"Very tasty! It was super quick and easy too. We had whole-wheat tortillas, so I just warmed them and made soft tacos. Nice, crunchy-ish filling with the cabbage. Will definitely make these often!"

—CWAZ23, TASTEOFHOME.COM

DILLY CHICKPEA SALAD SANDWICHES

This chickpea salad is flavorful and contains less fat and cholesterol than chicken salad. These make absolutely delightful picnic sandwiches.
—Deanna Wolfe, Madison, SD

TAKES: 15 MIN. • **MAKES:** 6 SERVINGS

- 1 can (15 oz.) chickpeas or garbanzo beans, rinsed and drained
- ½ cup finely chopped onion
- ½ cup finely chopped celery
- ½ cup vegan mayonnaise
- 3 Tbsp. honey mustard or Dijon mustard
- 2 Tbsp. snipped fresh dill
- 1 Tbsp. red wine vinegar
- ¼ tsp. salt
- ¼ tsp. paprika
- ¼ tsp. pepper
- 12 slices multigrain bread
- Optional toppings: Romaine leaves, tomato slices, dill pickle slices and sweet red pepper rings

Place chickpeas in a large bowl; mash to desired consistency. Stir in onion, celery, mayonnaise, mustard, dill, vinegar, salt, paprika and pepper. Spread over 6 bread slices; layer with toppings of your choice and remaining bread.

1 SANDWICH 295 cal., 11g fat (2g sat. fat), 7mg chol., 586mg sod., 41g carb. (9g sugars, 7g fiber), 10g pro.

ASIAN TOFU

This tasty tofu was the first meatless recipe my fiance made for me. It's a wonderful light protein and is so easy to pair with broiled or grilled veggies, such as eggplant, asparagus or even tomatoes.
—Emily Steers, Los Angeles, CA

PREP: 10 MIN. + MARINATING • **BROIL:** 10 MIN. • **MAKES:** 4 SERVINGS

- ¼ cup olive oil
- 3 Tbsp. reduced-sodium soy sauce
- 2 green onions, chopped
- 2 garlic cloves, minced
- ¼ tsp. ground cumin
- ¼ tsp. crushed red pepper flakes
- 1 pkg. (14 oz.) extra-firm tofu

1. Whisk together first 6 ingredients. Cut tofu lengthwise into ⅜-in. thick slices; cut each slice in half diagonally to make triangles. Place the tofu and marinade in a large shallow bowl; turn to coat. Cover and refrigerate 3-5 hours, turning occasionally.

2. Preheat broiler. Reserving marinade, place tofu in a 15x10x1-in. pan. Drizzle remaining marinade over top. Broil 5-6 in. from heat until lightly browned and heated through, about 10 minutes.

1 SERVING 208 cal., 18g fat (3g sat. fat), 0 chol., 440mg sod., 4g carb. (1g sugars, 1g fiber), 9g pro. **DIABETIC EXCHANGES** 3 fat, 1 lean meat.

NOTES

KIMCHI FRIED RICE

Forget ordinary fried rice! This dish is just as easy, but it packs a flavorful punch. It's a fantastic use of leftovers, and you can also freeze it for up to 3 months. When cooking your defrosted rice, add a little more soy sauce so it doesn't dry out.
—Taste of Home *Test Kitchen*

TAKES: 20 MIN. • **MAKES:** 4 SERVINGS

- 2 Tbsp. canola oil, divided
- 1 small onion, chopped
- 1 cup kimchi, coarsely chopped
- ½ cup matchstick carrots
- ¼ cup kimchi juice
- 1 garlic cloves, minced
- 1 tsp. minced fresh gingerroot
- 3 cups leftover short grain rice
- 2 green onions, thinly sliced
- 3 tsp. soy sauce
- 1 tsp. sesame oil
- 4 large eggs
- Optional toppings: Sliced nori, black sesame seeds and green onions

1. In large skillet, heat 1 Tbsp. oil over medium-high heat. Add onion; cook and stir until tender, 2-4 minutes. Add kimchi, carrots, kimchi juice, garlic and ginger; cook 2 minutes longer. Add rice, green onions, soy sauce and sesame oil; heat through, stirring frequently.

2. In another large skillet, heat the remaining 1 Tbsp. oil over medium-high heat. Break eggs, 1 at a time, into pan; reduce heat to low. Cook to desired doneness, turning after whites are set if desired. Serve over rice. If desired, sprinkle with nori, sesame seeds and additional green onion.

1 CUP FRIED RICE WITH 1 EGG 331 cal., 14g fat (2g sat. fat), 186mg chol., 546mg sod., 41g carb. (4g sugars, 2g fiber), 11g pro.

HOMEMADE MANICOTTI

These tender manicotti are easier to stuff than the purchased variety. People are always amazed when I tell them I make my own noodles. My son also fixed the dish for his friends, and they were impressed.
—Richard Bunt, Painted Post, NY

PREP: 70 MIN. + STANDING • **BAKE:** 40 MIN. • **MAKES:** 6 SERVINGS

CREPE NOODLES
- 1½ cups all-purpose flour
- 1 cup whole milk
- 3 large eggs, lightly beaten
- ½ tsp. salt

FILLING
- 1½ lbs. ricotta cheese
- ¼ cup grated Romano cheese
- 1 large egg, lightly beaten
- 1 Tbsp. minced fresh parsley or 1 tsp. dried parsley flakes
- 1 jar (26 oz.) meatless spaghetti sauce
- Grated Romano cheese, optional

1. Place flour in a bowl; whisk in milk, eggs and salt until smooth. Let stand for 30 minutes.

2. Heat a lightly greased 8-in. skillet; pour about 2 Tbsp. batter into center of skillet. Spread into a 5-in. circle. Cook over medium heat until set; do not brown or turn. Remove from pan. Repeat with remaining batter, making 18 crepes. Stack crepes with waxed paper in between; set aside.

3. For the filling, combine cheeses, egg and parsley. Spoon 3-4 Tbsp. down the center of each crepe; roll up. Pour half the spaghetti sauce into an ungreased 13x9-in. baking dish. Place crepes, seam side down, over sauce; pour remaining sauce over top.

4. Cover and bake at 350° for 20 minutes. Uncover and bake until a thermometer reads 160°, about 20 minutes longer. If desired, sprinkle with Romano cheese.

3 MANICOTTI 480 cal., 22g fat (11g sat. fat), 201mg chol., 1128mg sod., 44g carb. (17g sugars, 3g fiber), 27g pro.

FESTIVE FALL FALAFEL

Falafel is the ultimate Israeli street food. Pumpkin adds a light sweetness and keeps the patties moist while baking. Top these beauties with maple tahini sauce. You can serve them sandwich style, as an appetizer over a bed of greens, or with soup and salad.
—Julie Peterson, Crofton, MD

PREP: 20 MIN. • **BAKE:** 30 MIN. • **MAKES:** 4 SERVINGS

- 1 cup canned garbanzo beans or chickpeas, rinsed and drained
- ½ cup canned pumpkin
- ½ cup fresh cilantro leaves
- ¼ cup chopped onion
- 1 garlic clove, halved
- ¾ tsp. salt
- ½ tsp. ground ginger
- ½ tsp. ground cumin
- ¼ tsp. ground coriander
- ¼ tsp. cayenne pepper

MAPLE TAHINI SAUCE

- ½ cup tahini
- ¼ cup water
- 2 Tbsp. maple syrup
- 1 Tbsp. cider vinegar
- ½ tsp. salt
- 8 pita pocket halves
- Optional: Sliced cucumber, onions and tomatoes

1. Preheat oven to 400°. Place the first 10 ingredients in a food processor; pulse until combined. Drop by tablespoonfuls onto a greased baking sheet. Bake until firm and golden brown, 30-35 minutes.

2. Meanwhile, for the sauce, in a small bowl, combine tahini, water, syrup, vinegar and salt. Serve falafel in pita pockets with maple tahini sauce and optional toppings as desired.

2 FILLED PITA HALVES 469 cal., 21g fat (3g sat. fat), 0 chol., 1132mg sod., 57g carb. (10g sugars, 8g fiber), 14g pro.

VEGAN STIR-FRY

Quick and easy, fresh and tasty, stir-fries are the answer to the big "What's for dinner?" question on the busiest night! Even better, they're endlessly flexible—you can scale up or down easily to serve a couple or a crowd and add anything you like to suit your tastes.
—Taste of Home *Test Kitchen*

PREP: 20 MIN. • **COOK:** 15 MIN. • **MAKES:** 6 SERVINGS

- 1 cup vegetable broth
- ⅓ cup soy sauce
- 3 Tbsp. packed brown sugar
- 1 Tbsp. cornstarch
- 3 garlic cloves, minced
- 1 Tbsp. minced fresh gingerroot
- 2 tsp. sesame oil
- 3 Tbsp. olive oil, divided
- 4 cups fresh broccoli florets
- 2 cups fresh sugar snap peas
- 1½ cups julienned carrots
- 1 cup julienned onions
- 2 cups sliced fresh mushrooms
- 2 cups julienned sweet red pepper
- 1 cup canned whole baby corn
- 3 green onions, thinly sliced
- 1 Tbsp. sesame seeds
- Hot cooked rice, optional

1. In a small bowl, combine the first 7 ingredients until smooth; set aside. In a large skillet or wok, heat 2 Tbsp. olive oil over medium-high heat. Add broccoli, snap peas, carrots and onions. Stir-fry 5 minutes. Add mushrooms, sweet red pepper, corn and remaining 1 Tbsp. olive oil; cook 4-5 minutes longer or until the vegetables are crisp-tender.

2. Stir cornstarch mixture and add to pan. Bring to a boil; cook and stir until sauce is thickened, 1-2 minutes. Top with green onions and sesame seeds. If desired, serve with rice.

1 CUP 215 cal., 10g fat (1g sat. fat), 0 chol., 768mg sod., 26g carb. (16g sugars, 5g fiber), 7g pro.

NOTES

MUSHROOM BURGERS

Even the most stubborn meat-and-potatoes people have a change of heart when they bite into one of these flavorful, cheddary mushroom burgers.
—Denise Hollebeke, Penhold, AB

TAKES: 25 MIN. • **MAKES:** 4 SERVINGS

- 2 cups finely chopped fresh mushrooms
- 2 large eggs, lightly beaten
- ½ cup dry bread crumbs
- ½ cup shredded cheddar cheese
- ½ cup finely chopped onion
- ¼ cup all-purpose flour
- ½ tsp. salt
- ¼ tsp. dried thyme
- ¼ tsp. pepper
- 1 Tbsp. canola oil
- 4 whole wheat hamburger buns, split
- 4 lettuce leaves
- Optional: Sliced tomatoes, sliced Swiss cheese and mayonnaise

1. In a large bowl, combine the first 9 ingredients. Shape into four ¾-in.-thick patties.

2. In a large cast-iron or other heavy skillet, heat oil over medium heat. Add burgers; cook until crisp and lightly browned, 3-4 minutes on each side. Serve on the buns with lettuce and, if desired, tomato and mayonnaise.

1 BURGER 330 cal., 13g fat (5g sat. fat), 121mg chol., 736mg sod., 42g carb. (4g sugars, 5g fiber), 14g pro. **DIABETIC EXCHANGES** 3 starch, 1 medium-fat meat, ½ fat.

QUICK & EASY VEGETABLE POTPIE

This Meatless Monday superstar comes together quickly and is inexpensive as well. My 4-year-old always asks for seconds! You can substitute beans for canned lentils in this easy vegetable potpie. We also like using frozen edamame.

—Maggie Torsney-Weir, Los Angeles, CA

PREP: 30 MIN. • **BAKE:** 30 MIN. • **MAKES:** 6 SERVINGS

- 2 Tbsp. butter
- 3 cups frozen mixed vegetables, thawed
- 1 can (15 oz.) lentils, drained
- 2 Tbsp. all-purpose flour
- 1 cup vegetable or chicken broth
- 1 Tbsp. Dijon mustard
- 1 tsp. quatre epices (French four spice)
- ½ tsp. salt
- 1 sheet refrigerated pie crust
- 1 Tbsp. olive oil
- ¼ cup grated Parmesan cheese

POTPIE FILLING IDEAS

• For a smoky Spanish flavor, use lemon pepper and smoked paprika instead of the *quatre epices.*

• You can prepare the filling up to 24 hours beforehand or double the recipe and freeze half for another day.

1. Preheat oven to 375°. In a large skillet, melt butter over medium heat. Add the vegetables and lentils; cook and stir until heated through, 3-5 minutes. Stir in flour until blended; gradually whisk in broth. Bring to a boil, stirring constantly; cook and stir until thickened, 1-2 minutes. Stir in mustard, quatre epices and salt.

2. Transfer to a greased 9-in. pie plate. Place the pie crust over filling. Trim; cut slits in top. Brush with oil; sprinkle with Parmesan. Bake for 30-35 minutes or until golden brown. Cool for 5 minutes before serving.

1 SERVING 356 cal., 17g fat (7g sat. fat), 20mg chol., 705mg sod., 41g carb. (5g sugars, 9g fiber), 10g pro.

CAULIFLOWER ALFREDO

My family loves this quick and healthy cauliflower Alfredo sauce on any kind of pasta.
—Shelly Bevington, Hermiston, OR

PREP: 15 MIN. • **COOK:** 20 MIN. • **MAKES:** 6 SERVINGS

- 1 pkg. (16 oz.) fettuccine
- 2 vegetable bouillon cubes
- 1 medium head cauliflower, chopped
- 2 Tbsp. extra virgin olive oil
- 3 garlic cloves, minced
- 1 shallot, minced
- ¼ tsp. crushed red pepper flakes
- ⅔ cup shredded Parmesan cheese, plus additional for garnish
- Chopped fresh parsley

1. Cook fettuccine according to package directions for al dente; drain, set aside.

2. In a large sauce pot or Dutch oven, bring 4 cups water to a boil; add bouillon cubes, stir until dissolved. Add chopped cauliflower, cook 8-10 minutes or until very tender. Drain, reserving ⅔ cup cooking water.

3. Transfer the cauliflower to a food processor or blender. Process until pureed smooth, adding the reserved cooking water as needed.

4. In the same sauce pot, heat oil over medium-high heat. Add minced garlic and shallot; cook and stir for 1-2 minutes or until fragrant. Add red pepper flakes and cauliflower puree, heat through. Add pasta and ⅔ cup Parmesan, toss to coat.

5. Sprinkle with parsley and additional Parmesan cheese before serving.

1⅓ CUPS 371 cal., 9g fat (3g sat. fat), 6mg chol., 533mg sod., 60g carb. (5g sugars, 5g fiber), 16g pro.

BLACK BEAN & CORN QUINOA

My daughter's college asked parents for a favorite healthy recipe to use in the dining halls. This quinoa immediately came to mind.
—Lindsay McSweeney, Winchester, MA

TAKES: 30 MIN. • **MAKES:** 4 SERVINGS

- 2 Tbsp. canola oil
- 1 medium onion, finely chopped
- 1 medium sweet red pepper, finely chopped
- 1 celery rib, finely chopped
- 2 tsp. chili powder
- ¼ tsp. salt
- ¼ tsp. pepper
- 2 cups vegetable stock
- 1 cup frozen corn
- 1 cup quinoa, rinsed
- 1 can (15 oz.) black beans, rinsed and drained
- ⅓ cup plus 2 Tbsp. minced fresh cilantro, divided

GET TO KNOW QUINOA

Quinoa (pronounced KEEN-wah) is an ancient South American grain. It's often referred to as the perfect grain because, unlike others, it offers a complete protein. This makes quinoa an excellent choice for vegetarian and vegan meals, which can otherwise tend to be low in protein.

1. In a large skillet, heat oil over medium-high heat. Add onion, red pepper, celery and seasonings; cook and stir until the vegetables are tender, 5-7 minutes.

2. Stir in stock and corn; bring to a boil. Stir in quinoa. Reduce heat; simmer, covered, 12-15 minutes or until liquid is absorbed.

3. Add beans and ⅓ cup cilantro; heat through, stirring occasionally. Sprinkle with remaining 2 Tbsp. cilantro.

1¼ CUPS 375 cal., 10g fat (1g sat. fat), 0 chol., 668mg sod., 60g carb. (5g sugars, 10g fiber), 13g pro.

PUMPKIN LASAGNA

Even friends who aren't big fans of pumpkin are surprised by this delectable lasagna. Canned pumpkin and no-cook noodles make this comforting dish a cinch to prepare.
—Tamara Huron, New Market, AL

PREP: 25 MIN. • **BAKE:** 55 MIN. + STANDING • **MAKES:** 6 SERVINGS

- ½ lb. sliced fresh mushrooms
- 1 small onion, chopped
- ½ tsp. salt, divided
- 2 tsp. olive oil
- 1 can (15 oz.) solid-pack pumpkin
- ½ cup half-and-half cream
- 1 tsp. dried sage leaves
- Dash pepper
- 9 no-cook lasagna noodles
- 1 cup reduced-fat ricotta cheese
- 1 cup shredded part-skim mozzarella cheese
- ¾ cup shredded Parmesan cheese

1. In a small skillet, saute mushrooms, onion and ¼ tsp. salt in oil until tender; set aside. In a bowl, combine pumpkin, cream, sage, pepper and the remaining ¼ tsp. salt.

2. Spread ½ cup pumpkin sauce in an 11x7-in. baking dish coated with cooking spray. Top with 3 noodles (noodles will overlap slightly). Spread ½ cup pumpkin sauce to edges of noodles. Top with half mushroom mixture, ½ cup ricotta, ½ cup mozzarella and ¼ cup Parmesan cheese. Repeat layers. Top with the remaining noodles and sauce.

3. Cover and bake at 375° for 45 minutes. Uncover and sprinkle with the remaining Parmesan cheese. Bake 10-15 minutes longer or until cheese is melted. Let stand for 10 minutes before cutting.

FREEZE OPTION Cover and freeze the unbaked lasagna. To use, partially thaw in refrigerator overnight. Remove from refrigerator 30 minutes before baking. Preheat oven to 375°. Bake as directed, increasing time as necessary to heat through, until a thermometer inserted in center reads 165°.

1 PIECE 310 cal., 12g fat (6g sat. fat), 36mg chol., 497mg sod., 32g carb. (7g sugars, 5g fiber), 17g pro. **DIABETIC EXCHANGES** 2 starch, 2 fat, 1 lean meat.

CHICKPEA & POTATO CURRY

I make *chana masala*, a classic Indian dish, in my slow cooker. Browning the onion, ginger and garlic first is the key to making the curry taste amazing.
—Anjana Devasahayam, San Antonio, TX

PREP: 25 MIN. • **COOK:** 6 HOURS • **MAKES:** 6 SERVINGS

- 1 Tbsp. canola oil
- 1 medium onion, chopped
- 2 garlic cloves, minced
- 2 tsp. minced fresh gingerroot
- 2 tsp. ground coriander
- 1 tsp. garam masala
- 1 tsp. chili powder
- ½ tsp. salt
- ½ tsp. ground cumin
- ¼ tsp. ground turmeric
- 1 can (15 oz.) crushed tomatoes
- 2 cans (15 oz. each) chickpeas or garbanzo beans, rinsed and drained
- 1 large baking potato, peeled and cut into ¾-in. cubes
- 2½ cups vegetable stock
- 1 Tbsp. lime juice
- Chopped fresh cilantro
- Hot cooked rice
- Optional: Sliced red onion and lime wedges

1. In a large skillet, heat oil over medium-high heat; saute onion for 2-4 minutes or until tender. Add garlic, ginger and dry seasonings; cook and stir for 1 minute. Stir in tomatoes; transfer to a 3- or 4-qt. slow cooker.

2. Stir in chickpeas, potato and vegetable stock. Cook, covered, on low until potato is tender and the flavors are blended, 6-8 hours.

3. Stir in lime juice; sprinkle with cilantro. Serve with rice and, if desired, red onion and lime wedges.

1¼ CUPS CHICKPEA MIXTURE 240 cal., 6g fat (0 sat. fat), 0 chol., 767mg sod., 42g carb. (8g sugars, 9g fiber), 8g pro.

NOTES

how to cook ...
DESSERTS

CHOCOLATE PEANUT BUTTER CUPCAKES, PAGE 291

BANANAS FOSTER

Guests are always impressed when I ignite the rum in this delicious classic dessert. Use perfectly ripe bananas for best results.
—Mary Lou Wayman, Salt Lake City, UT

TAKES: 25 MIN. • **MAKES:** 4 SERVINGS

- ⅓ cup butter, cubed
- ¾ cup packed dark brown sugar
- ¼ tsp. ground cinnamon
- 3 medium bananas
- 2 Tbsp. creme de cacao or banana liqueur
- ¼ cup dark rum
- 2 cups vanilla ice cream

SUCCESS TIPS FOR BANANAS FOSTER

• Choose perfectly ripe, just-turned-yellow bananas or slightly underripe ones. They'll keep their shape during cooking.

• After heating, remove rum from the burner and use a long lighter to safely ignite it.

• Add creme de cacao for a hint of chocolate or banana liqueur for added richness. Or skip them entirely and just use rum.

• Keep a lid or extinguisher nearby. If preparing tableside, be sure the pan is free of table linens and decor.

• Scoop the ice cream and freeze it in its dishes so it's ready for the hot bananas as soon as they're finished.

• Remember, this dish was created at Brennan's in New Orleans in 1951, so channel that Big Easy flair as you cook.

1. In a large skillet, melt butter over medium-low heat. Stir in brown sugar and cinnamon until combined. Cut each banana lengthwise and then widthwise into quarters; alternately, cut into ¼-in. slices. Add to the butter mixture; cook, stirring gently, until glazed and slightly softened, 3-5 minutes. Stir in creme de cacao; heat through.

2. In a small saucepan, heat rum over low heat until vapors form on surface. Carefully ignite rum and slowly pour over bananas, coating evenly.

3. Leaving skillet or pan on the cooking surface, gently shake pan back and forth until flames are completely extinguished; serve immediately over ice cream.

NOTE Keep liquor bottles and other flammables at a safe distance when preparing this dessert. We do not recommend using a nonstick skillet.

1 SERVING 567 cal., 23g fat (14g sat. fat), 70mg chol., 224mg sod., 80g carb. (72g sugars, 2g fiber), 3g pro.

FRESH CHERRY PIE

If you're looking to learn how to make a cherry pie, this recipe is the place to start. This ruby-red cherry pie is just sweet enough, with a hint of almond flavor and a good level of cinnamon. I like to make a few of these cherry pies throughout the summer.
—Josie Bochek, Sturgeon Bay, WI

PREP: 25 MIN. • **BAKE:** 55 MIN. + COOLING • **MAKES:** 8 SERVINGS

- 1¼ cups sugar
- ⅓ cup cornstarch
- 1 cup cherry juice blend
- 4 cups fresh or frozen pitted tart cherries, thawed
- ½ tsp. ground cinnamon
- ¼ tsp. ground nutmeg
- ¼ tsp. almond extract

DOUGH

- 2 cups all-purpose flour
- ½ tsp. salt
- ⅔ cup shortening
- 5 to 7 Tbsp. cold water
- 1 large egg, beaten, optional

1. Preheat oven to 425°. In a large saucepan, combine the sugar and cornstarch; gradually stir in cherry juice until smooth. Bring to a boil; cook and stir until thickened, about 2 minutes. Remove from the heat. Add cherries, cinnamon, nutmeg and extract.

2. In a large bowl, combine flour and salt; cut in shortening until crumbly. Gradually add cold water, tossing with a fork until a ball forms. Divide dough in half so that 1 ball is slightly larger than the other.

3. On a lightly floured surface, roll out larger ball to fit a 9-in. pie plate. Transfer dough to pie plate; trim even with edge of plate. Add filling. Roll out remaining dough; make a lattice crust. Trim, seal and flute edge. If desired, brush with beaten egg.

4. Bake for 10 minutes. Reduce heat to 375°; bake until crust is golden brown, 45-50 minutes. Cool on a wire rack.

1 PIECE 466 cal., 17g fat (4g sat. fat), 23mg chol., 161mg sod., 73g carb. (41g sugars, 2g fiber), 5g pro.

COFFEE SHOP FUDGE

This smooth, creamy fudge has an irresistible crunch from pecans. The coffee and cinnamon blend nicely to provide subtle flavor.
—Beth Osborne Skinner, Bristol, TN

PREP: 15 MIN. + CHILLING • **MAKES:** 2 LBS. (64 PIECES)

- 1 tsp. butter, softened
- 1 cup chopped pecans
- 3 cups semisweet chocolate chips
- 1 can (14 oz.) sweetened condensed milk
- 2 Tbsp. strong brewed coffee, room temperature
- 1 tsp. ground cinnamon
- ⅛ tsp. salt
- 1 tsp. vanilla extract

READER REVIEW

"I've been using this recipe for years. It is a huge hit with my family and my co-workers. It's simple to make, but people think you are a genius for knowing how to make it."

—COLLEENBORDULA, TASTEOFHOME.COM

1. Line an 8-in. square pan with foil and grease the foil with butter; set aside. Place pecans in a microwave-safe pie plate. Microwave, uncovered, on high 3 minutes, stirring after each minute; set aside.

2. In a 2-qt. microwave-safe bowl, combine the chocolate chips, milk, coffee, cinnamon and salt. Microwave, uncovered, on high 1 minute. Stir until smooth. Stir in the vanilla and pecans. Immediately spread into prepared pan.

3. Cover and refrigerate until firm, about 2 hours. Remove from pan; cut into 1-in. squares. Cover and store fudge at room temperature (70°-80°).

1 PIECE 77 cal., 4g fat (2g sat. fat), 3mg chol., 16mg sod., 10g carb. (9g sugars, 1g fiber), 1g pro.

FROZEN GRAND MARNIER SOUFFLES

This delicious no-bake frozen souffle is perfect for summer and will impress just about everyone. It's a fantastic make-ahead dessert!
—Andrea Potischman, Menlo Park, CA

PREP: 30 MIN. + FREEZING • **MAKES:** 8 SERVINGS

- 6 large egg yolks
- ½ cup sugar
- ¼ cup orange liqueur
- 2 Tbsp. water
- 2 tsp. orange juice
- 1 tsp. grated orange zest
- 1½ cups heavy whipping cream
- 1 Tbsp. confectioners' sugar

1. In top of a double boiler or a metal bowl over simmering water whisk egg yolks and sugar until blended. Stir in liqueur, water, orange juice and zest. Cook over low heat until mixture is just thick enough to coat a metal spoon and a thermometer reads at least 160°, about 10 minutes, stirring constantly but gently. Do not allow to boil. Immediately transfer to a bowl.

2. Place the bowl in an ice-water bath for a few minutes, stirring the custard occasionally. Cool to room temperature.

3. Meanwhile, in a large bowl, beat the cream until it begins to thicken. Add confectioners' sugar; beat until stiff peaks form. Gently fold into cooled custard mixture.

4. Transfer to eight 4-oz. ramekins; smooth tops. Freeze until firm, at least 4 hours or overnight. Garnish with additional orange zest.

1 SOUFFLE 258 cal., 20g fat (12g sat. fat), 189mg chol., 18mg sod., 17g carb. (16g sugars, 0 fiber), 3g pro.

SOUTHERN SWEET POTATO TART

We love sweet potatoes, so I try to incorporate them in as many dishes as I can. My secret ingredient is the bourbon—that's what makes it so delicious.

—Marie Bruno, Watkinsville, GA

PREP: 1 HOUR • **BAKE:** 25 MIN. + COOLING • **MAKES:** 8 SERVINGS

- 1 lb. sweet potatoes (about 2 small)
- Dough for single-crust pie
- ¼ cup butter, softened
- ½ cup packed dark brown sugar
- 2 Tbsp. all-purpose flour
- 1 tsp. pumpkin pie spice
- ¼ tsp. salt
- 1 large egg
- ¼ cup heavy whipping cream
- 1 Tbsp. bourbon or 1 Tbsp. whipping cream plus ½ tsp. vanilla extract

TOPPING

- 2 Tbsp. butter, softened
- 2 Tbsp. dark brown sugar
- 2 Tbsp. dark corn syrup
- ½ cup chopped pecans

1. Preheat oven to 400°. Pierce potatoes several times with a fork; place on a foil-lined baking sheet. Bake until tender, 40-50 minutes.

2. On a lightly floured surface, roll dough to a ⅛-in.-thick circle; transfer to a 9-in. tart pan with removable bottom. Press onto bottom and up side of pan; trim edge to edge of pan. Refrigerate while preparing filling.

3. Remove potatoes from oven; increase oven setting to 425°. When potatoes are cool enough to handle, remove peel and place the pulp in a large bowl; beat until smooth (you will need 1 cup mashed). Add butter, brown sugar, flour, pie spice and salt; beat until blended. Beat in egg, cream and bourbon. Pour into the crust. Bake on a lower oven rack 15 minutes.

4. Meanwhile, for topping, mix butter, brown sugar and corn syrup until blended. Stir in pecans.

5. Remove tart; reduce oven setting to 350°. Spoon topping evenly over tart. Bake until a knife inserted in the center comes out clean, 8-10 minutes.

6. Cool on a wire rack. Serve within 2 hours or refrigerate, covered, and serve cold.

DOUGH FOR SINGLE-CRUST PIE (9 IN.)

Combine 1¼ cups all-purpose flour and ¼ tsp. salt; cut in ½ cup cold butter until crumbly. Gradually add 3-5 Tbsp. ice water, tossing with a fork until dough holds together when pressed. Shape into a disk; wrap and refrigerate 1 hour.

1 PIECE 477 cal., 29g fat (15g sat. fat), 85mg chol., 326mg sod., 52g carb. (27g sugars, 3g fiber), 5g pro.

LEMON-ROSEMARY LAYER CAKE

Tall and impressive, this unique dessert is a treat for the senses with flecks of lemon zest and fresh rosemary. Just wait till you taste it!
—Mary Fraser, Surprise, AZ

PREP: 20 MIN. • **BAKE:** 25 MIN. + COOLING • **MAKES:** 16 SERVINGS

- 1 cup plus 2 Tbsp. butter, softened
- 2½ cups sugar
- 4 large eggs, room temperature
- 1 large egg yolk, room temperature
- 4 cups all-purpose flour
- 3 tsp. baking powder
- 1½ tsp. salt
- ¼ tsp. plus ⅛ tsp. baking soda
- 1½ cups sour cream
- 6 Tbsp. lemon juice
- 3 tsp. grated lemon zest
- 3 tsp. minced fresh rosemary

FROSTING

- 2 pkg. (8 oz. each) cream cheese, softened
- 8¼ cups confectioners' sugar
- 3 tsp. grated lemon zest
- 2¼ tsp. lemon juice
- Optional: Candied lemon and rosemary sprigs

1. Preheat oven to 350°. In a large bowl, cream butter and sugar until light and fluffy, 5-7 minutes. Add the eggs, 1 at a time, and yolk, beating well after each addition. Combine flour, baking powder, salt and baking soda; add to creamed mixture alternately with sour cream, beating well after each addition. Beat in lemon juice, zest and rosemary.

2. Transfer batter to 3 greased and floured 9-in. round baking pans. Bake until the edges begin to brown, 25-30 minutes. Cool for 10 minutes before removing from pans to wire racks to cool completely.

3. For the frosting, in a large bowl, beat the cream cheese until fluffy. Add the confectioners' sugar, lemon zest and juice; beat until smooth.

4. Spread frosting between layers and over top and side of cake. If desired, decorate with candied lemon and rosemary. Refrigerate leftovers.

1 PIECE 756 cal., 28g fat (17g sat. fat), 146mg chol., 527mg sod., 119g carb. (90g sugars, 1g fiber), 8g pro.

READER REVIEW

"I used this recipe to make our daughter's wedding cake. The cake was moist and delicious, and it even impressed the caterer!"

—DDMYERS83, TASTEOFHOME.COM

CARAMEL APPLE CREME BRULEE

Here's the cream of the apple dessert crop. Fruit, caramel and cinnamon flavors enhance the rich, velvety custard. Served warm or chilled, it's a classic end to a meal.
—Cheryl Perry, Hertford, NC

PREP: 35 MIN. • **BAKE:** 1 HOUR + CHILLING • **MAKES:** 6 SERVINGS

- 3 medium tart apples, peeled and thinly sliced
- 6 Tbsp. caramel ice cream topping
- ¼ cup plus 4 Tbsp. sugar, divided
- ¼ cup packed brown sugar
- ½ tsp. ground cinnamon
- 2 cups heavy whipping cream
- 5 large egg yolks, beaten
- 1 tsp. vanilla extract

1. Place apples in a microwave-safe dish; cover with water. Cover and microwave on high for 3-4 minutes or until tender. Drain apples and pat dry on paper towel. Arrange apples in bottoms of six 6-oz. ramekins or custard cups. Top with the caramel topping; set aside.

2. In a small saucepan, combine ¼ cup sugar, ¼ cup brown sugar and cinnamon; stir in the cream. Heat over medium heat until bubbles form around sides of pan. Remove from heat; stir a small amount of hot mixture into egg yolks. Return all to pan, stirring constantly. Stir in vanilla.

3. Pour into prepared ramekins. Place the ramekins in a baking pan; add 1 in. boiling water to pan. Bake, uncovered, at 325° until centers are just set (mixture will jiggle), 55-60 minutes. Remove ramekins from water bath; cool for 20 minutes. Cover and refrigerate overnight.

4. If using a creme brulee torch, sprinkle remaining 4 Tbsp. sugar evenly over the custards. Heat sugar with the torch until caramelized. Serve immediately.

5. If broiling custards, place ramekins on a baking sheet; let stand at room temperature for 15 minutes. Sprinkle remaining 4 Tbsp. sugar evenly over custards. Broil 8 in. from heat for 4-7 minutes or until sugar is caramelized. Refrigerate 1-2 hours or until firm.

1 SERVING 504 cal., 33g fat (20g sat. fat), 280mg chol., 114mg sod., 50g carb. (33g sugars, 1g fiber), 4g pro.

TEST KITCHEN TIP

You can make your own caramelly mixture for this recipe by cooking the apples on the stovetop with butter and brown sugar. Spoon the caramel apples into ramekins and proceed with the recipe.

CHOCOLATE PEANUT BUTTER CUPCAKES

I've been baking cakes for years and enjoy trying new combinations of flavors and textures. Well, I blended two popular flavors peanut butter and chocolate. As soon as I took the first bite of these cupcakes, I knew I had created something divine! Most people who try them say they are the best thing they've ever eaten. They are definitely worth the time it takes to make them.
—*Ronda Schabes, Vicksburg, MI*

PREP: 55 MIN. • **BAKE:** 20 MIN. + COOLING • **MAKES:** 2 DOZEN

- 2 cups sugar
- 1¾ cups all-purpose flour
- ¾ cup baking cocoa
- ½ tsp. salt
- ½ tsp. baking soda
- ½ tsp. baking powder
- 1 cup buttermilk
- 1 cup strong brewed coffee, room temperature
- ½ cup canola oil
- 2 large eggs, room temperature
- 1 tsp. vanilla extract

FILLING
- ½ cup creamy peanut butter
- 3 Tbsp. unsalted butter, softened
- 1 cup confectioners' sugar
- 2 to 4 Tbsp. 2% milk

GANACHE
- 2 cups semisweet chocolate chips
- ½ cup heavy whipping cream

PEANUT BUTTER FROSTING
- 1 cup packed brown sugar
- 4 large egg whites
- ¼ tsp. salt
- ¼ tsp. cream of tartar
- 1 tsp. vanilla extract
- 2 cups unsalted butter, softened
- ⅓ cup creamy peanut butter
- Chocolate curls, optional

1. Preheat oven to 350°. In a large bowl, combine the first 6 ingredients. Whisk buttermilk, coffee, oil, eggs and vanilla until blended; add to the dry ingredients until combined. (Batter will be very thin.) Fill 24 paper-lined muffin cups two-thirds full.

2. Bake 18-20 minutes or until a toothpick inserted in the center comes out clean. Cool 10 minutes before removing from pans to wire racks to cool completely.

3. In a small bowl, cream peanut butter, butter, confectioners' sugar and enough milk to achieve piping consistency. Cut a small hole in the corner of a pastry bag; insert a small round tip. Fill with peanut butter filling. Insert tip into the top center of each cupcake; pipe about 1 Tbsp. filling into each.

4. Place chocolate chips in a small bowl. In a small saucepan, bring cream just to a boil. Pour over chocolate; whisk until smooth. Dip the top of each cupcake into ganache; place on wire racks to set.

5. In a large heavy saucepan, combine the brown sugar, egg whites, salt and cream of tartar over low heat. With a hand mixer, beat on low speed 1 minute. Continue beating on low speed over low heat until frosting reaches 160°, 8-10 minutes. Pour into a large bowl; add vanilla. Beat on high until stiff peaks form, about 5 minutes.

6. Add butter, 1 Tbsp. at a time, beating well after each addition. If the mixture begins to look curdled, place frosting bowl in another bowl filled with hot water for a few seconds. Continue adding butter and beating until smooth. Beat in peanut butter 1-2 minutes or until smooth.

7. Place the frosting in a pastry bag with large star tip; pipe onto each cupcake. If desired, top with chocolate curls. Store in an airtight container in refrigerator. Let stand at room temperature before serving.

1 CUPCAKE 498 cal., 33g fat (16g sat. fat), 69mg chol., 196mg sod., 50g carb. (39g sugars, 2g fiber), 6g pro.

WORK AHEAD

You can store frosted and decorated cupcakes in an airtight container in the freezer for up to 2 months. Let them thaw overnight in the refrigerator before serving. You can also freeze undecorated cupcakes and the peanut butter frosting mixture separately (this saves room in the freezer). Defrost both in the refrigerator overnight, then whip the frosting again until it regains its fluffy, pipeable texture.

CRAN-APPLE PECAN CRISP

Even folks who claim not to like cranberries rave about this dish. I cherish the recipe from my mother, who inspired my love of cooking.
—Debbie Daly, Florence, KY

PREP: 20 MIN. • **BAKE:** 40 MIN. • **MAKES:** 12 SERVINGS

- 1 cup sugar
- 1 Tbsp. cornstarch
- 3 cups chopped tart apples
- 2 cups fresh or frozen cranberries
- 1 cup old-fashioned oats
- ½ cup packed brown sugar
- ½ cup chopped pecans
- ⅓ cup all-purpose flour
- ⅓ cup cold butter

In a large bowl, combine the sugar and cornstarch; stir in the apples and cranberries. Transfer to a greased 2-qt. baking dish. In another bowl, combine the oats, brown sugar, pecans and flour; cut in butter until mixture is crumbly. Sprinkle over the apple mixture. Bake, uncovered, at 375° until golden brown, 40-45 minutes. Serve warm.

½ CUP 244 cal., 9g fat (4g sat. fat), 14mg chol., 56mg sod., 41g carb. (30g sugars, 3g fiber), 2g pro.

HOW TO MAKE ANY FRUIT CRISP

Use the basic recipe at left to inspire your own home-cooked creations.

CRAN-ASIAN PEAR

Substitute a few chopped Asian pears for the apples; add ground ginger to the filling.

CHERRY

Use 5 cups tart cherries. Sprinkle fruit with a little almond extract and vanilla, toss to coat and place in the baking dish.

PEACH & BLUEBERRY

Sub these fruits in for apples and cranberries. Dial back the sugar to as little as ⅔ cup.

APPLE

Use all apples instead of a berry-apple mix. Cut the sugar to ⅔-¾ cup. Add ground cinnamon to the filling and/or the streusel topping. Use walnuts instead of pecans if desired.

RHUBARB & STRAWBERRY

Sub these in for apples and cranberries, using at least 2½ cups of rhubarb.

BLACKBERRY

If using all blackberries in your filling, cut the sugar in half and the cornstarch to 2 tsp.

PINEAPPLE & BANANA

Sub these fruits in for apples and cranberries, using at least 3 cups chopped pineapple. Cut bananas into thick slices to help preserve their shape. Add shredded coconut to the streusel topping. Use chopped macadamia nuts instead of pecans.

GRANDMA'S SCOTTISH SHORTBREAD

My Scottish grandmother was renowned for baked goods; these chunky shortbread bars are just one example.
—Jane Kelly, Wayland, MA

PREP: 15 MIN. • **BAKE:** 45 MIN. + COOLING • **MAKES:** 4 DOZEN

- 1 lb. butter, softened
- 8 oz. superfine sugar (about 1¼ cups)
- 1 lb. all-purpose flour (3⅔ cups)
- 8 oz. white rice flour (1⅓ cups)

TENDER, CRUMBLY SHORTBREAD

Adding rice flour helps give this shortbread a crisp and crumbly texture. Since rice flour is gluten free, it delays excess gluten formation as you mix the dough.

1. Preheat oven to 300°. Cream butter and sugar until light and fluffy, 5-7 minutes. Combine flours; gradually beat into the creamed mixture. Press the dough into an ungreased 13x9-in. baking pan. Prick with a fork.

2. Bake until light brown, 45-50 minutes. Cut into 48 bars or triangles while warm. Cool completely on a wire rack.

1 BAR 139 cal., 8g fat (5g sat. fat), 20mg chol., 61mg sod., 16g carb. (5g sugars, 0 fiber), 1g pro.

PEACH COBBLER

I created this recipe myself with a few tips from my mom and grandma. Because it's so quick and easy, it can be made in minutes to suit any occasion. I've used it as a breakfast fruit dish, a dinner dessert and a little snack.

—Martha Betten, North Manchester, IN

PREP: 15 MIN. • **BAKE:** 20 MIN. • **MAKES:** 8 SERVINGS

- ½ cup butter, melted
- 1 can (15¼ oz.) sliced peaches
- 1¼ cups sugar, divided
- 1 cup all-purpose flour
- 2 tsp. baking powder
- ¼ tsp. salt
- 1 cup 2% milk
- Whipped cream, optional

1. Preheat oven to 400°. Pour butter into a shallow 2-qt. baking dish; set aside. Drain peaches, reserving ¼ cup juice. In a saucepan, bring peaches and reserved ¼ cup juice just to a boil.

2. Meanwhile, in a bowl, combine 1 cup sugar, flour, baking powder and salt. Stir in milk; mix well. Pour over butter in baking dish. Spoon hot peaches over batter. Sprinkle with the remaining ¼ cup sugar. Bake until bubbly and golden, 20-25 minutes. Serve warm and, if desired, with whipped cream.

¾ CUP 328 cal., 13g fat (8g sat. fat), 34mg chol., 282mg sod., 52g carb. (40g sugars, 1g fiber), 3g pro.

RICH & CREAMY TIRAMISU

Tiramisu is Italian for pick-me-up, and this one is definitely true to its name! My version of the classic Tuscan trifle has both coffee and espresso for layers of java flavor.
—Lauren McAnelly, Des Moines, IA

PREP: 15 MIN. + STANDING • **COOK:** 10 MIN. + CHILLING • **MAKES:** 16 SERVINGS

- 2 cartons (8 oz. each) mascarpone cheese
- 5 large egg yolks
- ½ cup plus 2 Tbsp. sugar, divided
- ⅓ cup plus 2 Tbsp. Marsala wine, Kahlua (coffee liqueur) or rum, divided
- ½ tsp. salt
- 1 cup heavy whipping cream
- ¾ cup strong brewed coffee, room temperature
- 2 tsp. instant espresso powder
- 1 pkg. (7 oz.) crisp ladyfinger cookies
- 1 Tbsp. Dutch-processed cocoa

TIRAMISU SUCCESS TIPS

• Whip the yolk mixture vigorously in a double boiler for a light, ribbonlike texture, but fold in the mascarpone gently. A few lumps are fine—they'll go away when you add the cream.

• Use espresso instead of strong coffee if you have it.

• If you're out of Marsala, swap in Kahlua, Grand Marnier or a different fortified wine.

• Dip ladyfingers for 1-2 seconds—long enough to moisten without making them soggy or fall apart.

• For the fluffiest texture, chill your bowl and beaters before whipping the cream.

• You can also make this tiramisu in a 9-in. square dish.

1. Stir mascarpone cheese; let stand at room temperature 30 minutes. Whisk egg yolks, ½ cup sugar, ⅓ cup Marsala and salt in the top of a double boiler until mixture is thickened (ribbon stage) and a thermometer reads 160°. Remove from heat; whisk in mascarpone until almost smooth. Beat the cream and remaining sugar until soft peaks form; fold into the mascarpone mixture.

2. Combine coffee, espresso powder and remaining 2 Tbsp. Marsala. Briefly dip 8 ladyfingers into coffee mixture and place in bottom of a 9-in. springform pan. Top with 1½ cups mascarpone mixture. Repeat 2 more times. Refrigerate, covered, 6 hours or overnight. To serve, loosen and remove rim; sprinkle with cocoa powder.

1 SERVING 280 cal., 21g fat (11g sat. fat), 123mg chol., 115mg sod., 19g carb. (14g sugars, 0 fiber), 5g pro.

JUMBLEBERRY CRUMBLE

A friend brought this delicious down-home dessert to church and everyone enjoyed it so much they showered her with compliments! She was kind enough to share the recipe. It's especially wonderful served warm with a dollop of creamy whipped topping.
—Mary Ann Dell, Phoenixville, PA

PREP: 10 MIN. + STANDING • **BAKE:** 45 MIN. • **MAKES:** 8 SERVINGS

- 3 cups halved fresh strawberries
- 1½ cups fresh raspberries
- 1½ cups fresh blueberries
- ⅔ cup sugar
- 3 Tbsp. quick-cooking tapioca
- ½ cup all-purpose flour
- ½ cup quick-cooking oats
- ½ cup packed brown sugar
- 1 tsp. ground cinnamon
- ⅓ cup butter, melted
- Optional: Vanilla ice cream or sweetened whipped cream

1. In a large bowl, combine strawberries, raspberries and blueberries. Combine the sugar and tapioca; sprinkle over berries and toss gently. Pour into a greased 11x7-in. baking dish; let stand for 15 minutes.

2. Meanwhile, in a small bowl, combine flour, oats, brown sugar and cinnamon. Stir in butter; sprinkle over the berry mixture.

3. Bake at 350° until filling is bubbly and topping is golden brown, 45-50 minutes. Serve warm, with vanilla ice cream or sweetened whipped cream if desired.

1 PIECE 290 cal., 8g fat (5g sat. fat), 20mg chol., 84mg sod., 54g carb. (36g sugars, 4g fiber), 2g pro.

BOURBON BRIOCHE BREAD PUDDING

My husband wasn't a fan of bread pudding until I had him try a bite of mine from a local restaurant. I replicated it with some added bourbon, walnuts and a different type of bread. It's a keeper!
—Cindy Worth, Lapwai, ID

PREP: 15 MIN. + STANDING • **BAKE:** 35 MIN. • **MAKES:** 6 SERVINGS

- ½ cup bourbon, divided
- ½ cup raisins
- 2½ cups cubed brioche bread, toasted
- ⅓ cup finely chopped walnuts
- 4 large eggs
- 1¾ cups heavy whipping cream
- ⅓ cup sugar
- 1 tsp. ground cinnamon
- 1 tsp. vanilla extract
- ½ tsp. ground nutmeg
- ¼ tsp. salt
- Optional: Confectioners' sugar and whipped cream

1. Preheat oven to 375°. Pour ¼ cup bourbon over raisins in a small bowl; let stand 5 minutes. Place bread in a greased 8-in. square baking dish. Top with walnuts, raisins and soaking liquid.

2. In a large bowl, whisk eggs, cream, sugar, cinnamon, vanilla, nutmeg, salt and remaining ¼ cup bourbon until blended. Pour over the bread; let stand until bread is softened, about 15 minutes.

3. Bake, uncovered, until puffed, golden and a knife inserted in the center comes out clean, 35-40 minutes. Serve warm. If desired, sprinkle with confectioners' sugar and serve with whipped cream.

1 SERVING 469 cal., 34g fat (19g sat. fat), 213mg chol., 218mg sod., 30g carb. (22g sugars, 1g fiber), 9g pro.

GOLDEN APPLE PIE

Pies are the dessert I like best to prepare. This one's the favorite for family get-togethers, and it has been awarded blue ribbons at a couple of local fairs.
—Theresa Brazil, Petaluma, CA

PREP: 30 MIN. + COOLING • **BAKE:** 40 MIN. + COOLING • **MAKES:** 8 SERVINGS

- 6 cups sliced peeled Golden Delicious apples
- ¾ cup plus 2 Tbsp. apple juice, divided
- ¾ cup sugar
- 1 tsp. ground cinnamon
- ½ tsp. apple pie spice
- 2 Tbsp. cornstarch
- ¼ tsp. vanilla extract

CRUST

- 2½ cups all-purpose flour
- 1 tsp. salt
- 1 cup cold butter
- 6 to 8 Tbsp. ice water

1. In a large saucepan, combine apples, ¾ cup apple juice, sugar, cinnamon and apple pie spice; bring to a boil over medium heat, stirring occasionally. Combine cornstarch and remaining apple juice; add to saucepan. Return to a boil, stirring constantly. Cook and stir 1 minute longer or until thickened. Remove from heat. Stir in the vanilla. Cool to room temperature, stirring occasionally.

2. For crust, combine flour and salt; cut in butter until mixture is crumbly. Gradually add water, 1 Tbsp. at a time, tossing with a fork until dough can be formed into a ball. Divide in 2 portions, making 1 piece slightly larger. On a lightly floured surface, roll out larger portion.

3. Line a 9-in. pie plate with bottom crust; trim even with edge of plate. Add filling. Roll out remaining dough to fit top of pie; place over filling. Trim, seal and flute edges. Cut slits in top.

4. Bake at 400° for 40-45 minutes or until crust is golden brown and apples are tender. Cool on a wire rack.

1 PIECE 480 cal., 24g fat (15g sat. fat), 61mg chol., 480mg sod., 65g carb. (30g sugars, 2g fiber), 5g pro.

NOTES

SPICED CHOCOLATE MOLTEN CAKES

Take some time to linger over this decadent dessert. There is nothing better than a gooey chocolate cake with a warm melted center.
—Deb Carpenter, Hastings, MI

TAKES: 30 MIN. • **MAKES:** 2 SERVINGS

- ¼ cup butter, cubed
- 2 oz. semisweet chocolate, chopped
- 1½ tsp. dry red wine
- ½ tsp. vanilla extract
- 1 large egg, room temperature
- 2 tsp. egg yolk, room temperature
- ½ cup confectioners' sugar
- 3 Tbsp. all-purpose flour
- ⅛ tsp. ground ginger
- ⅛ tsp. ground cinnamon
- Additional confectioners' sugar

1. Preheat oven to 425°. In a microwave, melt butter and chocolate; stir until smooth. Stir in wine and vanilla.

2. In a small bowl, beat the egg, egg yolk and confectioners' sugar until thick and lemon-colored. Beat in flour, ginger and cinnamon until well blended. Gradually beat in the butter mixture.

3. Transfer to 2 greased 6-oz. ramekins or custard cups. Place ramekins on a baking sheet. Bake until a thermometer inserted in the center reads 160° and sides of cakes are set, 10-12 minutes.

4. Remove from the oven and let stand for 1 minute. Run a knife around edges of ramekins; invert onto dessert plates. Dust with additional confectioners' sugar. Serve immediately.

1 SERVING 560 cal., 36g fat (21g sat. fat), 234mg chol., 200mg sod., 56g carb. (43g sugars, 2g fiber), 8g pro.

BANANA BARS WITH CREAM CHEESE FROSTING

I make these moist bars whenever I have ripe bananas on hand, then store them in the freezer to share later at a potluck. With creamy frosting and big banana flavor, this treat is a real crowd-pleaser.
—Debbie Knight, Marion, IA

PREP: 15 MIN. • **BAKE:** 20 MIN. + COOLING • **MAKES:** 4 DOZEN

- ½ cup butter, softened
- 1½ cups sugar
- 2 large eggs, room temperature
- 1 cup sour cream
- 1 tsp. vanilla extract
- 2 cups all-purpose flour
- 1 tsp. baking soda
- ¼ tsp. salt
- 2 medium ripe bananas, mashed (about 1 cup)

FROSTING

- 1 pkg. (8 oz.) cream cheese, softened
- ½ cup butter, softened
- 2 tsp. vanilla extract
- 3¾ to 4 cups confectioners' sugar

1. Preheat oven to 350°. In a large bowl, cream butter and sugar until light and fluffy, 5-7 minutes. Add the eggs, sour cream and vanilla. Combine flour, baking soda and salt; gradually add to the creamed mixture. Stir in bananas.

2. Spread into a greased 15x10x1-in. baking pan. Bake until a toothpick inserted in center comes out clean (do not overbake), 20-25 minutes. Let cool.

3. For frosting, in a large bowl, beat the cream cheese, butter and vanilla until fluffy. Gradually beat in enough confectioners' sugar to achieve desired consistency. Frost bars. Store in the refrigerator.

1 BAR 148 cal., 7g fat (4g sat. fat), 28mg chol., 96mg sod., 21g carb. (16g sugars, 0 fiber), 1g pro.

CARAMEL APPLE CHEESECAKE BARS

It's a caramel apple, cheesecake and streusel-topped apple pie all rolled into one irresistible dessert. If you can't resist a taste test before a party, just arrange them on a serving platter and no one will know a piece is missing from the pan!

—Katherine White, Henderson, NV

PREP: 30 MIN. • **BAKE:** 25 MIN. + CHILLING • **MAKES:** 3 DOZEN

- 2 cups all-purpose flour
- ½ cup packed brown sugar
- ¾ cup cold butter, cubed
- 2 pkg. (8 oz. each) cream cheese, softened
- ½ cup plus 2 Tbsp. sugar, divided
- 1 tsp. vanilla extract
- 2 large eggs, lightly beaten
- 3 medium tart apples, peeled and finely chopped
- ½ tsp. ground cinnamon
- ¼ tsp. ground nutmeg

STREUSEL

- ¾ cup all-purpose flour
- ¾ cup packed brown sugar
- ½ cup quick-cooking oats
- ⅓ cup cold butter, cubed
- ⅓ cup hot caramel ice cream topping

READER REVIEW

"These were delish! I made these as the recipe directed, and they turned out great. I like a lot of crust and topping, and this recipe had the perfect amounts for me. It's hard to beat all the great flavor and texture contrasts in this recipe, and the end result was YUM!"

—LVARNER, TASTEOFHOME.COM

1. Preheat oven to 350°. In a small bowl, combine the flour and brown sugar; cut in the butter until crumbly. Press into a well-greased 13x9-in. baking pan. Bake 15-18 minutes or until lightly browned.

2. Meanwhile, in a large bowl, beat cream cheese, ½ cup sugar and vanilla until smooth. Add eggs; beat on low speed just until combined. Spread over crust.

3. In a small bowl, toss the apples with cinnamon, nutmeg and remaining sugar; spoon over the cream cheese layer. In another bowl, mix flour, brown sugar and oats; cut in the butter until crumbly. Sprinkle over apple layer.

4. Bake 25-30 minutes or until filling is set. Drizzle with caramel topping; cool in pan on a wire rack 1 hour. Refrigerate at least 2 hours. Cut into bars.

1 BAR 191 cal., 10g fat (6g sat. fat), 40mg chol., 94mg sod., 23g carb. (12g sugars, 1g fiber), 3g pro.

FROSTED FUDGE BROWNIES

A neighbor brought over a pan of these rich brownies when I came home from the hospital with our baby daughter. I asked her how to make brownies like that, and I've made them ever since for family occasions, potlucks and parties at work. They're great!
—Sue Soderlund, Elgin, IL

PREP: 10 MIN. + COOLING • **BAKE:** 25 MIN. + COOLING • **MAKES:** 2 DOZEN

- 1 cup plus 3 Tbsp. butter, cubed
- ¾ cup baking cocoa
- 4 large eggs, room temperature
- 2 cups sugar
- 1½ cups all-purpose flour
- 1 tsp. baking powder
- 1 tsp. salt
- 1 tsp. vanilla extract

FROSTING

- 6 Tbsp. butter, softened
- 2⅔ cups confectioners' sugar
- ½ cup baking cocoa
- 1 tsp. vanilla extract
- ¼ to ⅓ cup 2% milk

1. In a saucepan, melt butter. Remove from the heat. Stir in cocoa; cool. In a large bowl, beat eggs and sugar until blended. Combine flour, baking powder and salt; gradually add to egg mixture. Stir in vanilla and the cooled chocolate mixture until well blended.

2. Spread into a greased 13x9-in. baking pan. Bake at 350° until a toothpick inserted in the center comes out clean, 25-28 minutes (do not overbake). Cool on a wire rack.

3. For frosting, in a large bowl, cream butter and confectioners' sugar until light and fluffy, 5-7 minutes. Beat in cocoa and vanilla. Add enough milk for the frosting to achieve spreading consistency. Spread over brownies. Cut into bars.

1 BROWNIE 277 cal., 13g fat (8g sat. fat), 68mg chol., 248mg sod., 39g carb. (29g sugars, 1g fiber), 3g pro.

CHERRY & ALMOND CRISPY BARS

A grown-up version of the crisp rice square will please the whole party. Everyone will agree it's delicious!
—Taste of Home *Test Kitchen*

TAKES: 20 MIN. • **MAKES:** 2 DOZEN

- 1 pkg. (10 oz.) large marshmallows
- 3 Tbsp. butter
- 1 tsp. almond extract
- 6 cups Rice Krispies
- 3 cups salted roasted almonds, divided
- 1½ cups dried cherries, divided

1. In a Dutch oven, combine the large marshmallows and butter. Cook and stir over medium-low heat until melted. Remove from heat; stir in extract. Stir in rice cereal, 1 cup almonds and 1 cup cherries.

2. Press into a greased 13x9-in. pan. Sprinkle with remaining 2 cups almonds and ½ cup cherries; gently press onto cereal mixture. Cool. Cut into bars.

1 BAR 205 cal., 11g fat (2g sat. fat), 4mg chol., 137mg sod., 25g carb. (13g sugars, 2g fiber), 5g pro.

NOTES

LAYERED TURTLE CHEESECAKE

After receiving a request for a special turtle cheesecake and not finding a good recipe, I created my own. Everyone is thrilled with the results and this remains a favorite at the coffee shop where I work.
—Sue Gronholz, Beaver Dam, WI

PREP: 40 MIN. • **BAKE:** 1¼ HOURS + CHILLING • **MAKES:** 16 SERVINGS

- 1 cup all-purpose flour
- ⅓ cup packed brown sugar
- ¼ cup finely chopped pecans
- 6 Tbsp. cold butter, cubed

FILLING

- 4 pkg. (8 oz. each) cream cheese, softened
- 1 cup sugar
- ⅓ cup packed brown sugar
- ¼ cup plus 1 tsp. all-purpose flour, divided
- 2 Tbsp. heavy whipping cream
- 1½ tsp. vanilla extract
- 4 large eggs, room temperature, lightly beaten
- ½ cup milk chocolate chips, melted and cooled
- ¼ cup caramel ice cream topping
- ⅓ cup chopped pecans

GANACHE

- ½ cup milk chocolate chips
- ¼ cup heavy whipping cream
- 2 Tbsp. chopped pecans
- Additional caramel ice cream topping, optional

1. Place a greased 9-in. springform pan on a double thickness of heavy-duty foil (about 18 in. square). Securely wrap foil around pan.

2. In a small bowl, combine the flour, brown sugar and pecans; cut in butter until crumbly. Press onto the bottom of the prepared pan. Place pan on a baking sheet. Bake at 325° until set, 12-15 minutes. Cool on a wire rack.

3. In a large bowl, beat cream cheese and sugars until smooth. Beat in ¼ cup flour, cream and vanilla. Add eggs; beat on low speed just until blended. Remove 1 cup batter to a small bowl; stir in the melted chocolate. Spread over crust.

4. In another bowl, mix caramel topping and remaining 1 tsp. flour; stir in pecans. Drop by tablespoonfuls over chocolate batter. Top with remaining batter. Place springform pan in a large baking pan; add 1 in. hot water to the larger pan.

5. Bake at 325° until center is just set and top appears dull, 1¼-1½ hours. Remove springform pan from water bath; remove foil. Cool cheesecake on a wire rack for 10 minutes. Loosen side from pan with a knife; cool 1 hour longer. Refrigerate overnight.

6. For ganache, place chips in a small bowl. In a small saucepan, bring cream just to a boil. Pour over the chips; whisk until smooth. Cool slightly, stirring occasionally.

7. Remove side of springform pan. Spread ganache over cheesecake; sprinkle with pecans. Refrigerate until set. If desired, drizzle with additional caramel topping before serving.

1 PIECE 495 cal., 34g fat (18g sat. fat), 124mg chol., 260mg sod., 42g carb. (32g sugars, 1g fiber), 8g pro.

TURTLE CHEESECAKE TIPS

Is a water bath necessary for baking cheesecake? A water bath ensures gentle, even baking by insulating the dessert from direct heat. This promotes a creamy texture. Some cheesecake recipes that contain flour do not call for water baths.

How can you prevent cracks in cheesecake? To avoid cracks, grease the pan—even if it's nonstick—so the cake doesn't stick and tear as it cools. Mix the batter gently to avoid adding excess air, which can cause cracking. Bake on the middle rack, and if the top browns too quickly, loosely tent with foil.

How do you know when turtle cheesecake is done? Tap the pan's edge with a spoon—if the cheesecake wobbles slightly in the center but not at the edges, it's done. A firm, crack-free top often means it's overbaked.

QUICK & EASY BAKLAVA SQUARES

I love baklava but rarely indulge because it takes so much time to make. Then a friend of mine gave me this simple recipe. I've made it for family, friends and co-workers, and they can't get enough. I'm always asked to bring these squares to special gatherings and parties, and I even give them as gifts during the holidays.
—Paula Marchesi, Lenhartsville, PA

PREP: 20 MIN. • **BAKE:** 25 MIN. + COOLING • **MAKES:** 2 DOZEN

- 1 lb. (4 cups) chopped walnuts
- 1½ tsp. ground cinnamon
- 1 pkg. (16 oz., 14x9-in. sheets) frozen phyllo dough, thawed
- 1 cup butter, melted
- 1 cup honey

1. Preheat oven to 350°. Coat a 13x9-in. baking dish with cooking spray. Combine walnuts and cinnamon.

2. Unroll phyllo dough. Layer 2 sheets of phyllo in prepared pan; brush with butter. Repeat with 6 more phyllo sheets, brushing every other sheet with butter. (Keep remaining phyllo covered with a damp towel to prevent it from drying out.)

3. Sprinkle ½ cup nut mixture in pan; drizzle with 2 Tbsp. honey. Add 2 more phyllo sheets, brushing with butter; sprinkle another ½ cup nut mixture and 2 Tbsp. honey over phyllo. Repeat layers 6 times. Top with remaining phyllo sheets, brushing every other sheet with butter.

4. Using a sharp knife, score surface to make 24 squares. Bake until golden brown and crisp, 25-30 minutes. Cool on a wire rack 1 hour before serving.

1 PIECE 294 cal., 21g fat (6g sat. fat), 20mg chol., 145mg sod., 26g carb. (13g sugars, 2g fiber), 5g pro.

DARK CHOCOLATE CREAM PIE

This is one of my favorite desserts to make for my chocolate-loving friends.
—Kezia Sullivan, Sackets Harbor, NY

PREP: 30 MIN. + CHILLING • **MAKES:** 8 SERVINGS

Dough for single-crust pie
1¼ cups sugar
¼ cup cornstarch
¼ tsp. salt
3 cups whole milk
3 oz. unsweetened chocolate, chopped
4 large egg yolks, lightly beaten
3 Tbsp. butter
1½ tsp. vanilla extract
Optional: Whipped cream and grated chocolate

1. On a lightly floured surface, roll dough to a ⅛-in.-thick circle; transfer to a 9-in. pie plate. Trim to ½ in. beyond rim of the plate; flute edge. Refrigerate 30 minutes. Preheat the oven to 425°. Line crust with a double thickness of foil. Fill with pie weights, dried beans or uncooked rice. Bake on a lower oven rack until edge is golden brown, 20-25 minutes. Remove the foil and weights; bake until bottom is golden brown, 3-6 minutes longer. Cool on a wire rack.

2. In a large saucepan, combine sugar, cornstarch and salt. Stir in milk and chocolate. Cook and stir over medium-high heat until thickened and bubbly. Reduce heat; cook and stir 2 minutes longer. Remove from the heat.

3. Stir a small amount of hot filling into egg yolks; return all to the pan, stirring constantly. Bring to a gentle boil; cook and stir 2 minutes longer. Remove from the heat.

4. Gently stir in butter and vanilla until butter is melted. Spoon into crust. Cool on a wire rack. Cover and chill for at least 3 hours. If desired, serve with whipped cream and grated chocolate.

DOUGH FOR SINGLE-CRUST PIE Combine 1¼ cups all-purpose flour and ¼ tsp. salt; cut in ½ cup cold butter until crumbly. Gradually add 3-5 Tbsp. ice water, tossing with a fork until dough holds together when pressed. Shape into a disk; wrap and refrigerate 1 hour.

1 PIECE 390 cal., 19g fat (10g sat. fat), 128mg chol., 218mg sod., 52g carb. (37g sugars, 2g fiber), 7g pro.

CARING FOR PIE WEIGHTS
Let pie weights cool before storing. Beans and rice may be reused for pie weights, but not for cooking.

VERY VANILLA CUPCAKES

My recipe is a vanilla lover's dream—it's a vanilla cupcake topped with vanilla buttercream frosting.
—*Michelle Dorsey, Wilmington, DE*

PREP: 15 MIN. • **BAKE:** 20 MIN. + COOLING • **MAKES:** 2 DOZEN

- ¾ cup unsalted butter, softened
- 1½ cups sugar
- 3 large eggs, room temperature
- 1½ tsp. vanilla extract
- 2⅓ cups cake flour
- 2½ tsp. baking powder
- ½ tsp. salt
- ¾ cup whole milk

FROSTING

- 1 cup unsalted butter, softened
- 3 tsp. clear vanilla extract
- 2½ cups confectioners' sugar
- Paste food coloring, optional
- Colored sprinkles and nonpareils

1. Preheat oven to 350°. In a large bowl, cream butter and sugar until light and fluffy, 5-7 minutes. Add eggs, 1 at a time, beating well after each addition. Beat in vanilla. In another bowl, mix flour, baking powder and salt; add to creamed mixture alternately with milk, beating well after each addition.

2. Fill 24 paper-lined muffin cups two-thirds full. Bake until a toothpick inserted in the center comes out clean, 18-22 minutes. Cool in pans 10 minutes. Remove to wire racks to cool completely.

3. For frosting, in a small bowl, beat the butter and vanilla until blended. Gradually beat in confectioners' sugar until smooth. If desired, tint with food coloring. Frost cupcakes. Decorate as desired.

1 CUPCAKE 278 cal., 14g fat (9g sat. fat), 62mg chol., 105mg sod., 36g carb. (25g sugars, 0 fiber), 2g pro.

NOTES

VERSATILE BUTTERCREAM FROSTING

This basic buttercream frosting has unmatchable homemade taste. With a few simple variations, you can come up with different colors and flavors.
—Diana Wilson, Denver, CO

TAKES: 10 MIN. • **MAKES:** ABOUT 3 CUPS

- ½ cup butter, softened
- 4½ cups confectioners' sugar
- 1½ tsp. vanilla extract
- 5 to 6 Tbsp. 2% milk

In a large bowl, beat butter until creamy. Beat in the confectioners' sugar, vanilla and enough milk to achieve desired consistency.

2 TBSP. 124 cal., 4g fat (2g sat. fat), 11mg chol., 40mg sod., 23g carb. (21g sugars, 0 fiber), 0 pro.

ALMOND BUTTERCREAM FROSTING
Substitute ½-¾ tsp. almond extract for the vanilla.

CHOCOLATE BUTTERCREAM FROSTING
Reduce confectioners' sugar to 4 cups and add ½ cup baking cocoa; increase milk to 6-7 Tbsp.

LEMON BUTTERCREAM FROSTING
Substitute 5-6 Tbsp. lemon juice for milk; add 1 tsp. grated lemon peel.

ORANGE BUTTERCREAM FROSTING
Substitute 5-6 Tbsp. orange juice for milk; add 1 tsp. grated orange peel. If needed, brighten the taste with a little lemon juice.

PEANUT BUTTER FROSTING Substitute peanut butter for the butter; increase milk to 6-8 Tbsp.

PEPPERMINT BUTTERCREAM FROSTING
Substitute ½-¾ tsp. peppermint extract for the vanilla.

COOKING REFERENCE

AL DENTE: An Italian term meaning "to the tooth." Used to describe pasta that is cooked but still firm.

BASTE: To moisten food with melted butter, pan drippings, marinade or other liquid to add flavor and juiciness.

BEAT: To mix rapidly with a spoon, fork, wire whisk or electric mixer.

BLEND: To combine ingredients until just mixed.

BOIL To heat liquids until bubbles that cannot be stirred down are formed. In the case of water, the temperature will reach 212°.

BONE To remove all bones from meat, poultry or fish.

BROIL: To cook food 4-6 in. from a direct, radiant heat source.

CREAM: To blend ingredients to a smooth consistency by beating; frequently done with butter and sugar for baking.

CUT IN To break down and distribute cold butter, margarine or shortening into a flour mixture with a pastry blender or 2 knives.

DASH: A measurement less than ⅛ tsp. that is used for herbs, spices and hot pepper sauce. This is not a precise measurement.

DREDGE: To coat foods with flour or other dry ingredients. Most often done with pot roasts and stew meat before browning.

FLUTE: To make a "V" shape or scalloped edge on pie crust with your thumb and fingers.

FOLD: To blend dissimilar ingredients by careful and gentle turning with a spatula. Used most commonly to incorporate whipped cream, beaten egg whites, fruit, candy or nuts into a thick, heavy batter.

JULIENNE: To cut foods into long, thin strips much like matchsticks. Used often for salads and stir-fries.

KNEAD: To work dough by using a pressing and folding action to make it smooth and elastic.

MARINATE: To tenderize and/or flavor foods, usually vegetables or raw meat, by placing them in a mixture of oil, vinegar, wine, lime or lemon juice, herbs and spices.

MINCE: To cut into very fine pieces. Often used for garlic, hot peppers and fresh herbs.

PARBOIL: To boil foods, usually vegetables, until partially cooked. Most often used when vegetables are to be finished using another cooking method or chilled for marinated salads or dips.

PINCH: A measurement less than ⅛ tsp. that is easily held between the thumb and index finger. This is not a precise measurement.

PULSE: To process foods in a food processor or blender with short bursts of power.

PUREE: To mash solid foods into a smooth mixture with a food processor, mill, blender or sieve.

SAUTE: To fry quickly in a small amount of fat, stirring almost constantly. Most often done with onions, mushrooms and other chopped vegetables.

SCORE: To cut slits partway through the outer surface of foods. Often required for ham or flank steak.

SIMMER: To cook liquids, or a combination of ingredients with liquid, at just under the boiling point (180-200°). The surface of the liquid will have some movement and there may be small bubbles around the sides of the pan.

STEAM: To cook foods covered on a rack or in a steamer basket over a small amount of boiling water. Most often used for vegetables.

STIR-FRY: To cook meats, grains and/or vegetables with a constant stirring motion, in a small amount of oil, or in a wok or skillet over high heat.

EQUIVALENT MEASURES

3 tsp.	=	1 Tbsp.	**16 Tbsp.**	=	1 cup
4 Tbsp.	=	¼ cup	**2 cups**	=	1 pint
5⅓ Tbsp.	=	⅓ cup	**4 cups**	=	1 qt.
8 Tbsp.	=	½ cup	**4 qt.**	=	1 gallon

FOOD EQUIVALENTS

Macaroni	1 cup (3½ oz.) uncooked	=	2½ cups cooked
Noodles, medium	3 cups (4 oz.) uncooked	=	4 cups cooked
Popcorn	⅓-½ cup unpopped	=	8 cups popped
Rice, long grain	1 cup uncooked	=	3 cups cooked
Rice, quick-cooking	1 cup uncooked	=	2 cups cooked
Spaghetti	8 oz. uncooked	=	4 cups cooked
Bread	1 slice	=	¾ cup soft crumbs, ¼ cup fine dry crumbs
Graham crackers	7 squares	=	½ cup finely crushed
Buttery round crackers	12 crackers	=	½ cup finely crushed
Saltine crackers	14 crackers	=	½ cup finely crushed
Bananas	1 medium	=	⅓ cup mashed
Lemons	1 medium	=	3 Tbsp. juice, 2 tsp. grated zest
Limes	1 medium	=	2 Tbsp. juice, 1½ tsp. grated zest
Oranges	1 medium	=	¼-⅓ cup juice, 4 tsp. grated zest
Cabbage	1 head	=	5 cups shredded
Carrots	1 lb.	=	3 cups shredded
Celery	1 rib	=	½ cup chopped
Corn	1 ear fresh	=	⅔ cup kernels
Almonds	1 lb.	=	3 cups chopped
Ground nuts	3¾ oz.	=	1 cup
Green pepper	1 large	=	1 cup chopped
Mushrooms	½ lb.	=	3 cups sliced
Onions	1 medium	=	½ cup chopped
Potatoes	3 medium	=	2 cups cubed
Pecan halves	1 lb.	=	4½ cups chopped
Walnuts	1 lb.	=	3¾ cups chopped

INDEX